CAROL BLY

Beyond the Writers' Workshop

Carol Bly is a critically acclaimed short story writer and essayist. She is the author of many books, including *The Passionate, Accurate Story*, a writing guide; *My Lord Bag of Rice: New and Selected Stories*, and an essay collection, *Letters from the Country*. She is also a frequent lecturer at conferences of the National Council of Teachers of English, Associated Writing Programs, and the National Association of Social Workers. She lives in St. Paul, Minnesota.

Also by CAROL BLY

Backbone

Changing the Bully Who Rules the World

Letters from the Country

My Lord Bag of Rice: New and Selected Stories

The Passionate, Accurate Story

The Tomcat's Wife and Other Stories

Beyond the Writers' Workshop

Beyond the Writers' Workshop

New Ways to Write Creative Nonfiction

CAROL BLY

ANCHOR BOOKS

A Division of Random House, Inc.

New York

FIRST ANCHOR BOOKS EDITION, APRIL 2001

 Published in the United States by Anchor Books, a division of Random House, Inc., New York, and simultaneously in Canada by Random House of Canada Limited, Toronto.

Library of Congress Cataloging-in-Publication Data
Bly, Carol.
Beyond the writers' workshop : new ways to write creative nonfiction / Carol Bly.— 1st Anchor Books ed.
p. cm.
Includes bibliographical references and index.
ISBN 0-385-49919-1
1. English language—Rhetoric—Study and teaching. 2. Prose literature—Authorship—Study and teaching. 3. Creative writing (Higher education) 4. Prose literature—Authorship. 5. Creative writing. I. Title.
PE1404 .B5896 2001
808'042'071—dc21
00-050233

www.anchorbooks.com

Illustrations by Stephen J. Brewer

Printed in the United States of America
10 9 8 7 6 5 4 3 2 1

This book is dedicated

to the four great teachers in my life:

Alice C. Sweeney

Jack Putterill

Chris Santella

Judy Halverson

Acknowledgments

I am grateful to Noah Lukeman for generously taking his valuable time to teach me how to conceptualize and organize a book proposal.

I was surprised and touched by the work of my editor at Anchor Books. Writers keep moaning, "Oh! for the days of Maxwell Perkins," but the fact is I can't imagine more generous or thoroughgoing help to an author than Tina Pohlman's to me.

I am indebted to Constance Brewer not just for first-rate manuscript preparation, but for her intelligent suggestions and queries, and for her wonderful enthusiasm.

Contents

Introduction

The mission of this book is to help creative nonfiction writers to use the writing process to find the meaning they want, to write as beautifully as they can, using the traditional and in many cases quite wonderful styles of conventional literature, and to avoid, as well as they can, those aspects of present-day American life that tend to diminish their individuality and lessen their bravery as writers. Bravery is the major difficulty for a sensitive writer in our time. More than anyone else except research scientists, who always run the chance that all their efforts will come to nothing, we writers need to brace ourselves over and over.

Nobody knows what creative nonfiction is, and therefore it can be nearly anything. You can write it the way Susan Griffin writes it, or you can write it the way Annie Dillard writes it. All you have to do is be truthful, tell things in your personal voice, and have your modus operandi be revealing your own life circumstances through anecdote or narrative and revealing the meanings you attach to those circumstances, rather than arguing a point. Creative nonfiction is basically about the author's wisdom. It is therefore like, but not the same as poetry, and it is like, but not the same as, literary journalism.

Creative nonfiction is the most democratic, most natural form of writing we have. It's the first form that any of us writes in. Our first- and second-grade papers are creative nonfiction. "What I Did over the Summer Vacation" is creative nonfiction. My diaries are creative nonfiction. I notice that most of my e-mail correspondence, flying back and forth on favorite subjects, grammarless and impermanent in that flitty, electronic way, are like creative nonfiction—collegial, but without frills, somewhat like first drafts of personal essays to their readers. Creative nonfiction is an easy form because no one has made up his or her mind that it must meet any peripheral specs for length or sound. Creative nonfiction doesn't even have to be succinct. (Much of it is gassy.) All it must do is be truthful.

Since it ties meaning to anecdote, creative nonfiction is a little like poetry. Oddly enough, poetry, especially the poetry written today, is more like creative nonfiction than like poems from the nineteenth century or the first half of the twentieth century; that is, the poet wants to reveal his or her take on some given episode, so he or she breaks up and left aligns the sentences, so what we see on the page is fractured. Why? The poet wants to slow down the reader.

There is great advantage in slowing down the reader. A hobbled reader cannot keep flying over the sentence tops looking merely for the gist. One can't frisk along, pacey and shallow, the way one can when reading prose. Slowed, nearly halted here and there at line ends, you, the reader, are automatically dropped into a contemplative, spongy frame of mind. You take up the author's feeling the way your shoes take up cold water when you wade in a stream, wading, like reading the poetic line, being a ponderous business. Poets who know nothing else about metaphor and sound do know this much: they break sentences to slow down the reader. When a poet knows nothing else about prosody, some of what he or she writes is the stuff of creative nonfiction. It is written in an informal spirit, with the profound hope that readers won't gallop along merely to identify the gist. Creative nonfiction, like poetry, is never written for gist.

Three problems threaten and erode creative nonfiction writing in our country. First: our current junk culture gives poor support to people who want to use writing to find meaning. Our culture offers scant prospect of making money on such writing. The very idea of using writing as a tool to become more deeply one's own particular self sounds nutty. Even English teachers begin to twitch when a writing student talks about such a purpose.

Most creative nonfiction writers I've known—the good ones—pay enormous, unremitting attention to the psychological dynamics of living in America in our time. They are torn. They know empire when they see it, but they also love the stars.

Half the skills that a present-day creative nonfiction writer needs to learn, therefore, are the skills of psychological sturdiness. (The other half are the skills of literary craft.) I am using the term *sturdy* with *psychological* because it pulls together two ideas that all of us need to see together. One is that psychology means understanding what our soul grapples with and making sure that our soul goes on grappling with it instead of pretending all is well, and all will be well, because all isn't well and all won't be well. And, two, learning some ways to strengthen ourselves so that we can keep writing literature.

The schooling of M.F.A. students is only two or three years. These students learn in a three-year period whatever it is they are going to learn about writing from their given college or university. If that college or university doesn't teach them how to be psychologically sturdy writers, they may not learn what they need most. A major problem for writers now is somehow to learn how to connect what leads us to love the universe with what leads us to wrath or despair, to write truthfully about *both*, and withal to go on seeing what is funny as funny and what is gorgeous as gorgeous. "Mood swings," ever a quality of good prose, are a form of psychological sturdiness.

A second problem of creative nonfiction writing is dishonesty. Whereas in the private sector and in the entertainment world dishonesty is acceptable much of the time, it is not acceptable in writing we trust to be "nonfiction." People read creative nonfiction expecting a kind of spiritual or psychological history, no matter how personal the history. We read someone's nonfiction to see how we might manage in that author's circumstances, or to learn from the author how we might give our own life more meaning—or if we are only in a mildly curious frame of mind, we read to note the author's circumstances and find parallels or nonparallels with our own. If the author has lied, however, about the events in a memoir—the memoir being a subset of creative nonfiction—then we haven't got true data to mull over. Unfortunately, a casual attitude toward lying in creative nonfiction is now being taught in American universities. I think it should be stopped. This book takes up problems related to lying.

The third major grief for creative nonfiction writers is that wherever in their lives they now are and wherever they've been—from day care to Little League to elementary school peer reviewing groups to high school peer reviewing groups to college peer reviewing groups to M.F.A. peer reviewing groups—creative nonfiction writers have spent thousands and thousands of hours *in groups.* Chapter 4 of this book focuses on the problem of how much solitude human beings need in order best to fulfill the potential of their minds. Serious helping professionals—Allen Ivey and Tom Kitwood and other social workers and psychotherapists and psychiatrists—warn us that human beings need solitude in order to take seriously their own ideas. Sadly, most Americans spend most of each day in groups.

We teachers and professors talk a good deal about the "dumbing-down of America." I am interested in removing, for creative nonfiction writers especially, as many of the influences and instruments or conventions that cause "dumbing down" as we can. I feel much hope about this. I am especially interested on behalf of creative nonfiction writers because they are the people who, as much as anyone, are committed to the idea of tying real life to real literature. They are not just technocrats. They are usually not just blithe hobbyists with literary flair. They consciously or unconsciously grope outward from that age-old idea of the pre-Socratics that if you go deeply inside what's visible you will find what's universal and invisible, and that the best way to go deeply inside what's universal and invisible is to look again at what is visible—namely our own day-to-day experience.

I have spoken favorably of creative nonfiction writers and praised them for wanting to find themselves and identify themselves. As writing students, however, they have signal weaknesses that may well be weaknesses that all of us share. One of these weaknesses is not being able to stick. Why do people want, quite passionately, to write? And then write down—still feeling inspired—a rough draft or a stanza of something. But next, they can't stick it.

There's a good deal of cant about writers' block and facing the blank page and other jetsam, but let me put it this way instead: writers often get stuck and then give up their writing projects because they want to practice the profession of writing, but at the same time they are anxious about whether the ideals they have and the life that they're leading are really worthy. They may not have read much excellent literature—most of us don't read nearly enough of the best—so they can't take collegial comfort from great authors. Some aspiring writers stay stuck after their first inspiration because they habitually cling to remaining neutral about most of what they see. They want a level deck to their ship, yet seeking a level deck means that you must sail in only the smallest of lakes. Clinging to neutral feelings is a dynamic that psychotherapists deal with in their clients first therapy sessions. People commonly, odd as it sounds, tell a therapist that they "don't want to be happy," that they "want to be contented." And the therapist has to ask them, "Why don't you want to be happy?" The client insists, "I just want to be contented." That is someone speaking who is clinging in terror, no doubt, to mere levelness of feeling—namely, contentment or neutrality, rather than outright happiness, for fear of what would happen if there were mood swings—mood swings that might take a person to unbearable unhappiness. The therapist's job is to make that tepid person sturdy enough so that he or she can then take a mood swing or two, strong enough to feel any lurking pain in order to feel any potential happiness. Once that's been done, of course, no one would dream of simply being contented again.

Writers need to be very sturdy. The sturdiness they need, however, is specifically *psychological* sturdiness. Yet most writers haven't studied psychology, so they don't know the modern ways of being sturdy.

All writing of any manuscript falls into three distinct stages. The first stage we're all familiar with—that is, inspiration. We dash down something onto paper.

The second is a long, middle stage, which I call the long, middle, *psychological* stage of a piece of writing. This stage is not even recognized by most creative writing teachers. Most creative writing students have not heard of this stage—not even once.

If a creative nonfiction writer clings to neutral feelings, then that writer's problems are not craft problems. Such a person can't make good use of the chapter called "Literary Fixes." That person has first to learn to do the hard psychological work of kindly nursing his or her own *strongest* feelings.

The third stage of the process is what I call "literary fixes," which I will discuss a little later.

The largest part of this book emphasizes how we can teach ourselves the psychological sturdiness and insight that we need in order to take our manuscript through its inevitable middle stage.

We may not call our travail "psychological," but that's what it largely is. Almost all of the psychological work, what's more, is done *after* our original inspiration. Psychological stamina is the most profound difficulty of our trade. I will break it into its parts and mention a few here.

We must deliberately keep intact *a general affection for the universe* no matter how dreadful the particulars we may be writing about. A few writers who have succeeded in just this way are Erich Remarque and Anne Frank and Tobias Wolff.

Writers must do the hard psychological work of recognizing that some things are not "just the way life is, I guess" but actually evil—whereas other things are neither "just the way life is, I guess" nor evil, but remarkably beautiful or remarkably just—worth praising. Stunning examples of people who have learned both to discern evil and to distinguish marvelous people when they see them are Denise Levertov and Allen Ginsberg and Edward Hoagland.

A writer has to do the hard psychological work of living with terrific mood swings, as already mentioned. That's logical enough, since the people who *don't* experience terrific mood swings are people who figure everything's more or less just the way it is. They remind me of Thurber's entrancing remark of a half-century ago: "Life is just one goddamned thing after another."

Writers do the hard psychological work of forming their opinions as resolutely as they can, while knowing at the same time that they may be totally mistaken. Say some new data came to light—so here we are—wrong about a tenet that we had such a proud stake in! Like a responsible scientist whose research conclusions prove to be mistaken, we must make ourselves *want the new truth more than we wish things had stayed the way we thought they were.* Writers have to keep their personal fear level as low as possible so we can hold a sturdy concept yet be willing to drop it if it proves false.

Writers do the hard psychological work of trying not to be ignorant; that is, if their table is spread in the presence of their enemies, they bravely eat at it anyway, and they *ask civil questions between mouthfuls,* too. I am referring here to that mysterious verse 5 of Psalm 23: "Thou preparest a table before me in the presence of mine enemies." Writers need to grasp every chance to learn more about others' lives. There is no dishonor in collecting information from enemies or in repulsive venues. One can always start a principled quarrel or fight later on. I've read a few exegetists' ideas about what that psalm means. None of their explanations makes much sense to me. Therefore I have summoned my courage to offer an interpretation of my own. If we live in a universe in which there is much evil and also much good, it's possible that we are *always* in the presence of both our friends and our enemies; that is, the beauty of the world, the love of those whom we love, and the hideous greed and predation of our own species and the cruelty practiced by those close to us whom we otherwise admire, are all present at the same time. It's possible that if our table is spread with those thoughts in our heads at all times, we must do whatever it is that keeps us alive. So possibly the key to being at a table spread in the presence of one's enemies is that you're supposed to eat at it, if eating is what's going on. And be brave, because one or another enemy is always in sight.

The third stage of writing any manuscript is one people are familiar with—I call it literary fixes. That is, you've gotten to the end of the manuscript, you've put almost everything into it that you want in it so far as you know, and now you're going to try to make it clearer and more succinct if you can, spruce up the language, and certainly correct the grammar if you can.

In the appendix are fifteen writing exercises that I have been using and amending over the last five to ten years. They are divided up into those that are comparatively simple, such as writing exercises on place; those that are not quite so easy (exercises 5–9); and those that require careful thought and reconsideration of one's own life and one's own opinions—namely, numbers 10–15, called "Elegant Exercises."

The appendix also contains material designed to help students be more analytical about their own and others' work. It contains material designed to help teachers as they work with beginning writers. At the very end of the appendix is an ethics code designed to help high school teachers as they work with young people.

Beyond the Writers' Workshop

1.
Taking on Three Demanding Situations First

So many creative nonfiction writers are disappointed or outright resentful of how they are being taught to write that they need to hear the bad news first. The bad news is what is on their own minds. I want to validate much of their confusion or disappointment or anger. Currently some teaching of writers is quite wonderful, or at least neutral, not damaging, but if we want to improve a practice, we don't write books affirming the good or harmless news about it. We need to do what people in both the private sector and the idealistic, not-for-profit organizations call a "needs assessment." A frank needs assessment is not full of idle complaints. The idea is to list what we think is wrong because we expect to change as much of the bad stuff as we can.

A note: writers or aspiring writers interested in publishing for mass-market audiences—those, for example, who want to write romances or best-selling novels—are not nearly so discontented with present-day courses and texts and writers' Web sites and professional conferences as are those people who want to write literature. For literary people, marketability may run a close second, but is not a primary goal. So many creative writing students in the United States are irritated by the guides and instruction offered them that I think we had better identify whatever we think is being done wrong as well as we can.

I see three troublesome features in much of the teaching of creative writing. (I use the word *troublesome*, not *bad*, because some of what appears to be bad has a bright underside to it.)

1. The cultural deprivation of thousands of Americans;
2. The mission of present-day writers—which is very different from the mission of student writers half a century ago;
3. The skimpy, conventional teaching of creative writing.

Cultural Deprivation

Americans and their culture are now significantly "dumbed down." Having said that, let me immediately recognize and point out the exception: that is, a few thousand American English majors and writing students have been taught by elementary teachers to be expressive. They have been read good books and learned to love them. They have been guided by high school teachers to make connections between the stories and poems they read and the stuff of their own lives. They have been taught to stand apart from both life and literature enough so they can make judgments based on their own tastes.

But they are the exception. Most Americans have been "dumbed down," and the sooner we realize it the sooner we can give our attention to the problem. As the secretary of education under Richard Nixon said, if this low level of American schooling had been laid on us by a foreign country we'd have gone to war against that country.

With particular reference to literature, what does it mean to be dumbed down? It means that the schools American children go to are not so good as the schools that European and Asian children go to—not by a long shot. American children learn far less in public high schools than they learned half a century ago. Some even graduate illiterate. Most children today graduate from high school without having been asked any questions about ideas, and therefore without having experienced the exhilaration of conceptual thinking. They learn mechanical data, but they don't learn the connective principles behind those data. They have been left out of the struggle to identify the organizing principles behind information.

Even those who want to write read astonishingly few books. In the main, this leaves beginning writers still reading only for sense impression, rather than for the ancient balance of both sense impression and contemplation. The mix of sense impression and consulting one's own mind is an acquired taste that comes from reading literature.

Further, some adult creative-writing teachers are horribly ignorant of the sciences—not just of the abstract, conceptual sciences such as physics and chemistry, but even of the descriptive sciences such as botany and biology.

American writers tend to know and use minuscule vocabulary. American writers' prose has fewer and fewer words. To use an anthropologist's expression, we are experiencing a partial *extinction* of language. And syntax, the logical spine of sentences, is losing variety. For example, the elegant subjunctive mood is vanishing. "If he wouldn't have dropped the ball," the announcer tells us, "the pass would have been complete"—using a double conditional instead of the subjunctive and conditional on the teeter-totter opposite one another.

So much for the dumbing down of the culture. The surprising underside is that literature is coming from voices largely unheard half a century ago. The hard knocks that were the schooling for African Americans and other minorities, women, and the poor did what schools of hard knocks can do—provided the blows that are received aren't so bad that they discourage the soul, and provided that someone will listen at all: The products of this hard-won learning have infused post–World War II literature with intense, everyday psychological insight. Minority voices have replaced a lot of neutral vagary and pitty-pat aestheticism with no-nonsense tragedy. Pain has been America's cultural teacher since 1945.

I am sorry that pain is a great teacher. I wish decent literature could be made prettily and laid across the mind's roof like snow. It can't. The moment the author puts in a metaphor, the metaphor does what metaphors do: it shafts down in the mind and makes its dozens of connections. One can escape such sadness only by using fewer and fewer metaphors, somewhat the way a very smooth diplomat can manage a cocktail party at which natural political enemies have a pleasant time: the trade-off is that all the talk must be small talk.

Most present-day writers have not given way to small talk (or pretty phrasing instead of sober feeling). Americans have learned that their own country has a disgraceful foreign policy. We have finally got it through our heads that our own country has been unfair to African-Americans and Asian-Americans for years and years and years. Our society is still horribly unfair to women. Our country has started more than one illegal or extralegal war since World War II with neither congressional approval nor apology. Sanctions by our country are killing Iraqi children under five years old at a rate of 6,000 to 7,000 a month.[1] It is painful to know such things about one's own country.

But once we accept bad news, our tapestry of sadness makes us smarter. In a psychological sense, an educated American today is much smarter than an educated American of 1945. In 1945 you could not have civilly discussed in someone's living room, without host or hostess throwing a fit, whether or not twenty- and twenty-one-year-old crews of B-17s and B-24s ought or ought not to have been sent up over Germany day after day after day to kill large numbers of civilians.

People are steadily getting more stalwart about facing shameful news without denial. In October of 1999 Americans learned that our soldiers had massacred hundreds of Korean civilians—women and children—at the Bridge of No Gun Ri. The army had covered up this massacre for forty-seven years.[2] Americans have had to learn again that our army will lie to us over and over and over.

Present-day young people of privilege are not nearly such fools, in the sense of being conscious of ethical rage, as their opposite numbers in 1945 and 1950. (I consider it an extraordinary privilege for young people to attend a private high school with its tiny classes and cordial but frank discussions.) With regard to the world of literature, let me give as an example *The Paris Review*, the excellent little magazine founded in 1953 by George Plimpton. Its Contributors' Notes used to read that such and such a contributor "prepared at Groton" or "prepared at St. Paul's" for Harvard or Yale. Nowadays no literary magazine would say that a contributor had "prepared at Groton" because, at last, Americans are aware of the millions who prepared at Nisei camps and workers' towns like those near the mighty hotels of Florida.

A curious social-class fight carries on between those who mainly mourn the old canon of American literature and those who mainly welcome the wide new canon. We need both. I am sorry to see people sneer at dead white males. So many dead white males have written such profound literature, usually enabled, of course, by so many dead white, yellow, or black other people who did their scutwork for them. Dead white males were able to promote their beautiful literature while no one paid much attention to dead white females' writing, no matter how ecstatic, troubling, and insightful it often was. The only sensible practice is for twenty-first century writers to read *all* the good books they can. And I am delighted that Asian-American and African-American and Hispanic literature is so widely read now.

A second, less obvious form of cultural deprivation is bad character modeling by people of privilege. It may be fashionable to jeer at any mention of noblesse oblige, but noblesse oblige, in corporate leadership, is infinitely preferable to no noblesse oblige. Gift giving has dropped. Feelings of responsibility for the community on the part of privileged people is less, head by head, than it has been at other times in our urban history.

What's more, large corporations are sponsoring violent and boring TV shows with frequent commercial interruptions, seemingly oblivious or indifferent to the prospect that such programming does psychological and intellectual (not to mention spiritual) damage to young audiences. Apparently it has never occurred to corporate sponsors that they have a serious role to play in promoting culture and learning for the public good.

Ours is in general a selfish society with pockets of idealists fighting against the avarice. Whenever idealists are forced into pockets, their voices sound shrill. The bad news is that the idealists are a minority. The good news is that at least *someone* is shrill. Here is a passage from a good interpreter of our culture, Gerald Graff:

> [T]he type of society which has emerged since the end of World War II, for all the overpowering weight of its technology and its bureaucratic organization, is a more elusive and shadowy entity. It is a society where boredom is more conspicuous than poverty and exploitation, and where authority encouraged hedonistic consumption and a flabby, end-of-ideology tolerance. Such a society does not present the type of sharp resistance requisite for individual self-definition. In say-

> ing this, I do not mean to imply that censorship and repression would be desirable, but rather that the patronizing of diverse viewpoints in contemporary society is a reflection of contempt for ideas, which are seen as impotent, and not of a disposition to take them seriously. Though there is some truth to the complaint that this society "processes" and "indoctrinates" individuals, the typical product of this processing is not the indoctrinated conformist of anti-utopian science fiction and radical folklore, but a diffuse, unfocused, protean self which cannot define issues in any determinate way. A confused self is as good as an indoctrinated self from the ruling-class point of view—though the situation is complicated by the fact that the "ruling class" itself often shares the confusion.[3]

I regard this problem of "hedonistic consumption and flabby, end-of-ideology tolerance" as a problem of *character*, not simply as a free-standing evil that somehow, mysteriously, has alighted among us. If American corporate leaders had wanted to exert themselves to eschew one-one-hundredth of the gigantic profits they have licked up off our system, they could have done so. If American corporate leaders wanted to stop violence in America, those who sponsor salacious TV shows could refuse to sponsor them. I bring this up because so much liberal objection to cultural deprivation is vague. It is so chicken that it won't even name specific predators, and thus those specific predators go free.

But this book is mostly about solutions of the kind that we creative writers and teachers of creative writers can ourselves bring about. I point at evils caused by corporations or by government or by universities first, only because we should stay aware of which evils are *not* caused by creative-writing teachers. Here is a rough example: college-level English teachers frequently blame high school language arts teachers, in print, for not assigning their students writing projects and not reading teenagers' writing. But the classes that public high school teachers must teach are usually so populous that if each student wrote a paper a week and the teacher allowed ten minutes to comment on each, that teacher would have to spend 150 hours every weekend on students' work. Therefore, those high school language arts teachers are struggling to teach in a fraudulent workplace for which the United States Congress, not the teachers, is to blame.

The second reason this book pays attention to societal evils is to recognize the mission of the largest enclave of American student writers—namely, nontraditional writing students. Societal evil of several kinds is typically part of these adults' conscious grist. A central goal in these writers is to expose public evil.

The New, Nontraditional Mission of Present-Day Writers

The traditional students in creative-writing classes wanted to become authors. Half a century ago these candidates for the literary life or profession were well-read before they entered privileged venues like the Iowa Writers' Workshop. They had read the best literature. They duly hoped to write the best. They conferred with each other. They wrote letters to each other giving each other tough criticism, because everybody wanted to do excellent work. For most of these aspirants, collegial love meant outspoken comment, the discipline being always literature—*its* mores, *its* treasures of the past, *its* aesthetic ideals.

Of course, there are still writers like that, but a new kind of population is making up more than half of creative-writing students in universities as well as in summer programs and weeklong retreats. This new kind of writer is an adult whose primary interest is looking for meaning in life. This person usually is trying to get free—at least for a week if not for a full term—from the American junk culture.

We may each define American junk culture differently. Let's not stumble over that, because the telling psychological reality here is that if you are wanting to get *free* of something, it means that you are struggling within the tentacles of that thing. The majority of students in personal-enrichment courses (writers' retreats, evening writing courses, and the like) are *of* the culture, yet trying to leave it.

A lot of writing teachers, including me, love to teach such meaning-and-freedom seekers. They can be awfully hard to approach, however.

The younger ones typically did not do much reading during childhood. Their Saturday mornings were spent watching a television genre called "cartoons," which is, in fact, a genre full of not humor but violence. According to research conducted in the early 1970s, "By 1969 there was a violent episode at least every two minutes in all Saturday morning cartoon programming, including the least violent and also commercial time. The average cartoon had nearly twelve times the violence rate of the average movie hour."[4] What was normalized to them as "just cute kids' stuff" was solid violence, with solid trickery as the humor mode. I mention this because people who watched cartoons in the 1970s are at risk of not being able to discern moral qualities well. A second psychologically and cognitively damaging outcome of such television watching is the assumption that *any* kind of cute stuff could be a good steady diet for kids. Most of the new, growing population of writers are people over twenty-five. They are the first generation who spent hundreds of childhood hours in day care, and further hundreds of childhood hours engaging in a level of entertainment (the cartoons) often much coarser than any entertainment their parents would put up with for themselves. They tend to be highly unconscious of the kind of culture that has been visited upon them.

They can be initially hard to teach because of this unconsciousness. They can be hard to teach if the teacher is attuned to liking literature, because such students generally aren't much interested in English or American or any other literature. They don't know Toad and Mole or Eeyore or Anna Karenina or Hamlet. Most students of writing courses not only have not read *Hamlet,* but they don't mean to read it in the future, either.

We writing teachers split into two very different factions in answering the question: how do you teach a habitual nonreader and nonwriter how to write? One faction says you must absolutely, on the first day of the class, make it clear to students that they can never learn to write *unless they read*—read, and read the very best. These lively teachers then hand their students a list of the best in whatever genre the course is about and try not to feel desperate.

The other faction, which I belong to, and may be a founding member of, believes in asking the adult would-be writer a lot of questions about what he or she would like to do in the writing course. I have a preconceived idea, myself. My conviction is that if one is raised in the

United States without any particular experience in literature, and in a culture in which nice words such as *cartoons* are used to cover up the modeling of brutality—and despite that, this person wants to write, then this person has some particular moral taste and some bravery. He or she wants to leave the herd—that's good moral taste; ask anyone from Pythagoras to Wittgenstein—and they are actually doing it, going out on a limb to take a writing course, and who knows what treatment they might get. That takes bravery. So I feel respectful.

But my first questions get tepid, conventional, peripheral sorts of answers. Human beings who have never been asked any searching questions tend to be unconscious. They don't give deep answers. They may want to keep a serious record of some kind. Their chosen form is creative nonfiction. They may count on the evening class or the week's or six weeks' course to be a setting where thought and feeling can clamber toward one another more closely in their minds than they have so far. They may be sick of secular, kidding American life. They may be hungry for the conjunction of feeling and thinking—well, hungry for earnestness, anyhow.

But do they say any of that? No.

They announce that the reason they have joined this class is that they'd like to write a history of their grandmother. They have heard a lot of talk about "roots." They therefore suppose that they want to write about their roots. When I ask them a few questions about this goal—roots writing—it turns out that a few, indeed, do want to write about their roots, but the majority actually do not. They already know about their roots, and what they really want to write about is this question: what meaning can my own life have? Shyness drives them to the clichés of our time: "I want to find my roots." Or they say, "I want to find out who I am." They generally drop the clichés as soon as they feel they have permission to drop them. Groups don't give such permission, but writing teachers do, or they should.

The adult writer wants to find meaning, but another force in his or her life is terrible, terrible boredom. Liberals too blithely support the notion that only the corporate culture is dull. Actually, arts organizations and writers' clubs can be tremendously dull. Anyplace where people have accepted pop-culture clichés as their own truth and where people talk in the slow jell of dull language can be dull. I consider it a curious mark of our times that so few writing students say, "I want to be a writer," while so many others say, "I want to get in touch with my creativity." I take "getting in touch with my creativity" to mean, "My mind feels both bruised and idle." Nontraditional writers are often refugees from a dull culture.

Dullness in the corporate life drives stockbrokers and executives of one kind or another in two very noticeable directions. One is to continue their ordinary, profitable work by day, but by night to attend large meetings where charismatic speakers describe ways to examine and practice life with more spirit. The businesspeople feel immensely grateful to these leaders for talking about spiritual things. They sponge up new, absolutely genuine confidence and bravery from such charismatic leadership.

Next morning, they return to their profitable work. Their "high" the evening before does not ruin their efficacy at work the next day. They are refreshed.

But soon they need to go to the charismatic leader again, or to another one. They must physically see and hear him or her again because they are experiencing mentoring as a sensuous pleasure, and therefore not taking meditative notes. They are experiencing the remarks of this wonderful person as exquisite, sensuous nourishment rather than partly as sensuous nourishment and partly as new philosophies to be mulled over—categorized and recategorized—by their own minds.

Businesspeople—probably all people busy working in organizations, in the nearly constant presence of other people addressing practical issues—have not exercised the classical process of relaying all new ideas to their own brain sites of old ideas and consciously comparing notes. That process benefits from habitual exercise. If one is too busy or too merely-practical or too given to looking only outward for stimulation, one simply won't do such inward relaying and reevaluating and trying and retrying any new edicts against old thoughts of one's own.

Such trying and retrying new impressions against our own old, rich, meaning-laden thoughts may be the central pleasure of philosophy—but it is a quiet occupation, an acquired taste, and you need the habit of it. If you haven't that habit, you nevertheless may yearn for meaning in life. This makes you vulnerable to becoming a follower of charismatic leaders. You eagerly submit yourself for sluicing by the leader's wonderful enthusiasm and hopeful pronouncements. Such a sluicing is like a great wash under a waterfall, an immediate inundation of pleasure.

That is the pleasure of a follower, not of someone who is what used to be called "his own man" or "a person in her own right."

One result is that followers do not take notes at the lecture, or if they take them they don't take good ones. They write exultant exclamations. They are hungry for mental ecstasy and now that they have it they give themselves over to it for the whole evening. They are not annoyed at drumming or dancing, because drumming and dancing heighten the sensuous, uncritical pleasure of ritual—a very opposite pleasure to the joy of reflection. No wonder drumming is such a good prelude to going to war: the pleasure of it deafens one to meditative thought, so the more broad-brush excitement of being shoulder to shoulder with others of the same species and the excitement of risk-taking sluice over the critical process. People experiencing charismatic onslaught don't internalize any very complicated ideas. Muddling through their own thoughts seems like very small beer to them.

Thus today people can exercise the role of being a mentored person by night, while functioning as a competent businessperson by day. Some cunning businesses hire the charismatic speakers to come perform by day right in the corporate meeting rooms—hence so many guided meditations with formats that are curiously free of any rational thought about evil and good. Typically, at a corporate workplace meditation one is asked, eyes shut, to go to a peaceful, joyous place of one's own imagining. What is the implication? The implication is that you, the employees, are conscientious workers in the organization whom the top brass honor. Company leaders realize that employees need relaxation time, so they are glad to pay for this pricey team of facilitators to take workers through half a day of guided relaxation.

The devilish outcome here is that the message given and taken in is that there are no ethical griefs in the world; there is only stress. If I am told that stress is not a function of moral anxiety or of meaninglessness, and that by doing some group relaxation I will feel gratified. I will be a mollified employee, too grateful for this relaxation session to want to become a personnel problem of any kind.

A second, and vastly wiser, direction in which the dullness of corporate life drives people is toward writing. Writing is neither sociable nor relaxing. Nor does the initial thrill we feel upon being inspired stay with us. Then why is it such a life-giving activity?

Writing essays—creative nonfiction, including memoir, autobiography, poetry, or any form that is utterly true to life so far as the writer knows—has a psychologically opposite effect to that of going to hear charismatic speakers or sitting in guided meditation sessions. That is because a writer must *think*, not fantasize, and a writer must write *alone*, not in a group. The writer must look at the outside world.

I think people are wise to flee the junk culture by means of weekend and weeklong and six-week-long writers' courses. They may or may not learn something about literature at these night courses and summer conferences, but they always learn something about philosophy if they are writing nonfiction: they learn to get apart from the herd and to decide that they respect their own minds.

Schiller's vehemence on just these points is lovely: "But how is the artist to protect himself against the corruption of the age which besets him on all sides? By disdaining its opinion. Let him direct his gaze upwards, to the dignity of his calling, to the universal Law, not downwards towards Fortune and the needs of daily life."[5]

Adult nontraditional students generally wander into some poorish writing classes because there are so many poor writing programs about. No matter how scant the program or banal or lazy or ignorant the teacher, however, a writer does better to take classes than to take none.

If you are starting to take classes in writing, you may meet up with bad teaching. The next part of this chapter is devoted to exploring various kinds of bad teaching, the idea being that you recognize them, gladly take whatever advisories seem useful, and elude those that might do harm to your mind or your self-confidence.

Eight Elements of Bad or Scanty Teaching of Creative Writing

In the following pages we discuss bad teaching as a function of poor preparation, negative attitudes, selfishness on the part of teachers, and poor working conditions brought on by underfunding of educational institutions. Here are the eight elements of scanty teaching:

1. Bad teaching as low-level sadism
2. Scanty teaching owing to ignorance
3. To market, to market . . . jiggety jig
4. Teaching corrupted by nihilism
5. Teaching corrupted by inappropriate affiliation
6. Teaching corrupted by sloth
7. Teaching corrupted by wixelism
8. Teaching spoiled not by instructors but by government or university policies

I will take up bad teaching of creative writing in reverse order of importance. That is, I will discuss first the evils of rare occurrence—and then those of large incidence and therefore large influence.

Bad Teaching as Low-Level Sadism

I remember very clearly the first time I saw a student undergoing a "workshopping" of his manuscript. I had heard of "workshopping manuscripts" all my adult life, but I hadn't actually seen it done.

The procedure: A student feels that his or her manuscript is ready for some peer evaluation. The student "puts it up for workshopping." The student's creative-writing instructor schedules the workshopping for a particular day. The student sees to it that each classmate receives a copy of the manuscript in advance. Everyone prepares some remarks to help the student writer.

The class meets on the appointed day. The writer is expected to sit still and say nothing while each critique giver makes comments, in turn. I wasn't ready for this. I was amazed to observe the frozen, very courageous, oddly silent student whose work I had read and begun to critique. As I spoke he said nothing. I asked him some questions about his underlying ideas and themes. He looked nervous but wouldn't answer. Clearly he was focused on bearing up well. He didn't expect any discourse with me.

At last someone explained that those being workshopped were not allowed to talk lest they argue with instead of listen to their peers.

I then noticed two points: first, the room was filled with the smell of fear, and second, I didn't care for the expressions on the other students' faces. They had the look of cats near a mousehole. I couldn't quite identify it at the time, but in retrospect and with much experience since, I know that at least one dynamic in that room, whether conscious or unconscious, was low-level, mild, politically sanctioned sadism.

In the field of psychotherapy, low-level, half-conscious or unconscious sadism is so well identified and understood that reliable training programs regularly provide a "control" for student therapists. The old hand who has agreed to be a control frequently sits in on sessions between the student therapist and his or her clients. The control also listens between the lines as a student therapist discusses a present case. The control is watching for many things, among them the gleam of a power trip. Such a gleam can flash and vanish, reappear and vanish, like a shark near trustful swimmers.

A mentor or teacher has such tremendous power! And he or she has no trouble finding prey. Wanting a mentor at all, any kind of mentor, is a major, elegant passion of life. What's more, this wanting mentors is a passion that knows no sociological barriers. A social worker makes the rounds through ghettos: when he or she comes to visit their house, little boys and girls who know the worker grab onto the worker's clothes. They want to go along with him or her on that day's round.

People are starved for leaders. When anybody is starved for anything—for any gift that *you* have to give—you automatically become a powerful person, thereby especially at risk for allowing yourself little power trips.

Power can make silky and dangerous an otherwise agreeable creative-writing teacher.

The most horrible literary kind of meanness I know of had to do with Robert Lowell. In his memoir *The Bread of Time*,[6] the poet Philip Levine describes coursework he undertook at the famous Iowa Workshop with Robert Lowell. Lowell was already famous. He had won a Pulitzer. Robert Lowell gave As to some people, and lower grades to others. Philip Levine got a B. He was a painstaking young poet, yet at the end of the next grading period he got only another B.

Levine went along to Lowell to inquire about his grade. Lowell said, "You have come the farthest." Philip Levine asked Lowell why, then, he had received only a B. Lowell said, "I've already given out the As." Grading on the curve—so many As, so many Bs, and so forth—is corrupt in itself. (I offer a fresh way to grade M.F.A.-level creative writing in Chapter 10).

Unfortunately, the very questions that writing students ask teachers can ignite a negative power trip like the one Lowell visited upon Levine. Being asked to prophesy is a kind of ego entrapment. Students ask for prophecy. And a psychologically naïve teacher pinkens and becomes a prophet—"Yes, I think you might well become a writer," or "I think you should plan on just writing for family and friends or your own pleasure."

Anyone trained in clinical psychology or in decent administrative practice knows enough never, ever, to prophesy. A proper response to a student's request for a prophecy is along the lines of "Look—throw your heart and soul into your writing and let God take the foremost."

Creative-writing teachers usually have neither clinical skills nor administrative discipline, so they are at risk, when asked for advice or assessment, to swell a little, like Toad describing Toad Hall. Too bad, because the result is little to do with truth and much to do with low-level hurting of other people's feelings.

Scanty Teaching Owing to Ignorance

In both high schools and colleges, people are teaching both short fiction and creative nonfiction who have themselves written nothing or almost nothing of either genre. People who have written nothing but entries in their journals (to which they make no revisions) are hired to teach creative nonfiction. People who have written only nonfiction—

journal entries or memoirs or autobiography—are teaching people to write short stories.

This last phenomenon especially galls me, because although memoir writing is about whatever is or was going on in a particular person's life, and needs no other unifying principle, story at its classical, full potential, is poised across a universal theme and includes *at least two realized characters.* Its events are symbolic. A short story trembles with suffused meaning. The short story is a difficult art.

Adjunct and sometimes even faculty core instructors typically don't teach most of the possibilities in a short story at all: instead, they settle, if they are kindhearted, for encouraging their students to "fictionalize," as the wretched expression goes, some occasions in their own lives.

Five years pass. The memoir fictionalizers have now grown up into adjunct instructors who in turn will teach short-story writing. (Five years is approximately one generation in college-level pedagogy.) They cannot show writers how a full story is designed to bear meaning that goes well beyond the sensate stuff of one's own life. They may well never have heard of the concept.

To teach creative nonfiction as expanded journal entries or to teach the short story as tampered-with autobiography is like going out to the airport, getting into a handsome 757, and then teaching a student pilot how to taxi it back and forth, crossing to the outer tarmac, keeping the nosewheel pinned on the yellow line for parking the aircraft—all because no one told you that a 757 can *fly.* We would growl if medical schools allowed their second-year students to practice medicine the way college programs in creative writing invite second-year graduate students who have never published any essays or short stories to teach essay and short-story writing.

Let me give a specific example of procedural ignorance in nonfiction-writing teachers so you will see that this isn't just vituperation. An inexperienced creative-nonfiction-writing teacher will frequently tell student writers to outline their essays. Sometimes he or she will even ask to see what are called "rough drafts," thus too soon stiffening the skin of the subject. Few writers can alter their central, most delicate thinking once they have passed in a rough draft. By asking for advance outlining and the passing in of rough drafts the instructor shows that he or she doesn't grasp the actual dynamics of writing a piece of literature.

Teaching of writing by people ignorant of and unpracticed in teaching of writing is not, however, the fault of the teachers themselves. I never realized that until I was asked to teach a poetry-writing class. I have published five poems in my life, none of which is anything better than prose in long dress or white tie: none of my poems turns on metaphor; none of them turns on plot; and the language is uniformly earnest but banal. I love my own poetry—I reread it to myself once in a while—my poems are rhetoric on my favorite shrieky subjects—but the fact is they aren't real poetry. So I absolutely refused to teach the course. The hirer exclaimed, "Oh, but if you don't teach it, we can't offer the course."

It is the fault of the Congress, which won't provide enough money for public schools to hire enough teachers of the liberal arts. It is the fault of state legislatures that won't assign monies to their universities so they can hire artists to teach the literary arts. Please see the section of this chapter entitled "Teaching Spoiled Not by Instructors but by Government or University Policies."

A last point, lest my assessment seem gratuitously fierce: adjunct instructors and teaching assistants often do an apparent kindness to their students on the first day of a course. They typically say, "Look, we're in this together. I will be learning right along with you." Such warm collegiality and modesty are encouraging to writing students.

Nonetheless, we need to imagine the medical equivalent. What if a second-year medical student were authorized and paid—underpaid, perhaps, but paid—to operate on us? What with one thing or another, presurgical untranquilized patients have a tendency to look a little dispirited in the best of circumstances. Let us say the med student notices it.

Out of kindness, therefore, this second-year medical student wanders over to our gurney and looks down kindly. He or she tells us that we are in this thing together, and he or she will "be learning right along with us."

It is ridiculous for a writing teacher, whose ministrations we pay for, to "be learning right along with us."

To Market, To Market . . . Jiggety Jig

I mention the commercial mission in creative writing only because it is a reality. Commercialism is writing in which one colors both content and tone to suit a perceived market. This perceived market is usually considered by the commercial author to be a little less educated than the author takes himself or herself to be. "You have to have a hook," such authors tell themselves—as if the reader were a leghorn to be culled for today's pot. "You have to I.D. the audience and give them what they want . . . whatever it is."

Several decades ago Peter Elbow wrote eloquently against letting any thought of *audience* shape a piece of creative writing. He discussed this topic in several lights—the brightest of which is that if the soul is thinking *audience*, *audience*, *audience* it cannot at the same time be inquiring of itself, kindly but firmly, "What are we doing here?" I commend Elbow's classical defense of aiming for truth, letting profit leach away if it will.[7]

We have very little pressure in universities to write for a market other than literary or professional journals. Only a few high school teachers, probably those who find themselves teaching writing without any literary background, stumble into teaching people to aim at a market because they—the teachers—consulted commercial how-to books in good faith. They sincerely took *Writer's Journal* for the definitive basis of teaching. Almost every course or interactive site or message board for "writers" that I have seen on AOL or the Web advises the student writer about how to contrive something that will be salable in a large market. M.F.A. candidates at reputable universities are not taught to put such considerations of market before those of art.

Teaching Corrupted by Nihilism

Nihilism commonly takes two forms in creative writing: indifference to the *content* of a work of literature and disbelief in the possibility of teaching creative writing at all. Chapter 7, "Seven General Issues in Teaching Creative Writing," discusses both anticontent teaching and cynicism about whether or not writing literature can be taught at all. I mention the two forms of nihilism here only because both belong on any list of pedagogical corruptions.

Teaching Corrupted by Inappropriate Affiliation

I laughed the first time I heard Ted Solotaroff, then senior editor at HarperCollins, use his phrase "blurb sluts." He was speaking of people who send round their book galleys to one another to solicit a blurb. Soon they all owe each other. It is difficult to maintain a friendship, even a friendship of long standing, firmly built on the sand of both people being writers if one of you refuses to write a blurb for the other. So unwillingly you go ahead and agree to write the blurb. But then your friend writes a dull book. You will feel constrained to praise it, drivel or not. So you go ahead and praise it in order to save the friendship. Some authors even write blurbs without reading the work all the way through.

Blurb prostitution may not be a major form of corrupt affiliation, because much of the time literary friends *do* like each other's work. Similar taste is part of the reason they are friends. I suggest we look at the following kinds of corrupt affiliation and decide for ourselves how much of it is serious.

1. Graduate students truckle to their instructors because they need those instructors' recommendations in the future.
2. Members of the Associated Writing Programs of America sometimes promote one another for pleasant positions, rather than new, unknown people to whom they ought to be giving more ear.
3. Some students deliberately take coursework with famous people in order to get a recommendation from that instructor. The instructor may write a more positive recommendation than otherwise if that student has previously been a student of an associate who in turn might do the esteemed faculty member a favor (or a disservice, as the case may be).

I don't regard the problem of young-boy and young-girl network and old-boy and old-girl network as nearly so corrupting as it could be.

Reports from creative writing departments don't suggest anything like the rot we read in news releases about scientists promoting one another's work—sometimes, amazingly enough, even after the given piece of research has been proven to be spurious.

I mention corruption by affiliation only to remind people who will be teachers not to recommend your colleagues for publication before you have made yourself remember the beautiful work done by relatively *unknown* authors: *they* are the makers of literature who need all the who-you-know benefits you can possibly give them. A trick that works: keep a list of essays, stories, poems that you have briefly or greatly liked in magazines, as well as the copyright page information, so that

- you can take four or five minutes to write this author about your enthusiasm, and
- you have your note to that person in your file in case you might be able to offer him or her a leg up sometime in the future.

Other than ignoring more deserving people, the only harm done by heavy, mutually beneficial over-affiliation among writing teachers is a tendency to further mediocre literature. But if we have third- or fourth-class abilities we have a right to pursue our writing careers at third- and fourth-class levels. I shall never write a short story so exciting, exquisite, and moral as D. H. Lawrence's "The Rocking-Horse Winner" but I have the right to do as well as I can. And besides, all of us make such appalling failures of judgment. An American author whose work I tremendously respect told me that he couldn't get through *Anna Karenina* because he couldn't see that Tolstoy was really going much of anywhere with it.

Teaching Corrupted by Sloth

There are so many things I despise about the Roman Catholic Church—its ongoing authoritarianism and its history of torturing people—that it is hard for me to be fair. Still, I honor the fact that sloth made it into the Church list of mortal sins—lack of industriousness, not showing up for work, not being a warm body where needed, not doing the job you are paid to do. Sloth is far and away the most widespread and the second most horrible predation on people trying to learn how to do creative writing. I say second because the refusal of the Congress of the United States to fund new schools, to split our huge classrooms in half and to provide new and more teachers for each half, so that public school students can have the experience that goes on in our private schools, is the *most* horrible thing. (Besides, overlarge classrooms are a crime perpetrated against children, whereas the crime of sloth operating in our universities works against people who are already eighteen years old and may have some psychological immunity to it.)

First of all, most teachers know that peer reviewing doesn't teach anybody anything profound. Teachers keep using this teaching method for three reasons. One, it's what they've been doing, and mammals, including us, will keep doing what they've been doing if nothing waylays them. Two, they don't know what they'd do if they didn't do it—how would they run a class? And, three, they do it because it saves them hours and hours of time. It gets the students to do the teacher's job—that is, teaching each other.

The second form of sloth that teachers most commonly fall into is not reading students' work *midcourse*. It's quite common in creative-writing departments for a faculty member to announce that there will be a final paper for the course. Everyone works on his or her final paper throughout the term. That sounds like a very generous and very trusting arrangement. It sounds like independence. It sounds as though nobody's going to bully students about their material and that they'll work at their own speed, and so on. What finally happens, however, is that students hand in a final paper only at the end of the course, and the faculty member is or is not constrained to write comments on it. Perhaps the faculty member actually reads the paper through and does write some comment, in which case, even so, it's too late for the teacher to help the students with the rewriting or re-envisioning of their papers. A worse aspect: we have only that faculty member's word for it that he or she really did read through the paper at all.

A slothful teacher will make it very difficult for students to have a conference with him or her. Many creative-writing teachers do not respond when students send an e-mail saying, "When can I have a conference?" Such teachers do not return telephone calls. They don't want to have a conference with a student because there is little harder work than conducting a one-on-one conference with an intelligent student.

And here is a very peculiar psychological aspect of sloth—a psychological dynamic worthy of Clausewitz (the classical German psychologist on war) or of Machiavelli: some slothful creative-writing teachers actually whine to their students about finding time to do "their own work." Teachers should never take this tack with students. Students pay a thousand dollars or more to take a writing course. If the teacher bleats about finding time to do his or her "own work," students feel guilty about asking for what are their prepaid *rights* in the course. The teaching was contracted for. This practice of making students commiserate with faculty griefs, unprofessional at best, is so common that it sounds shrill to inveigh against it. An odd parallel is the very common practice of bullies, especially wife-beaters, to ask for pity from the very person they've been bullying. I am sorry that teachers beg students to sympathize with *them* for *their* having chiseled on their contract with students.

A slothful teacher commonly lies and breaks promises about the service that will be rendered to the student. The classic cases are the very rich writing teachers whom I will describe in further detail under the section of this chapter entitled "Corruption by Wixels." Wixels (David Ehrenfeld's nickname for World Class Scholars) may take $80,000 or $100,000 or $150,000 a year, for example, to drive out of New York one day a week to teach at a university. A frightful case: in the 1960s a famous writer (now deceased) lived in Manhattan and drove one evening a week to an outlying university to teach a course. He saw his SUNY students *only* during the weekly class period. The writer lied, claiming that he had read their M.A. theses. When cornered, he shrugged, merely remarking that if he had read those papers it would spoil his lifestyle. How such cavalier sloth got normalized seems very strange, but it did.

Slothful teachers often promise, then fail, to serve writing students by following through with common subsidiary responsibilities. In the America Online Writers' Club a now well-known teacher of writing reported that her core advisor for her doctoral committee told her that he was going to nominate her dissertation for a couple of awards. Later she found out, after direct, not very delicate inquiry, that he had missed both deadlines for submitting the nominations. As she pointed out on the message board of the AOL Writers' Club, she'd have been happier if he had never promised to do her that favor: then she wouldn't have felt the sting of his casual defection. Such forgetfulness is so common that M.F.A. students, being helpless to do anything more pointed, sometimes call up or e-mail the instructor near the time at which some sort of recommendation letter needs to be sent in. The poor students use an array of 1990s schmooze tactics for reminding power figures of their responsibilities to themselves—non-power figures: "I'm calling just to ask you if you have any questions that I can help with—any concerns about the recommendation at all." Shockingly, often the student finds that the task has clearly gone out of the head of the professor. Good thing the student made the call.

In some M.F.A. programs, graduate students can scarcely find anyone willing to be their advisor. Their program guarantees them an advisor, but as they make the rounds of all the appropriate faculty, and ask one after another to be their advisor, each faculty member is perfectly free to say he or she hasn't got time and can't take them on. If there are several universities in the same city, a university can circumnavigate this problem by saying, "Well, you can choose someone across town who is in a parallel position." Then the students are chasing down advisors in other colleges around the city while the university from which the student will get the degree has ducked out of its responsibility to provide an advisor. Those who ought to have advised the student in the first place are simply let off.

Worse, sometimes the director of a creative-writing program may even tell the students, "You must *make* this faculty member serve you." Sometimes this suggests that the director is so afraid of the slothful teacher that he or she won't do the necessary policing. That is grossly unfair. A graduate student shouldn't be expected to face off an authority figure who is already complacently settled into the habit of clipping students. The director of the creative-writing program himself or herself should be able to make a faculty member do the job he or she was hired to do.

Teaching Corrupted by Wixelism

> For who would bear the whips and scorns of time,
> Th' oppressor's wrong, the proud man's contumely . . .
> the insolence of office.
>
> —Hamlet 3.1.69–70

Professor David Ehrenfeld is a biologist at Rutgers University, where he teaches ecology and conservation. He is the author of several books, and he is a gallant idealist when it comes to preserving knowledge for future generations as well as teaching students to think. Ehrenfeld, as mentioned earlier, uses the term *wixels* to refer to world-class scholars who think they have the right not to teach beginning courses. They feel they may skimp on what teaching they do, and that they can be disrespectful of students' intellectual needs.

> Despite the starvation of teaching, universities are receiving and spending money as never before. Where is it going? The answer varies from school to school—at one it will be computer science, at a second genetic engineering, at a third high-energy physics—but in all cases the money is going to hire "world-class scholars" at world-class salaries, and to set them up in business. At my university, as at many others, world-class scholars have become a kind of academic consumer item, like fancy computer systems; our administrators refer to them as WCS's, or wixels. They are purchased on the open market. One wixel can cost tens of millions of dollars by the time the university is finished providing the building, space-age equipment, and numerous support personnel that the wixel has been promised. Wixels don't have time to teach, except for occasional cameo performances; they don't even have time for graduate students.
>
> Eventually, every asset that the university can lay hands on is hocked to pay for these wixels. Teaching budgets are slashed, teaching laboratories are converted into research space, and the salaries of professors who were foolish enough

> to teach or whose research is not in one of the glamorous areas are seized when these professors retire or, if untenured, inevitably fail to gain promotion. Soon, the only way the university can afford to keep its teaching program afloat is to hire a flock of temporaries. Not only are they cheap, but if they complain they can be fired.[8]

Being a slouch on the job is very attractive to social climbers, however. Slouching on the job and getting away with it shows others that you are top dog. Even as a child I noticed how senior officers or visiting potentates from another country love to amble past lines and lines of rigid soldiers who have to hold a brace. That the soldiers must be rigid and unnatural shows that they are minions. They move their rifles with staccato snap to parade rest or port arms or they rigidly cross their hands exactly perpendicular to their weapons by way of salute. But the reviewing officers lounge and stagger along. It's amazing they don't scratch themselves. Somehow *they* have the right not to look hardworking and unnatural.

Being proud of not working is the very core of wixelism. In creative-writing teachers, wixelism means that the teacher has the right to prepare casually for classes or to come late, not to answer letters or calls from students, not to attend student conferences. Wixels are famous and everyone should be glad that they are there at all. These world-class scholars give the university serious cachet. The students must get their kicks from admiring the teacher instead of getting their kicks from learning how to write.

I bring up this appalling situation because commonly—especially in corporations where the top brass openly, splendidly, leave early to play golf—but also in academic institutions, where the top brass spend minimal time on students' concerns—there is a lot of respect for authority and power—the power specifically *not* to do serious, gracious, generous work.

I have tried to think up various suggestions for how students might deal with wixels. None has worked so far. We need, therefore, a new, forceful solution to get a day's work out of these high-end sloths. In the meantime, here they are, in their dozens, teaching, and an M.F.A.

student needs some patchy ways to manage. Please see Navigating Creative-Writing Programs, on p. 29.

Teaching Spoiled Not by Instructors but by Government or University Policies

The principal predators of creative-writing teaching in America are, first, the United States Congress, and, second, our universities. The Congress keeps chipping away money from public education. The Congress indirectly frightens state legislators, who in turn chip money away from the liberal arts in their own universities. We need to consider this hypothesis: the Congress may well be the main predator of American children, and less directly of American college-age students.

I have taught children in private secondary schools—most recently at Andover and Shattuck–St. Mary's School. Twelve or fewer students sit in a room together: their teacher discusses course issues with them respectfully. They are not crowded forty-five or fifty in a room with a teacher who feels depraved by hopelessness.

Congress could divide every American public school classroom at least in half. How heavenly it is for someone to learn creative writing at the age of sixteen or seventeen *in a small, polite group*! I once visited a class of twelve students at Milton Academy. A student raised his hand and said in a courteous, relaxed voice, "Ms. Bly, would you please say that again, what you just said, in other words, so I can tell whether you're doing fuzzy thinking or whether I didn't get your meaning right?" What a wonderful thing for a student to say! He spoke politely, but his easy frankness said that he trusted that he was in a civilized environment where serious discourse could take place. Therefore, he didn't have to act tricky, surly, or indirect. Instead he was direct (plenty direct) and courteous. With enough funding, every American public school writing class could have twelve or fifteen class members. In the current classroom environment teachers don't know who is bright and who is not bright and who has possibilities and who does not. If we have twenty million students in ghetto schools we can't tell whether or not nineteen million of them might be wonderfully educable people.

So I do not forgive the Congress for ruining public school settings by failing to spend money on kids.

Universities classically gather prestige by how much *research* they produce, not how well they teach. A university takes great pride in being known as a research university and not a teaching university. A teaching university is sometimes dubbed a "nonresearch university." Funding pours into the research maws of this academic food chain. Because grants usually require expensive, partial matching by the receiving institution, they actually cost the university money. The university must conserve budget somewhere. Where?—usually in liberal arts courses where legislators tend to chintz anyway, and to which the armed services never give any money. The university then hires cheap help, made up of the teaching assistants, or TAs, and adjunct faculty members.

Navigating Creative-Writing Programs

Given the mix of wixels (discussed earlier) and TAs and adjunct faculty members, how should students make their way through creative-writing programs?

a. Be sensible about hotshot teachers. A world-class hotshot teacher may give writing students a marvelous experience. He or she may read aloud from elegant literature or from the latest quarterlies to which students might not otherwise be exposed. I would look over any famous faculty member's syllabus ahead of time, then visit the course for two sessions to see if anything on the syllabus is really going to happen in class. Watch to see if the famous, star-system professor is going to allow any open discussion. Don't automatically withdraw from an all-lecture class. We don't need a good back-and-forth discussion process all the time. If you need much more acquaintance with the charm or the craft of literature, one or two straight lecture courses might be the right idea.

On the other hand, be alert to whether or not this star teacher is going to conduct all the conversation simply about his or her own career, enriched with nostalgic anecdotes or trivia about other famous authors or professors. There is almost no cognitive use to being suffused with stories about famous writers, although the ambiance—as one listens—is literary and one feels let in on some inside circle. If that's going to be the talk, I would withdraw quickly. But first you need to think about this: if that professor *loves literature,* both American literature and foreign literature, and is going to read to you and point you toward beautiful books, you should stay the course. It's worth it to learn from someone who loves the field. In reading and writing, a teacher's love of literature should carry more weight than his or her vaunting egoism. That is an infuriating truth, of course.

b. Be sensible about posers. If your prospective teacher announces to you, following the current fad, that creative writing simply "cannot be taught," I would leave the course. What that teacher is really saying is that with whatever pedagogy he or she has in hand, creative writing cannot be taught. Leave, because you need someone who *does* know useful methods.

c. Be sensible about adjunct faculty. Sometimes adjunct faculty members teach wonderfully because they are true lovers of literature who are scrounging to make a living. They may well regard themselves as vastly but honorably underpaid. Occasionally, however, teaching by adjuncts is a travesty.

If you find yourself in a class taught by a TA or an adjunct teacher who apparently can't help you much, try for a better section. Failing that, I would resign myself to taking comfort *from the class itself.* After all, any room of fifteen or twenty people who, like you, want to write serious nonfiction is potentially a pleasant place. Every one of these people has somehow escaped their family members, their neighbors, and their clergy because they want to speak from deeper inside themselves than family members, neighbors, and clergy have stomach for. Your classmates are potentially good company, and so, usually, is the teacher. You might want to keep your writing to yourself, but ask all the questions you can. There might be some kind of wonderful eccentric genius in the room: if the TA fails to discern the genius's presence, then you may be the one to point it out. One word of warning: try to avoid using low-key language even if your instructor and everyone else in the room is using it. Low-key, desultory language can erode your own inner feeling. In some sense, your brain trusts your mouth, which of course is its mouth, and the only mouth it has.

There are a few reasons for being kind to a TA or an adjunct teacher. Viciously underpaid as they are, they are expected to do the work cast lightly aside by the wixels in the department. Adjuncts find the university system of hiring adjunct teachers handy in the same way that people who work for McDonald's are glad to pick up low-paid work when they need it. A subset dynamic of adjunct writing teachers is that they're likely to feel righteous about the hours and hours they put in, even if the service they provide is incompetent, if kindhearted.

Such teachers are usually young, and, therefore, if they are Americans, they may have spent thousands of hours of their formative years in groups. They have been heavily socialized. Life has taught them to adapt amiably to others. Very likely they regard such adaptation as a virtue. They are at risk not to recognize the historical moment—that is, not to recognize originality or excellence here and there in their students' manuscripts. This should be some small comfort: we creative writers don't suffer so much from group drowning as do students in theological schools. Freshman classes in seminaries are full of people who are socialized rather than virtuous; that is, they are very kind about getting along with others. They suffer fools impressively. They blend well. They generously share their nearly neutral insights. They are team-builders. If they ever met up with people of such noncollaborative leadership styles as Jesus or the Buddha, their response would be civility, not gratitude for prompting.

No matter how a generally oversocialized adjunct faculty is at risk to read all the students' papers without noticing that one of them is extraordinary (since oversocialized people don't believe in the extraordinary), this teacher is still a creature standing apart from the junk culture. Unlike most theological students, writing teachers really do *believe in originality*. They know literature is a practice involving originality, and they *want* to praise it when they see it. But preprofessional writing teachers want to be encouraging without making distinctions. With hearts full of goodwill they slather encouragement over *all* of the manuscripts. Sometimes their students feel caught between a slug and a soft place.

Adjunct writing teachers are always working in haste. They may teach four courses at once in order to make a decent living. Some of them may have read so little literature themselves that intense beauty or fervor of thought or bright shock of wit may be literary values they have never developed even the slightest taste for. Whoever demonstrates beauty, fervor, or wit in their manuscripts may not receive appropriate encouragement.

Finally, adjunct faculty and TAs cannot be expected to know modern teaching concepts such as the psychological logic of asking open-ended questions versus asking yes-or-no questions about a student's intuitions or intentions in a given manuscript. This is absolutely not the fault of the TA or the adjunct instructor. After all, everybody is ignorant of any given methodology until he or she learns it. The job of writing teachers and prospective writing teachers, then, is to learn all the methodology we can if we are writers, and practice it for our own benefit. Later, if someone wants to hear about it from us, we can teach it to them.

2.

A Fundamental Mistake in How We Learn to Write: Skipping the Long Middle Stage of Writing

> It is no use thinking, however, that the writing of poems—the actual writing—can accommodate itself to a social setting; even to the most sympathetic social setting of a workshop composed of loyal friends. It cannot. The work improves there and often the will to work gets valuable nourishment and ideas. But, for good reason, the poem requires of the writer not society or instruction, but a patch of profound and unbroken solitude.
>
> This is the reason. The poem, as it starts to form in the writer's mind, and on paper, can't abide interruption. I don't mean that it *won't* but that it *can't*.
>
> —**Mary Oliver, "Solitude," in *A Poetry Handbook***

When I lived in the country, I took my car to be repaired by a man named Dick Larson, outside the small town of Madison, Minnesota. One of my children had let the car float into another car at a stop sign. I wanted the door knocked back out to its original shape. I expected Dick would wrap a hammer up in some soft cloth and bang on the door fabric from the inside until the whole thing looked right. Instead, he brought out an odd-looking device that *pulled* the exterior door fabric until it was perfectly straight.

I said, "That's a strange-looking thing. Look how fast it did it. You didn't have to hammer on the door."

"It's a door-straightening jack," he said.

I said, "Well, where'd you get it from?"

Modestly, he gave me to understand that he had invented it. I asked around a bit, the way we do in a small town. Someone told me he'd heard that Dick Larson's door-straightening jack was being used all over the world. Then I happened to mention the tool to another man. I said, "Did you know that Dick Larson has invented a thing called a door-straightening jack that's really good for fixing up wrecks, and it's being used all over the world?"

And he said, "Where's he doing that?"

I said, "His body shop, south of town on the east side of U.S. 75."

The man said, "No," with a long, drawn-out *o*, and added, "He hasn't invented anything like that."

I said, "Yes, he has too. I saw it."

And he said, "No" again, ending with that long, drawn-out note—with a tone of great confidence. "No," he repeated in his tone of infinite satisfaction, "I drive by that place all the time, and if there was anything going on in there I'd know it."

This man made two wondrous assumptions: first, that you can see ingenuity right through the slap-up steel walls of a pole building, and, second, that originality isn't much anyhow. I was informing him of a very original invention, but he chose not to ask me even one question about it. He chose not to know about it. In fact, he insisted on not knowing about it. *Place* interested him, as in something going on or not going on on the east side of U.S. 75, but *idea* did not interest him.

I have read little theory about why some people feel threatened, even indignant, at the prospect that an original invention has been created somewhere *near* them. An invention in Paris does not offend somebody from western Minnesota. But when people learn of an invention right in their own town, not everyone will be glad that the ingenious fellow—in this case, Dick Larson the auto-body expert—is from their town. Others will insist he didn't invent anything and there is no such invention. I don't understand all the psychological dynamics of people's disliking originality, but here are some guesses: if a townsman thought up an invention, it makes me feel inferior. Therefore I will pretend that he did not think up an invention so that I can go on feeling I'm just as good as he is. Another possibility: there is something socially wrong with inventiveness, just in itself. If being different from others is a gaffe, then a kind neighbor would do you the favor of keeping the news of your originality hushed up for you.

An instance of such a kindhearted gesture touched me some years ago. The property assessor came on a periodic check around our farmhouse and barn to inventory our buildings. Her job as assessor meant she needed to see what kind of a herd we had and what shape the barn was in. She had to make sure that on our ten acres of what's called "farmstead property"—that is, property that's not working fields or woods—we hadn't put up any new buildings not listed on her clipboard.

As soon as she got near the barn she saw my enclosure with our five sheep. She looked them over and she glanced at me with increased respect. "Ah," she said in a deep tone, "you've got sheep."

The assessor happened to be a sheepherder. She loved sheep. Since you who read this are probably writers, and fewer than 2 percent of the population of the United States still makes a living farming, you may not know that to people who only casually raise sheep—as I was doing at the time—"a sick sheep is a dead sheep"; that is, we second-rate lamb raisers don't know enough about sheep to save their lives. But to a born sheep woman like this property assessor, every sheep is a very interesting issue.

I took her to see and count our few Shropshires. Her eyes lighted up. The sheep milled about. I knew those sheep. I'd raised them, but I didn't like them because as animals go they were extraordinarily stupid. The assessor bent into a little crouch: her face was suddenly vigilant, like the face of someone with an eye pressed to a microscope. She said, "That one sheep's sick, that ewe outside to the right."

I said, "Yeah, is that right?"

"Yes, it is," she said. "That one sheep's sick. You ought to do something about that."

Then she looked at me with great camaraderie. She repeated, in the warmest way, "I didn't know you raise sheep."

Our family didn't usually get much respect from property assessors. We were among the last people in the county to get plumbing up to our house. Our buildings were poor, and we owned no stock—except a few leghorns and these five sheep, one of them sick.

After the property assessor got though outdoors she came into the house. She noticed that our walls were lined with built-in bookcases. She did not fail to notice that the bookcases were built by me—she ran a deft finger over where I had missed toenailing the upright supports into the shelves. The bookcases were only pine. They were nicked.

She looked around the room with the professional deadbeat expression of property assessors. At last she said, "Ja, well, how many books have you got then?"

I said, "I think it's between five thousand and eight thousand."

She said, "Well," and now she was writing on her clipboard, "I'll put you down for no books."

I said, "But we've *got* all those books. Why do you put us down for no books? Listen, that's the one thing we *do* have. We haven't got a television set, but we've got all these books."

I didn't want to be taxed on those books, but a person likes to be known as a person of *property*, as Galsworthy would have appreciated.

The woman's response was mysterious to me then, and it still is. She said, "Nobody else has any books. Why should you?"

Her disrespect for diversity didn't come of being threatened or envious. She knew that owning all those books was improper. She didn't want me to look ridiculous in the eyes of anyone who would find out that we had between five thousand and eight thousand books in our house.

These anecdotes about the door-straightening jack and the books illustrate how resistant some people feel to whatever isn't yet part of a given community's conventional wisdom. Both examples are classically rural. An urban person might well say, "Yes, well—that's rural life for you—cozy, friendly, convivial, rigid, and utterly without intellectual curiosity."

But awful psychological dynamics cross all classes and demographics. Scrupulous scholars are wise to be skeptical of an as yet unproved theory, but if they resist the theory without asking any questions about it, their resistance is obduracy. We blithely associate obduracy with provincials or with Prussian militarists, but obduracy is the mulish behavior of anyone of any background who fears new energy and ideas entering into his or her field of expertise. How dullish parents hate it when the exciting aunt comes to visit! Our children hang on her every word. Worse, the aunt gives us fine-tuned insights into our children that we hadn't thought of. "You've done wonderfully with Hillary!" she exclaims. "No wonder she has such a sharp ear for nuance!"

We give as starry and sparkling a smile as we can while we think to ourselves, "What's this 'nuance' drivel, and what's it got to do with our Hillary?"

And what is this drivel about a manuscript being written in three stages?

The Three Stages of Writing a Manuscript

The conventional wisdom has it that to write a piece of literature, first you have the inspiration, and then you do literary fixes on it. But that skips a long middle stage in which the expertise needed involves psychological, not artistic tools. Why is it that the very idea of there being this middle, psychological stage meets instant resistance—no questions asked—from writing teachers but not from writing students? A proper skeptic, it seems to me, would ask: "If there is some long middle stage of manuscript writing that we haven't been bothering with, what are the assumptions and methodology of it?"

For the most part, though, writing teachers muddle along using ineffective, even damaging pedagogy because they don't learn anything else to do. Even if they accepted the idea of this long middle stage in every piece of writing for which one needs psychological, not critiquing skills, they wouldn't know which psychological skills are wanted and where to go to get them.

The skills of deepening oneself (in solitude), never mind showing others how to deepen themselves, are very different from the skills of orchestrating group critiquing.

The three identifiable stages for doing any work of literature are inspiration, spiritual deepening, and literary fixing.

Inspiration: Taking a Notion to Put Something Down on Paper

For decades, since 1942, the conventional interpretation of the cave drawings at Lascaux and Altamira was that by painting on those cave roofs the Stone Age human beings somehow magically could control the animal population for the next year. Such underestimation of other people's imagination and numinous inventiveness is a folk habit, the habit of being incredulous about or indifferent to other people's *inner* life.

I never had any idea why Paleolithic humankind made those paintings until I pretended I was a Paleolithic person.

It was much harder work to paint those ceilings than one might think. The artists had to work perched on high, ten- to fifteen-foot scaffolding. The cave roofs were much higher then than they are now, because stalagmite formation had not yet built up the floors. Stone Age artists used sophisticated paint, what's more. They didn't grab up a handful of mud from the cave floor and make colors from it. They didn't use dirty old lampblack or vegetable dyes. They actually ground manganese oxide for black; iron oxide for red, brown, yellow, and violet; porcelain clays for white; and copper oxide for blue. Their blue was perishable and doesn't survive the millennia to our time as did the other colors, but they did make blue paint. They took pains grinding these minerals, then mixed their paints with limestone water from the cave floors to make the colors adhere to the statues or walls or ceilings.

These old Stone Age people were using the highest technology they had in the service of a very impractical cause—namely, creating beauty or praising animal beauty. They painted pictures and made statues thousands of years before human beings made pottery, and it would be actually tens of thousands of years before they decorated pottery with such paint. Thus the artistic drive—their inspiration, their taking the notion to put a picture onto the ceiling—predates their handicrafts. Wanting art, wanting to express our spirit, goes way back with us. Unlike other interests of Stone Age people, this one is still with us.

I was furious as a youngster and as a young adult when I read the usual texts in archaeology that said that Paleolithic man wanted to control the animals by making those paintings—as if his aims were merely practical. In my middle age I finally had the sense one day deliberately to pretend I was a Paleolithic painter who had just killed an animal, dragged it to the cave entrance, and meant to eat it later. But I noticed the gloss lost from its coat and that its upward-turned eye was going to stone. I felt bad about the sight, but inside my cortex were two realizations: I was still glad I had killed the beast, and I would be delighted to eat it. What's more, in a few days, I meant to kill again. So, therefore, to sum this up in the brief if flavorless style of psychotherapists, I felt five feelings at once: pity and shame for my prey, pride in being able to make the world give me a meal, gratitude for the beauty of the animal I had killed, and resignation: I had no intention of becoming a vegetarian. I would kill again, and soon.

I think it very possible that each of us wants to make art, feels inspired, and hides from the ironical family and the coarse neighbors in order to write or paint. And we must make a living as well. We love the beauty of the creatures we come across, and we are sorrowful we will kill them, but we are not hopeful about changing our own behavior. There is just the right tension among those feelings to drive a homo sapiens to art.

Having contradictory feelings doesn't lead to either governance or theology. It leads to art. Our ideas about government have blessedly changed since Stone Age chiefdomry. Our ideas about theology, if we have them, are much less anthropomorphic and totemic. But our ideas about art have scarcely changed at all. We still find the universe and our fellow creatures beautiful, but we still wreck or kill it and them for profit. Or we are attractively pensive but unprotesting while others wreck and kill because we own shares of a firm that is wrecking and killing for profit. We experience some of the same tensions the Paleolithic cave painter would seem to have felt.

I can't know exactly what any other person's first inspiration is to write something. But all of us have this much in common: once we start to write, we are blown clear of either the low-hearted nihilism or the jaunty nihilism that lie like a heavy gas in the low pockets of our ordinary day.

The Long Middle Stage: Spiritually Deepening Your First Draft

Good teachers know intuitively that one must develop and develop and develop the original inspiration before starting to do any traditional "literary" fixes. Nonetheless the majority of creative-writing teachers allow a student to "put up for workshopping" work that is still so close to the original inspiration that the student's mind has not yet lived it through. Even elementary-school writing teachers ask their youthful writers to share what they've done in small groups. The group or the teacher and the writer and the group all together then conspire to do literary fixes on a student's partly developed inspiration.

Here is the crux of what to do versus what *not* to do just after an inspired first draft: if we take our manuscript into a social and sociable situation, kind-minded others will suggest *adding* to the inspiration. "Oh, put in more! Give us more!" they will say. Even if we feel oppressed by the language of the group—phrases like "writer's block" and "flesh it out," this last being a phrase that takes me straight to a slaughterhouse—the group is unmistakably right: our first draft wants *more*, but not more added on top: it needs more from underneath.

The problem is: how, exactly, does one "develop and develop and develop" the first inspired draft of two minutes ago or a week ago or a year ago? We know some attractive end results we may want—metaphors instead of reiterated bald statements (if we are writing poetry or nonfiction); an anecdote evoking a vivid scene—in any case, *more*. More feeling, more idea. Developing our inspiration means not only returning to our first inspiration, but, if possible, taking a mental swim *beneath* that first inspiration.

Here is our first inspiration.

Here is the metaphor our psyche picks up when a group of peers suggests that we add more to our manuscript.

But whatever we add should go *under* the original inspiration, not piled on top of it. Let me change the metaphor to show how different going beneath something is from adding to the top of something: This time let's see our inspiration as a ship.

A group of peers suggests we add more.

The sea is stuff of the mind, much of it unconscious. But never mind the sea for the moment. We are diving down to look at something enchanting and scary—namely the underside of the hull of the inspiration ship. The hull is scary, gliding hugely along in the half dark as it does. The underside of a ship may, indeed, be built from the bottom of the keel up, but it is designed *never to be seen in the course of everyday use.* Its job is to move through a heavier and many times more sonorous element than our element.

If our first inspiration needs to be looked at from below, we needn't add supercargo to improve on that inspiration. We need to examine what lies below, from inside and out.

Peer critics are usually polite, considerate colleagues, so they offer what they can. "I'd like to know more about such and such," they tell us. No one has told them to ask why the hull was built to such-and-such a draft or such-and-such a strength.

In fact, middle-class life is short on conversations that buck us up to dive overside and examine our mind's inventions while holding our breath. American living rooms don't ring with talk about one's inner love of truth, or inner love of beauty, or inner love of goodness or one's inner hatred of meaninglessness or inner despair over or inner fear of cruelty. We count on preaching in churches or the encouragement from elementary and high school English teachers, or courses in philosophy, or the skilled encouragement of psychotherapists both to light and to preserve our inner fires, if inner fires are to be lighted and preserved.

Those outer resources are still there, but they are there only for ever smaller and smaller numbers of people. Fewer and fewer teachers are teaching in situations where they're even able to attend to the minds of their students, never mind help them develop any inventiveness. Most Americans have never had a chance to write literature. Even clergypeople, who even in Kierkegaard's day were a scattershot source of learning, are now less devoted to helping parishioners figure out their mind-sets than in trying to create feelings of sweetness and sociability and belonging across their parish committees. Few clergypeople set themselves to helping an individual person to dive into *difficult* feelings and thinking. Very few Americans, only people with deep enough pockets, use philosophically inclined psychotherapists to help them deepen the meaning of their lives. Only educated people benefited from Viktor Frankl's logotherapy.

This inaccessibility to wisdom leaves English teachers to pick up for children, young people, and, now in the thousands, older people, the work of protecting their inspirations.

Perhaps writers need to learn how to protect their own inspirations. Here's a scenario. We should try saying to ourselves, "Stage one was my first inspiration, and I am going to protect it throughout stage two of my working on this manuscript. I am not going to do any public literary fixing until I know the underside of my idea. I promise myself not to be distracted by the slightest practicality if it shows its head. I certainly will keep clear of friends and loved ones. (Note: there are now several books out by authors who say they showed their work to a trusted love one. The loved one made some dispassionate remark—usually some sort of suggestion about craft—and the young writer then wrote nothing for *years*. Moses was a moral genius, so he saw the good of a burning bush. Most people live so suffused with practicality they would have taken Moses's bush for a brushfire and doused it. Our tendency is to douse our own fires.)

A word about how I came to see that a first inspiration must be kept private. Like so many others, I was on the receiving end of the affectionate little put-downs of my first work that family members and close friends dole out. Then, purely by mishap, I started psychotherapy. For the first time in my life I was asked a question about what lay *beneath* something I had just said. The conversation did not move on. It stayed *there.* I felt nearly faint with hope for something I'd never known existed. Usually when we fervently *want* something, it is something we've seen or at least heard of. I had never seen basic empathy practiced, and I didn't know anybody who had even heard of it. People in my life didn't say, "I certainly hope Santa Claus brings me a fifty-minute experience of being listened to and then being asked to go *underneath* what I just thought. And I want another human being's *silence* and attention while I try to do it."

A happy side effect of being asked to go deeper is that we begin to believe we do have a deep idea underneath the idea we so excitedly blurted out or jotted down as a first stanza or paragraph. Most people, even writers, believe that they themselves are shallow. No one has behaved in any way that would make them believe they weren't shallow. No one has asked them minutely to revisit what they just said and state the feelings they had at the moment they said or wrote it.

This kind of revisiting is not a skill of traditional literary criticism. It is a skill of 1990s interpersonal communications. The greatest and most life-changing of communication skills is empathic inquiry. We need it for creative-writing pedagogy. I will explain it in Chapter 3. We can use this process to help ourselves and others through the long middle stage of any literary manuscript.

Literary Fixing

The third stage of the writing process starts when we decide that all the drafts we've labored over somehow now contain all we can hope for from this piece of writing. Now we want to make the writing sensible and beautiful. We want no loose ends—no loose ends of argument or of characters or of settings. If it's fiction, we want all of the characters' fates to have been solved one way or another. If it's nonfiction we want the arguments and the metaphors to be as clear and gracious and pungent as we can make them. We want our work to be more metaphorical than adjectival. Symbol, after all, is deeper than anecdote.

No matter which form our work seems to be taking—poetry, nonfiction or fiction—we want the piece to be as brief as it can be without losing any fine tendrils; that is, no paragraph should duplicate a literary effect achieved in an earlier paragraph or stanza.

A word on brevity: brevity closes the gap between exposition and direct revelation. Some of the best literary fixing one can do involves combining exposition with strong feeling.

Here is exposition by itself: "It was a wonderful day so I spent it raking the lawn."

Here is exposition in which strong feeling has been brought into the work so early that the manuscript gallops into revelation just as fast as it accomplishes the exposition. "I was amazed to find myself so angry all the while that I raked. I had gone outside to rake because it was a wonderful day. But the anger at [such and such a horrific event—whatever it is] made me rake with a vengeance."

Those examples aren't numinous, but they illustrate a major difference between beginning prose writers and mature prose writers. Beginners usually tackle one thing at a time—usually an extrovert's sort of thing, such as fine weather. They want to say something and make sure the reader knows it. An old hand wants to work in some of the deeper, central feeling of the essay, so that the reader will get dropped right into the very core of the piece while still being given the mere stage business—nice day, leaves, rake. That's a case of achieving brevity.

In this third stage, making literary fixes, a writer is not harmed by having a group there to help him or her with it. On the other hand, I can't help noticing that groups aren't really much good at doing literary fixes. Students, too, report impatience with the halting pace of group critiquing. Seldom do groups of fellow writers suggest a change that hasn't been suggested a thousand times. Groups commonly miss, or at least give too little attention to, the subtle points of a writer's prose. Members of a group balk at saying anything unusual, lest they look like fools.

There are dozens of good books about how to make literary fixes. Please refer to Chapter 6, Literary Fixes, for a more in-depth discussion of this stage of the writing process and for the names of authors and guides to help you in this stage of your writing.

3.

Using Empathic Questioning to Deepen Your First Draft

> *Sempre con sentimento e espressione, Gesangvoll mit der innigsten Empfindung, Sehnsuchtvoll.* (With constant feeling and expression, songfully with the most inner feeling, soulfully.) Those were not orders Minnesotans gave one another.
>
> —**Bill Holm, "The Uses of Beethoven in Western Minnesota"**

These are also not exhortations commonly given in either the tough or the supportive kind of workshop. Writing "songfully" or "with the most inner feeling" is not advice most groups give their members at any time.

Nor is it the advice that the more superficial parts of our brain give the deeper parts of our brain. Anyone will agree that rural people don't advise one another to speak or to play music or to write with strong inward feeling. Rural people usually give each other practical advice. Beginning writers need to realize that workshop members, too, in fact cheerful colleagues, members of groups of any kind, will consciously or unconsciously bend us away from our strongest feelings.

But why would these kindly disposed people, our colleagues in the enterprise of becoming writers and of helping other writers, *not* steer us to our strongest feelings? I think the answer lies in the nature of working groups—or "intentional" groups, to use the social-work word for people gathered especially to do a particular task.

Such groups want, first of all, to strike a *general affectionate tone.*

Just looking at the others' friendly faces around the U-shaped table softens our hearts. We feel collegial. If we have come from families who wittily discouraged us or even outright sneered at our writing, we are all the gladder to be with like-minded people—our writers' group, if that's what we are, or our classmates' group, if we are in an academic program. We are in this thing together. We say one thing or another gently to one another. We pass along to one another some insightful comment from a new writers' manual. Someone answers, "That resonates with me, all right." Someone else says, "I am so glad that you are experiencing the same literary etc. and psychological etc. that I am struggling with." Others join in. Someone says, "And yet, I find that at the same time I etc., etc."

Conversations about process are sincere enough. I object to them only because like oil poured on water, they do not allow whatever swims up from the deeps to breathe. Habitual conversation about process kills the *adventuresomeness* we need to feel not five percent of the time but nearly *all* the time.

We are going to have to be adventurous because after we have jotted down an inspired rough draft or two on our own we must continue to keep clear of the others. Each of us must ask our own mind, "What else are you feeling? What are the many, many other separate ideas in there? What is going on for you in there?" This is where the empathic inquiry technique comes in.

Many beginning nonfiction writers, like poets, can break out of too narrow an emotional scope by simply asking themselves an empathic question or two. Writers can learn to open the connections between quite inconsonant passions in their own mind.

Empathy is an "intentional" *procedure*, designed only *to help a person identify, and follow up on, his or her own feelings and ideas*. By definition empathy *cannot be corrupt*. If you are conducting a conversation designed to make another person compliant, what you are practicing isn't empathy but *industrial psychology*—a very different animal. Or if you are conducting a conversation designed to make the speaker reverse his or her opinions so that he or she will agree with *yours*, then what you are practicing is not empathy but philosophical debate, like Socrates's conversations—again a very different animal.

All the questions that we ask when we use an empathic inquiry format on our own minds are designed both to deepen our original idea and to give ourselves credit for having had an idea with a lot more to it than the few words we've slapped down so far. We assume that underneath our original impulse to write was at least one particular emotion or vision.

We are going to treat that original impulse as if it were a decent-looking stranger in our own mind. We will ask it inviting questions. Another way to put it: we will regard this stage of the writing process as a *massive psychological project.* After we have questioned ourselves about the deeper subject lying just under the subject we have written down so far, we want to wake up all connections between this deeper subject and other deeper feelings firing about here and there in our terrific memories. This last part—the tracking of small fires—is what leads poets and also nonfiction writers toward metaphor. Such outcroppings of fire look like *symbol* to theologians. And to children, who love mind play at least as passionately as do thoughtful adults, making funny connections is literally an exquisite pleasure.

Empathic Inquiry

We may all be sick to death of the word *empathy*, since it is not just overused but wrongly used. Empathic questioning is an exact skill, not just some sort of high-end sympathy, although a lot of people probably will take it for that. The process is not some vague conversation that is especially sympathetic, although empathy is never unsympathetic.

The model offered here, which is called *basic empathic questioning* by most people who use it, is *not a healing model.* For that reason it is not a tool that psychotherapists use *on its own.* Please be very clear that our endeavor, in this middle stage of working on a manuscript, is not a healing or therapeutic endeavor. Our project is literary: we will use a few tools from healers to help us through this phase of the writing process. We pick up their tools because they are plainly better for helping writers elucidate their own minds than those we are in the habit of using.

A Five-Step Format for Basic Empathic Questioning

1. The first step (often completely missed!) is deciding to hear our own thoughts or others' at all. Our usual experience is this: Someone starts talking, and, being nice people, we listen for a minute or two. Then we decide we know what he or she is saying, or "where they're coming from," so we quit listening. If we have good manners we let him or her go on talking, but in our hearts we are really just waiting for the other person to quit so we can talk.

2. The second step is emptying yourself of *your own point of view* or of any association of *yours* that comes to mind as the speaker speaks.

> *Bad Example 1*: Say the speaker says, "I got a little bashed up in the hockey game." Sometimes people respond to a remark like that with "Yeah? Well, I nearly broke two fingers in volleyball, and *that* was just in *practice*, forget a game."
>
> *Bad Example 2:* The speaker says, "Jesus told a great story about an older son who got it about property values but didn't get it about love [the Prodigal Son]," to which the other person replies, "Well, there have always been a lot of storytellers around. Buddha told stories a good four hundred years before Jesus did."

In both of these examples, the listener rushed into contributing slants of his or her own, instead of staying with the speaker's remarks. The dullest human conversation is constructed this way.

3. Ask the person who just spoke (or yourself) some open-ended (not yes-or-no) questions about what he or she just said. Most Americans have *never once* been asked to enlarge on, or refine, anything they have just said. Here is where we get a sense of how manipulative Socrates let himself be with those yes-or-no questions, designed half to help readers think and half to show us up for being inconsistent. Empathy is *nothing like Socratic questioning*. The usual aim of empathy, at this point, is to collect further *data* from the speaker, further reported *feeling*, and further reported *meaning attached to the reported feelings*. Why? To help the speaker himself or herself pull up the data, pull up the feelings involved, and be

conscious of the meaning he or she attached to it all back then—and the meaning he or she attaches to it now. (This approach is the opposite of industrial psychology!) The empathic questioner helps others become more like themselves. The empathic questioner does *not* help people slide into agreement with the questioner.

4. In your own words, paraphrase what the person has just said, as you understand it. Ask the person if you have it right, and give him or her a chance to correct what you have said. Sometimes the speaker says, "Oh, you have it right, all right, but now that I hear you saying it aloud in *your* voice, I realize it isn't exactly right. I *thought* I meant that, but what I see *now* is . . ."—in which case the emphatic listener starts all over again with the speaker, because here is a new idea.

Here is a simple but clear example: The empathic listener has just remarked, "Is this right? In your experience two plus two makes at least three if not more?" The original speaker answers: "Yes, I did say that. I think that's what I meant, all right, but now that I hear *you* say it aloud, in *your* voice, I've changed my mind. I think two plus two just plain unequivocally makes four. I am willing to commit to that idea."

5. Here is the part of the empathy format that few outside of social workers and existential therapists know about: it is that the empathic person helps the speaker look *forward* and *plan ahead* free-spiritedly. The empathic person says something along the lines of "OK. Given those data, feelings, and meanings you've just reported, what do you see as a good direction to take from here? What might some of your goals be for now and for the future?

When we use empathic inquiry in writing creative nonfiction we ask these questions of our various selves. (If we were writing a story, we would ask these questions of our characters.)[1]

Teachers do well to practice empathic inquiry with student writers, but the most valuable process is for writers to practice empathic questioning with themselves. If we writers learn to do this, we can do it all our lives. We won't then have to keep returning to writing classes for another fix.

Psychotherapists and clinical social workers often start off with a basic empathy format like the one I describe here, but they are ready at any second to interrupt that process with a "confrontation" or an "intervention." They do that in order to help someone swiftly cut through some stubborn knot in their thinking or feeling.

We writers and teachers of writers never practice confrontation or intervention for any reason. In fact, if an English teacher or creative-writing teacher does practice confrontation or intervention, that teacher is being intrusive and inappropriate. Our purpose is to awaken, and to give confidence to, *the imagination*—imagination being the connection-making aspect of human intelligence.

When we set about waking our own imaginations we hit harsh rubble. Say that we have been bullied all our lives. Say we have been culturally deprived in any way. If we are over four or five years old we may already have taken some bullying or incorporated some anti-intellectual circuitry right inside our personalities. We may sneer at our own deeper thoughts. Children jeer at themselves. Adults jeer at themselves. Sneering at ourselves is a copycat crime. We have what the pop-psych people call "internalized" the bullying that was visited upon us years ago from outside. Our habitual mind-set may bully our inner nature. Empathic questioning is a kind, cool-handled tool, not just to encourage our imagination, but to fend off all enemies of our deeper selves, enemies that include our *shallow* selves.

A great blessing of empathy is that when we use it to help ourselves in any kind of creative writing, the process shows that yes, we may have the emotions we thought we had but we have others at the same time. Here's a coarse example: a writing student exclaims, "Get off my back. I just want to write salacious sex and salacious violence and make money." When asked empathic questions, that writing student might respond, "Yeah, I really do want to write violence and junk to sell, but I will admit, a part of me would kind of like to write up a wonderful character and put him or her in some wild circumstances." In other words, that student writer saw for the first time that he or she was capable of having genuine but different motivations at the same time—for example, in this case, 90 percent junk purpose and 10 percent artistic purpose. Cognitively speaking, that writer just made a very desirable leap forward.

What is a classic way in which writers of literature can use empathic inquiry? Say we have just said to ourselves, "As I look over this first draft, I don't feel much. I am going to highlight all of the *plu-*

ral nouns and all the *generic* nouns so I can see if there are a lot of them. I might change at least some of them to singular and specific nouns."

Psychotherapists often ask their clients to break down "plurals and generics." They know they can make a client revisit the actual event or scene if they can (1) sharpen up that client's memory and (2) make the client brave enough to state the single and specific points *aloud*. Social workers and psychologists call that sharpening up "partializing"—becoming aware of parts instead of wholes of things. (If you find yourself wincing at their jargon, it helps to remember some of ours, such as *writerly* and *craft-oriented*. Every field has its own ghastly jargon, and the best thing to do is to take whatever wisdom we can from the best practitioners of the field and forgive the language.)

We writers benefit from making the same two demands of ourselves that therapists ask of their clients.

1. What was the singular of that noun? What would be a specific example of that generic noun I just put down?
2. Am I courageous enough to put anything clear and unevasive down on paper or not?

Following are two examples of what happens when we change plurals and generics to singulars and specifics.

Plural and generic: Night after night I pigged out and then joined friends for recreation.

Singular and specific version of the above: On October 14, 1987, I pigged out on two fried bananas, one orange, and a half a dried apricot I found at the Higgins Quicky Counter. Then Joanne, Merv, Belcher, and I met under the marquee. We sat through *Anna Karenina* twice.

The second example is more striking.

Plural and generic: Old age is a diminished circumstance unless one converts former physical prowess into psychological or spiritual acumen. In fact, the more decrepit people are physically, the more elevated their souls need to become.

Singular and specific:

An aged man is but a paltry thing—
A tattered coat upon a stick unless
Soul clap its hands and sing, and louder sing
For every tatter in its mortal dress.[2]

Another way that writers can make good use of basic empathy is by asking ourselves, as we look at something we just wrote, "I seem to have said such and such—that *x* is true—but is that what I really feel, or was I just going along with the usual conventional opinion?"

A teacher of carpentry makes certain assumptions. He or she assumes, for example, that the apprentice carpenter has hands strong enough to drive home a roof nail in two blows. The carpentry teacher also assumes that his or her apprentice can concentrate well enough to either do the math or apply the pattern to lay up rafters.

We creative writers have to make assumptions. One of them is that we writers or student writers are grown-up enough to love life despite the evils life brings us. If we have gotten far enough in our development to be nursing a small, genuine love of life, then empathic questioning may let loose the wonderful animal of literary surprise. When a human being is being encouraged by being asked empathic questions for the first time in his or her life, he or she will feel a happiness. Such a flash of surprise happiness sometimes can give us writers the playfulness we need to make metaphor. I told my own story about this experience in Chapter 2.

Others who report this effect, by the way, are teachers of *art*. Artists tell beginning art classes to draw their own hands. If you are right-handed you are told to draw your left hand. You may not look at your paper as you draw. During this exercise the beginners, according to the art teachers I have talked to, typically make the best drawings they will do for the next year. It sounds nutty, but the reasoning behind it is that this is the first time these students have been given orders *to look with great attention at something that up until then they have ignored.* Since they are not allowed to see what they are drawing, their conventional minds cannot take back or amend what their fingers are doing.

Empathic inquiry can serve writers in a like way: we can take note of what we have been unconscious of. Once we have done that, we cannot erase the fresh impression.

I have said a good deal about the love of life—whether one feels it consciously or doesn't feel it, or whether one's only beginning to feel it. I have also said that what members of writing groups tell one another is not helpful. I do not mean that such conversations are mediocre or low-key *by choice.* Small talk doesn't happen by choice. I think we are an appalling species in a number of ways, but our diversity of ideas, our range of feelings, and our surprising linkage of feelings are elegant. We can get over our socialized habits of group behavior. Most of us are socialized to act only lightly interested in ideas. Everything profound is said only *im passim,* so we won't be seen to come on too heavy. Very few of us ask anyone about what that person has just said.

An example: I recently took part in a panel of Midwest MLA writers who had had breast cancer. I had dreaded the event. I was afraid it would be a sop. I feared members of the panel would say nothing that hadn't been said in every single women's support group on the Web and in oncology waiting rooms.

What took place was a hundred times worse than earnest repetition of stale ideas: a number of people made fascinating remarks *and no one questioned them.* Those speakers' ideas went out into the air like smoke. That odd incuriosity, that failure to question people—that accidie—reminded me of a painful parallel I once noticed in the Church of England.

For several years I admired a man named Father Jack Putterill, the vicar of Thaxted, in Essex. He was an anticlassist. He despised bullying. I experienced in this village priest someone with some moral force who actually used metaphor. So many of us never get shown the knack of it. Jack constantly gave us mental images. When he lectured about St. Paul he noted that most of us feel annoyed with the man for a number of reasons, but that St. Paul got some things right. One of those things was Paul's advising us to "put on the whole armor of God." Jack pointed out to us that no one knows what in the world the whole armor of God would look like, but that Jews at the time of Jesus knew only too well what the armor of the Roman army of occupation looked like. Jack described a centurion's battle dress—fascinating, with all the scary, glamorous accessories—leather leg bands, thongs, the famous short sword, kit that clanked and reminded you of sharp edges.

One day I drove down the high street of Thaxted in our Volkswagen van. It was fitted up for Americans. The driver sat on the wrong side of English streets, so I could pull right up to the paving where a pedestrian was walking and talk face-to-face without leaning across a passenger space.

Along swung the priest in his black cassock, past the baby pink and white and baby blue emulsion-painted village shop fronts. I came up alongside him and said, "Father Jack!" He stopped and smiled. I said, "You know, I have figured out what your life is like." "Oh, have you," he said. "And what is it like?" "I used to think that you gave these great sermons, and we came from all over the world to hear you." (As, indeed, we did—people took pains, enduring the awful East Anglia train service, to come down from London, over from Germany, and from other European countries. Americans came. Hundreds visited Thaxted to hear Jack.) "I used to think that we all come to listen to your sermons and then we return to our various countries or to the English countryside and we change the world in some of the ways you tell us to. Now I realize what really happens. We listen to your sermons all right, mass in the morning, Evensong Sunday night, and we are thrilled, and I even take notes, but then nothing happens. Everything goes on exactly the same. No one changes."

He gave me a look of good humor. He said, "Exactly. You've got it exactly."

That doesn't mean that people don't *want* to change the world. People grieve a lot about the problems of the world. What it does mean is that we are heavily socialized to waste anything that is invisible, the whole armor of God or our own feelings or whatever else may not show at the waterline. We are socialized not to follow up on intelligent counsel given, not to ask searching questions, because moral excitement is invisible.

As I listened to MLA participants talking about breast cancer but saw that no one was asking appropriate questions, I thought, this is mere habit—socialized habit. If anyone in this conference room had been taught the art of empathic inquiry, we wouldn't be wasting one another's intelligence like this.

Most human beings have not been taught how to engage in empathic inquiry. Considering how fleeting the focus we give anyone else's invisible ideas, it's amazing we communicate any ideas with each other at all. No wonder our starved, ideal-loving minds incline us to glom onto charismatic leaders with such avidity. Charismatic leaders generally hand off the same message: "Please find and act on your more intense emotions instead of moldering about with your flaccid emotions." We are charmed to hear that! Half secretly, even the most lethargic of us knows that we have intense feelings *somewhere* inside ourselves. But never having been asked particularizing questions by anybody, we are afraid that those intense invisible feelings inside us are not psychologically correct.

No one today would be so pushy as St. Paul as to dare say aloud, "Today I am going to put on the whole armor of God." We get so little encouragement for inner contemplation that we wouldn't even whisper it to ourselves.

A few insights from sociology are helpful. First, people adapt to whatever the going system is. Let's say the system is the grade school in which the elementary student is writing, or it's the high school in which the high school student is writing, or it is the graduate school or university where the college student or M.F.A. candidate is writing. People will adapt—or, to put it baldly, capitulate—to the next larger system in which their system (their *self*) lies. You yourself are a system, a human organism with literary intent, but you are also a member of a group belonging to the larger system, your writing class, your writers' group, or the university, or the school. A writing student will capitulate to the writing-class custom. You will probably feel that you ought to submit to the edicts of that larger group. Otherwise you might be thrown out. Good point: you might. Aristotle left town fast so that he wouldn't fall victim to the same fate as Socrates got at the hands of Athenian jurors.

I suggest, therefore, that you look over this empathic inquiry process and try it discreetly with yourself and with any friends who are interested in having a go at it with you. If you are tempted to propose to an instructor that your class try empathic inquiry, bear in mind that people in professional authority never get more defensive than when someone suggests that they are using outmoded pedagogy.

As an illustration of the use of empathic inquiry, let's look at an example of an author who was too intense and original for most group life. Her genius never did lend itself to cordial, desultory group discussion. Her poem, "Like Loving Chekhov," can be used to illustrate the use of empathic questioning.

The genius of Denise Levertov lies in the surprising *amount* of love she has for the universe. She could not have acquired this capacity from working in a group, nor would she ever learn in a group that such an affection is a mark of genius.

In her poem "Like Loving Chekhov," Denise Levertov describes how, logically enough, she admires Anton Chekhov for his generosity, for his kindness to people of less privilege than he, for his willingness to travel across the dangerous Tatar Strait and Sea of Okhotsk to give medical care to the prisoners on the Isle of Sakhalin. But as if she were engaging in empathic inquiry, suddenly she says (I am paraphrasing), "But there's also a man whom I'm in love with, whom I've just met, and I want him, too. And I don't want him because he is like Chekhov. My admiration for Chekhov may remind me of how much I admire *this* man because like Chekhov he's not going to be a bore. But I want him because my body wants him and it wants him *now*—" and Levertov says, "Our bodies have given each other pleasure—and our bodies are resentful that we've been kept apart." (Apparently one of them had to go out of town on a business trip.) Levertov said, "I want him right here and now, too." She didn't want him in the afterlife, and the only way that her lover resembles Chekhov (she said) is that "the ache of distance between me and a living man I know and don't know grips me with pain and fear, a pain and fear familiar in the love of the unreachable dead."[3]

Levertov's poem illustrates intensity. It illustrates something else that empathic inquiry can elicit from less stunning writers: it illustrates how one can start with one idea and then ask one's own mind, "Well, what else have you got to say about love?"

Let's pretend we are Levertov.

1. First we thought we'd write an elegant ode to Chekhov. (We take the high ground.)
2. Then, after we've praised Chekhov for a while, we interview our

own mind, asking, "Well, is that *it* for you? What else might you know about love?"

3. Then our mind, glad to be asked, zooms in on its present, joyful desire for a temporarily absent lover— and thus we have the rich *second* half of the poem.

Some Final Thoughts

Don't spend even a minute criticizing yourself for having been conventional first time round in any piece of writing. We have to be proud, not ashamed, about our changes of heart. Changes of heart are the huge glad beasts in the forest of the writing process.

We may be bored by the phrase "the writing process," but it is a wonderful process. When you have written some inspired draft, it has found a home *outside* you—*on paper.* Having that draft *outside* your head gives the brain new perspective. Your brain, behind your eyes, looks at what you've written. It sees ways to deepen or to contradict the text. Let it. Let the brain do this wonderful work.

A final check, especially for nonfiction writers: have you served or have you betrayed your innermost self in what you've written here?

Social workers keep going back to the *values* of their clients. They use empathic questioning to help people find their own backbone. Writers need to check in with *their* values, especially in our culture where we might go for weeks or years without anyone asking us to state our values and why they're important to us and how our values are doing.

"Here I have written this bit of memoir," writers can say to themselves. "Which value of mine does it come from?"

Bill Holm reminds us that we ordinary people have not been told to be *sehnsuchtvoll* (soul searching). The whole point of basic empathic questioning is to help writers, indeed everybody, to find and stick with their "*innigsten Empfindung*"—innermost feeling.

4.

How Stage-Development Philosophy Serves Writers

> Now, in the make and nature of every man, however rude or simple, whom we employ in manual labor, there are some powers for better things: some tardy imagination, some torpid capacity of emotion, tottering steps of thought, there are even at the worst: and in most cases it is all our own fault that they are tardy or torpid.
>
> —**John Ruskin, from *The Stones of Venice*, 1851–1853**

A Basic Overview of Stage-Development Theory

Ruskin's creed above is the succinct and heartbreaking remark of a natural stage-developmentalist. Stage-development theory is the idea that people are not immutable types, but instead they grow and change in an elegant procession of stages. Everyone has the potential to achieve self-actualization, the highest stage in any hierarchy, though bad psychological luck can block millions from reaching some of the upper stages. People go through given stages at different speeds—some as fast as night—but no one skips a stage as far as they develop. The stages are sequential: one goes, however long or short one's progression, through each stage in order. There are as many theories about the number, duration, and definitions of stages as there are stage-developmentalists, but they are agreed on the above concepts.

Of the many stage-development theorists, the best known are Harry

Stack Sullivan, Ferenczi, Erik Erikson, Jean Piaget, D. Ausubel, Eric Fromm, David Riesman, R. Adorno, Lawrence Kohlberg, and Jane Loevinger. Most stage-developmentalists are psychologists or educators, but some scholars who have written stage-developmental theories are better known for other accomplishments, such as Alexander Bain, known as an economist, and Adam Smith (*The Wealth of Nations*).

As do experts in any field of interest, stage theorists ponderously explain the differences between their own and others' theories. They generally agree, however, on the very democratic ideas expressed by Ruskin. No one is an immutable *type* of person. Regardless of their culture, people's personalities develop in sequential stages. No one skips a stage, although, as Ruskin said, bad treatment might well retard the imagination, or make for a tepid heart or a vacuous intellect.

In addition to the ingenious constructs of scholars in the social sciences, there is a surprising literary heritage of stage-developmental philosophy that most writers have never heard of: for example, two famous authors, the poet and playwright Friedrich Schiller in 1801 and the novelist and essayist George Orwell in 1946, wrote out their own philosophies of development. Both noted a key sequence: people develop as lovers of beauty before becoming people who have concerns larger than their own lives. Neither Schiller nor Orwell could have heard of anything called "stage-development theory," but both intuitively chose to think in developmental terms. We will look at their ideas in the last section of this chapter.

That two such extraordinarily imaginative authors should consider it valuable to lay out orderly, numinous perspectives on invisible things buoys me up: it invites us all to arrange whatever we know of life in orderly, numinous perspectives of our own.

Stage-development theory is *philosophical* theory. That is, it concerns itself with universal ideas about what humankind is born with and where we can or can't go from there. Philosophers are people who ask us to look at their various explanations for why we either succeed or fail in becoming civil, open-minded, intellectually excitable human beings with a taste for justice and kindness.

There were faint wisps of developmental theory in the thinking of Indians and ancient Greeks. Indians divided a man's life into four psychologically logical stages: first one is a learner of one's own culture; next, a rebellious, deliberate tester of the wider or forbidden ways of the world; next, one marries; and fourth, one becomes a philosopher.

Socrates tells Protagoras that if he wants his son to be brave he can't take him at age one to look at the Spartans at Thermopylae. A child picks up on things visible before things invisible—self-sacrifice is invisible. In the dialogue Meno, Socrates says things have to be learned in a certain order—not too soon and, presumably, not too late.

Socrates lacked a virtue that is a core value of stage developmentalists, however: he wasn't democratic. He assumed some people simply couldn't be taught to be philosopher kings. This subclass of people had to be told what to do all their lives. Thus Socrates accepted what in animals is called pecking order and in human beings the class system. All cultural class typing is anathema to stage-developmentalists, who believe that all children have the potential of the species—unless the brain is damaged.

As you look over the discussion of stage-development theory here, I suggest weighing each of its ideas against what you recall of your own life as you have gone along and against how you perceive your life as you go along now.

It's no good trying to understand any psychological theory without trying it on for fit. No sooner did I begin reading Lawrence Kohlberg, a leader in moral stage-development thinking, than I found I could tie the stage idea to my own life, to myself, and to people I know. The scheme below is mine, greatly influenced by Kohlberg and by the ego-development scholar Jane Loevinger.[1]

I. One is at a premoral utterly selfish stage.
II. One is still selfish, but at least one sees that there are others out there, and one decides they have a right to be selfish, too.
III. Whatever seems to win strokes from the crowd is the highest good.
IV. Whatever authority says is right is right.
V. One has developed one's own code of rights and wrongs, which one applies *universally*—such as honesty, hospitality, murder: one sup-

Table 1. Some Milestones of Ego Development

Stage	Code	Impulse Control, Character Development	Interpersonal Style	Conscious Preoccupations	Cognitive Style
Presocial			Autistic		
Symbiotic	I-1		Symbiotic		
Impulsive	I-2	Impulsive, fear of retaliation	Receiving, dependent, exploitative	Self vs. nonself Bodily feelings, especially sexual and aggressive	Stereotyping, conceptual confusion
Self-protective		Fear of being caught, externalizing blame, opportunistic	Wary, manipulative, exploitative	Self-protection, trouble, wishes, things, advantage, control	
Conformist	I-3	Conformity to external rules, shame, guilt for breaking rules	Belonging, superficial niceness	Appearance, social acceptability, banal feelings, behavior	Conceptual simplicity, stereotypes, clichés
Conscientious-Conformist	I-3/4	Differentiation of norms, goals	Aware of self in relation to group, helping	Adjustment, problems, reasons, opportunities, (vague)	Multiplicity

Conscientious	I-4	Self-evaluated standards, self-criticism, guilt for consequences, long-term goals and ideals	Intensive, responsible, mutual, concern for communication	Differentiated feelings, motives for behavior, self-respect, achievements, traits, expression	Conceptual complexity, idea of patterning
Individualistic	I-4/5	*Add:* Respect for individuality	*Add:* Dependence as an emotional problem inner life from outer	*Add:* Development, social problems, differentiation of outcome	*Add:* Distinction of process and
Autonomous	I-5	*Add:* Coping with conflicting inner needs, toleration	*Add:* Respect for autonomy, interdependence	*Add:* Vividly conveyed feelings, integration of physiological and psychological, psychological causation of behavior, role conception, self-fulfillment, self in social context	Increased conceptual complexity, complex patterns, toleration for ambiguity, broad scope, objectivity
Integrated	I-6	*Add:* Reconciling inner conflicts, renunciation of unattainable	*Add:* Cherishing of individualism	*Add:* Identity	

Note: "*Add*" means in addition to the description applying to the previous level.

Table I. Some Milestones of Ego Development, on pp. 24 and 25 of *Ego Development: Conceptions and Theories,* by Jane Loevinger with the assistance of Augusto Blasi, 1987: San Francisco. Jossey-Bass Publishers.

*This same table of milestones appears unchanged but with E-level code numbers in two subsequent books: *Paradigms of Personality* published by W. H. Freeman & Co., and *Technical Foundations, for Measuring Ego Development,* published by Lawrence Erlbaum & Associates, Mahway, N.J.

poses that everyone in every culture should be honest and hospitable and eschew killing people. (Stage V people may be cultural relativists so far as *styles* of honesty and hospitality are concerned, but the content, the underlying principles, apply to all.)

VI. One has to disobey one's own code of rights and wrongs in order to make the best judgment in a given predicament. For example, one would lie to Gestapo in order to save innocent lives. One can't remain a clean-cut Girl Scout.

A reader will notice straight off that the first two levels aren't moral at all. The person in Stage I or II is still only practical, thinking of what works as opposed to what is conscientious. The second two levels are conventional: the person is taking his or her cue from others in the social or national group. Only the final two stages have any aspect of what people nowadays call "taking responsibility for yourself" or "being accountable," and, especially important for our suffering globe, people in the last two stages have philosophies spacious enough to consider everyone.

In order that this chapter not be offering only ideas at second hand, here is a scheme from Jane Loevinger's Ego Development.[2] Dr. Loevinger's elegant four-column scheme lets us track a person's growth in four areas—character development, interpersonal style, main concerns or priorities of contemplation ("Conscious preoccupations"—an especially ingenious offering, I think), and cognitive style. We can think across, as well as vertically.

I suggest that writers first acquaint themselves with my all-purpose mongrel development scheme above. Next, read over, vertically column by column, Loevinger's format, testing it against your own life. Last, read Loevinger laterally. It is interesting to note that when one is at the "autonomous stage," for example, one can handle conflicting inner needs and also, in terms of cognitive style, one can handle complicated ideas. One can make out the patterns that lie behind phenomena. One can study life "objectively" —not feeling one's own ego threatened at every turn. The "vividly conveyed feelings" of Loevinger's listing are one of any author's main occasions.

Assumptions of Stage-Development Theory

As people develop cognitively their ideation gets less viscous or tepid, more passionate. They are developing the ego, the wonderful part of us characterized by conscious will. The ego leads us to distinguish not only between one or another visible thing but between one or another invisible thing as well. Here is what may be surprising to some: as our ego develops our ability to attach values to such ideas as we have picks up pace. We wiggle free of mere practicality. Children are born utterly practical at first—values-free, though their minds are already growing values, such as altruism. Early twentieth-century scientists assumed that one met one's physical needs first and then and only then began to develop civilized or idealistic goals. More modern research now suggests that all the human goals get going at the same time. Even as a child howls for breast milk, that child's brain cells are making the moves—even amazing migrations—that will find homes for that child's complex, inner, idea-inspired life.

Whichever stage you are in is an all-purpose philosophical stage—that is, it describes a simplicity or sophistication of thought that will inform your imagination and behavior while you're in that stage. It will tell a lot about the kind of response to life that you make while you're in that stage. A stage frames the whole personality for the moment. It is not specific to any one task we're doing. You don't act like a Stage IV person today because you're at school but act like a Stage II person at home because you're at home. You are either in the general mode of Stage II or of Stage IV and you have that level of philosophy about life that goes with that stage.

Stage-development is definitely and blessedly hierarchical. Things get more difficult as you go up through any stage-development scheme. But the stages get better as you go up. People get morally, as well as cognitively, more elegant as they develop. That is, like Iago, who indicated as much of himself, in *Othello*,* a person can distinguish between honorable and dishonorable behavior but that doesn't necessarily mean choosing to behave honorably. Our thinking gets

* Act I sc i, speaking to Rodrigo

more elaborate and more refined. In every philosopher's or educator's or psychologist's stage system that I've looked at, one becomes more altruistic, less tribal, more open-minded, more anxious to contemplate species-wide or even planet-wide ideals, less quick to anger without thinking things through. Almost all the stages give as their top levels two particular qualities: the ability to absorb painful information without denying it (a quality very dear to psychotherapists, heads of governments, and military commanders in the field) and the ability to delay taking instant action or making some sharp, all-inclusive remark, for the sake of gathering still more data, sad or not, before deciding on a course of action—a quality much admired and needed in ships' captains, clergypeople, and especially authors.

The scope and quality of one's thinking are irreversible. Once you know that human beings can disinterestedly want justice for people you may never meet—such as, say, justice in hiring practices for people in a different part of the country—then you can never go back to believing that only your own family or your own townsfolk have a right to fair employment practices. In your mind you know that if fairness is good for anyone it is good for all. Once you have grasped a concept you cannot go back and unthink it. True, you may never actually help, by vote or by protest, those faraway people struggling for fair employment, but that is simply a question of your having decided not to give time to their cause.

Stage-development philosophy also says that how people grow is universally ordered. The stages are not culturally relative, as was briefly mentioned on page 60. The style of a certain level of development may vary from culture to culture, but the essence or content is universal to everyone who has developed to that stage. A rough-hewn example: no newborn baby has developed the value we call hospitality. If you tell that baby some needy babies have come to visit its home, so would it please share its customary breast-feeding with them, the baby won't get it. Later the baby will learn hospitality, since we all do. Hospitality is an absolute, cross-cultural value, varying from culture to culture only in style. (A seventeenth-century president of Harvard College would not lend his wife to a weekend drop-in, though an Inuit chief of the same century might.)

I go into this because Lawrence Kohlberg has been repeatedly accused by cultural relativists of describing stages that applied only to middle-class American males. It isn't true. His cross-cultural studies of non-American, non-middle-class children revealed the same stage hierarchies, only with different "content." How this ingenious thinker was made a whipping boy by gender specifists has been much discussed over the past thirty years. I mention it here because I defend the idea that women as well as men traverse the same cognitive and ethical stages, and women, like men, as Mary Oliver says in her handbook about writing poetry, need solitude, not cozy groupings, in order to be authors.

Not only are the stages of development universal, but their sequence is unvarying. Later stages are either built on earlier stages, or our arrival at a later stage depends on our succeeding in abandoning constrictive tenets of an earlier stage. For example, if we are in a tribal-loyalty level of love where we feel and practice no mercy on anyone who isn't part of our family or church, we have to abandon that we-versus-all-others orientation before we can feel any creature love for others on our planet. Anyone refusing to donate to any cause except one's own church has to expand such ideation before he or she will feel the force of any genuinely philosophical, universal idea.

One's habitat may, of course, help one speed through the bottom stages faster. Conversely, a habitat that deprives a person of any peaceful contemplation, time alone, access to a mentor, and so forth, may stall or block a person's development. Kohlberg's cross-cultural studies, for example, suggested that children in non-middle-class villages stayed stuck in concrete thinking longer than children of middle-class backgrounds. The middle-class kids were better acquainted with narrative and with abstract language. Since abstractions were a normal experience for them, their minds got and enjoyed the knack of categorizing what they knew of life. They liked putting things in abstractions. Those lucky children spent less time stuck in concrete thinking, but even they *didn't get to skip* the stage of concrete thinking. Conversely, just because very poor Central American villagers appeared to be limited to only the most concrete kind of thinking, that doesn't mean that all their children were "concrete thinkers." Stage-developmentalists don't call any child a "type."

So stage-developmentalists are never stereotypers. They think of people as cognitively on their way to fulfillment. Individuals may progress at different speeds. Some will get as far in gracious inner life as any human being can. Others' minds seem to get blocked or foreclosed. But the most important assumption of stage-development theory is that everyone has the potential, if not necessarily the ability, to achieve the highest stage. The genome itself specifies very little of what we become—yet we can become, and become, and become—so stage-developmentalists are not genetic determinists. They take a dim view of all reductive philosophies.

They see the old stimulus/response mind-set, most notably B. F. Skinner's determinism, as wretched and archaic. Stimulus/response philosophy says that if you give type *x* stimulus to a human being or a rat, it will behave (or think) with type *y* response. Stage developmentalists say, instead, if you give someone a type *x* stimulus, that person's mind will take *x* aboard, weigh it against what other ideas (memories) are in the mind, and make a symbolic new idea from it—thus actually changing that person's mentality forever. I will give a specific example because the idea of the mind changing in this lightning way may be new to some readers.

Let us pretend we have just received, while reading, some new insight that doesn't square with previous assumptions of ours. This new insight feels wrong. But our eyes dutifully send news of it into the visual cortex, where it makes its case with the circuitry already there. This outside stimulus—that is, the new contradictory insight—will not change us. What changes us is our own active seeking for connections to that stimulus. We poke back through our previous takes on the subject or near the subject, and then, with the new insight before us, we amend our old categories. It is this amending of the old categories that changes us—a very active process.

A specific example: Let us say we always supposed that the last Ice Age, ending about eleven thousand or ten thousand years ago, killed the large mammals in North and South America. Now we read that Clovis humankind, not the climate, actually killed those large mammals. We people wiped them out. This is the lively argument of some archaeologists, among them Richard Leakey and Paul S. Martin.[3] This new idea is unpleasant. If we take it aboard, we have increased our personality's ability to believe and not deny unpleasant truths. Therefore, our personality is different—stronger than before. The famous early-stage developmentalist Jean Piaget called it "adding a structure." The poet Richard Wilbur called it "correcting the cave." This is the very core of what Wilbur tells us in an amazing poem called "The Mind." The mind, Wilbur says, in its "very happiest intellection . . . may correct the cave."

There are several possible ways of interpreting the idea that "an error" would bring about improvement. Here is one of the most charming. Let us say your mind has settled for several conventional interpretations of some subject. But one day it fails to follow its usual routing: instead it charges into some fiery tangles it has never ventured into before. This new, particular fiery connection is a thousand times more intelligent and exciting than the old flight plan. Such sudden insights (or graceful errors in the old set of insights) come even to dull-seeming people sometimes. It suggests that originality, at least some originality, is a potential for each of us, at least occasionally. The idea is that however rarely we sense it happening, the mind is constantly revising its opinions. It is constantly reeling in or letting out the spinnaker of its own philosophies, all because it constantly mixes what it hears just this moment with what it has heard and assessed before. That constantly changing mix of old idea and new impressions is what gives us fresh attitudes that weren't ours before.

THE MIND

The mind in its purest play is like some bat
That beats about in caverns all alone,
Contriving by a kind of senseless wit
Not to conclude against a wall of stone.

It has no need to falter or explore;
Darkly it knows what obstacles are there,
And so may weave a flitter, dip a soar,
In perfect courses through the blackest air.

And is this simile a like perfection?
The mind is like a bat. Precisely. Save
That in the very happiest intellection
A graceful error may correct the cave.[4]

How Two Authors Offer Us Stage Philosophies That Are Especially Pertinent to Writers

"Letter 24" of Schiller's *On the Aesthetic Education of Man*[5] offers a three-stage theory of the growth of consciousness. The theory is psychologically intricate. Schiller has a realistic grasp of how a person starts out just practical and indifferent to beauty, next learns love of beauty, and only then—*after* learning to love beauty—arrives at strong feelings about goodness or public virtue.

Schiller's Three Stages

1. You are inclined to physical practicality.
2. You get the idea you could plan to make your own life beautiful. Your mind focuses on beauty.
3. You deplore what is horrible and become interested in governance in order to correct one or another cruelty.

In the first, "physical," stage, then, you are an instinctual, conventional creature jolting along with everyone else, thinking nothing much, really, neither reflecting nor judging, but reacting case by case to whatever difficulties nature or society hands you.

In Schiller's second, aesthetic, stage, it occurs to you that you could and might as well design your own life. You could invent plans and at least try to implement the plans. You could make your life beautiful, so that your life gives you the pleasure generally called "enjoyment of beauty." You are still self-oriented, but now you have ideas you are implementing. You are using some idealistic willfulness.

In the third stage you are what both neuroscientists and clinical psychologists call "socialized." You wish to change what is unfortunate, unkind, or horrible—in nature or in society. Governance means joining other human beings to make improvements. You have now entered a *moral* condition. Once you're morally aware, according to Schiller, you can never again become unaware. A similar observation about human development fascinated Jean Piaget and Lawrence Kohlberg: once we human beings have learned how to generalize from a series of specific impressions, and thus can do that invigorating work called "predicting," you can't talk us into going back to having a mindless series of sense impressions just for their own sakes. We will always want to fit whatever we notice into a pattern. Schiller realized a century and a half before George Orwell talked about it that love of beauty is a lot more accessible to very young people and inexperienced thinkers than is love of fairness. Love of natural beauty and dance and the mere rhythm of poetry appeal to us well before we have any strong feelings of the kind that make us shout about anything, "*That* certainly isn't fair!" It would be 160 years after Schiller before Lawrence Kohlberg would do what Schiller had done—define the desire for justice as an upper level of thinking in a set of developmental stages.

Orwell's Four Stages

We think of George Orwell first as a political moralist. We honor him for writing *Animal Farm, The Road to Wigan Pier, 1984,* and "Politics and the English Language." He says of himself, however, in a sharp little essay called "Why I Write,"[6] that he is someone who arrived at moral, political caring only after he had moved up through three earlier stages. I expect this hater of every kind of bullying who also hated pretentious, Latin-based language would be infuriated by being called a "stage-development thinker" or a "precursor of stage-development philosophy," even if Schiller visibly gleamed in the same showcase.

In "Why I Write," George Orwell lays out the four stages of his psychological motivations with regard to writing. If we think about our own lives as we're looking over Orwell's four stages we might say, "Oh yes, I remember being in that stage," or "No, I'm different from Orwell in this way because I don't recall such a stage," or "None of this stage theory makes sense to me because for me it was like . . ."

1. Vanity or careerism
2 Pointless love of and efficacy in things aesthetic
3. Interest in reportage
4. Dislike of injustice

His four stages were: first, *vanity*, or in his words "sheer egoism." He wanted to be published; he wanted to be a writer. This is a stage of both commercial writers and writers of literature. What we call market-guided writers are people who stay in Orwell's stage one. For the decades of their adult lives they contemplate the market, figure out its demands, and discipline themselves to fit the need.

Everyone seems vulnerable to remaining in Orwell's stage one. The yearning to be published is so strong that I have often wished I had some force majeure to get all my writing students published in famous magazines and by famous book publishers immediately, just to propel them past the smoking, scorching drive to get published. A beginning writer's vanity is aggravated by the fact that the world, especially siblings and relatives, neighbors, clergy, and as often as not teachers, can't help the writer. Therefore we writers feel the more lonely. The loneliness itself increases the wanting to be published.

The second of Orwell's four writing stages is like the second of Schiller's thinking stages: the love of beauty. Orwell complained vividly about his awful prep school. In *Such, Such Were the Joys*, he tells about the Head's crookedness and the systemic cruelty at the boarding school where Orwell prepared for Eton. Orwell got a poor boy's view of the English class system. But both his awful prep school and his later public school put crisp and salient English into his ears and taught him to write it. He and other boys of poorer and untitled families were no doubt psychologically abused, but they learned to recognize good prose. Orwell knew the conventions of poetry and English criticism. What's more, his education was classical. Given that leg up, Orwell could manufacture very quickly, he said, any number of kinds of poetry and essays for the publication he ran at Eton. Orwell said it was astonishing how easily he wrote, how *much* he wrote, how quickly he wrote. Looking backward, he said, "I see that it is invariably where I lacked a *political* purpose that I wrote lifeless books and was betrayed into purple passages, sentences without meaning, decorative adjectives and humbug generally."

Writing decorative humbug is a stage at which most M.F.A. students work and typically get stuck. They are proud to learn gorgeous phrasing. They are refugees from U.S.A. junk language. If they have any literary instincts at all they are delighted to write as beautifully as they can. They want to coil themselves around such beauty.

What's more, the majority of their mentors (instructors) are themselves escapees from the U.S.A. junk culture—escapees from what C. S. Lewis in "The Abolition of Man" called "the cold vulgarity" of culture. Such teachers encourage their students to write beautifully. I have never heard instructors or professors of M.F.A. candidates say, "Write beautifully and also morally," but they do bid everyone "write beautifully." Aesthetically minded teachers do not literally say, "Keep on writing humbug," or "Stay stuck in Schiller's and Orwell's stage two," but they offer much more praise for felicitous phrasing than they offer warnings against humbug—or warnings against writing—"just gas" (another Orwellian label). No writing teacher wants to be intrusive. Besides, one person's humbug may be somebody else's religion.

M.F.A. students usually think of writing as a craft. When they go to their workshop groups or when they have a conference with their creative-writing teachers, the talk spirals woefully downward to craft and craftsmanship. If the teacher "respects the student's goals" for a piece of writing, this respect of the student's goals usually leads the teacher not to ask the student what those goals are. Apparently to that faculty member the *content* of the student's writing doesn't count for much. If all the conversations a student writer hears are about craft, he or she is likely to languish in Orwell's stage two—enthusiastically pounding away—writing craftfully. Writing humbug mostly.

Orwell's third stage is journalistic writing. You have found yourself in some corner of the world where you have access to information other people need to know. You want to share your perspective, especially through poems or essays. This is the stage at which most members of minority groups and previously silenced people—such as women—and most idealists come into their powers.

Members of minority groups realize that they should tell those in the majority what it's like for people living in the minority situation. In this stage it is intensely important that the writer not lie at all. If you are writing a memoir about a particular episode in your life, such as, let us say, a memoir about incest as criminal assault, it's important that everything you say be true. No character, under any circumstances, should be combined with another character into a composite. No events should be "conflated." Why the fuss? If you are representing the minority experience in your writing, reporting on the physical or psychological or spiritual truths about your corner of the universe, you need to provide exact documentation to jolt your readers to imagine *other.* If (stage-three) journalism is written truthfully, it gives readers psychological insights they might spend decades getting to if they had only their own lives to learn by.

Orwell's fourth stage is the moral stage. Having realized what the world is like, a fourth-stage nonfiction author says, "Some of this is not good. I am going to have to inveigh against it. I will use literary representations—that is, characters, argument, story, plot, plays, metaphor—to show the cruelty or the fairness or the admirability of such and such a human behavior."

Most writers don't reach stage four. We get "validated," as the pop-psych people say, by giving our best attention to *craft.* We are terrified of being unattractive to our colleagues. Being unattractive means being earnest. Being unattractive means valuing content as much as technique.

I have gone into these observations about growth by stages because stage-development philosophy encourages us to move toward ever more complex thinking. Complexity of thought brings with it not just culture—we all know that—but also morality and *enthusiasm* for the tiniest as well as the major things in life.

If we look at the great similarity between Schiller's stage three and Orwell's stage four, we find that both men thought that as a full-grown person you should care a great deal about whether or not you belong to and are participating in a fair or unfair government. Such caring is certainly not the strongest wind blowing today. Our habit in learning how to write books today is to pay only the slightest attention to any ethical goals—those of Schiller's stage three or Orwell's stage four or Loevinger's I-5.

What's more, literary history is commonly written up as though some of our most conscientious citizen writers had not given agonized thought to just and unjust government. Our teachers present great moral leaders who also happen to be literary craftspeople as if they were *only literary craftspeople.* That is because by far the majority of teachers, cultural critics, and literary pundits live their lives at the *craft*, or how-to, stage. I will take up this issue in Chapter 12, "Some Issues of Aesthetics and Ethics of Writing Literature."

The folk wisdom in the United States is that if one is uneducated one will enjoy the simple pleasures more than if one is educated. I am sorry about this lie. Those who contemplate life at Loevinger's "autonomous" stage, for example, clearly are able to experience more joy in life than those who are stuck at the concrete thinking phase.

Most of my adult students who happen to be beginners at writing suffer horribly from this folk wisdom: they are sure, because various groups keep passing these advisories about, that they *will* find meaning in sense impressions, noticing a leaf, but *not* in imagination (meaning making connections in the mind). They are sure, because they have heard it said especially by careless preachers, that they will be happier and better writers if they stick to really simple ideas, rather than complex, delicate ideas.

The result of this anti-intellectual fad is that adults by the hundreds, perhaps the thousands, are censoring the most wondrous tendrils of ideas from their own heads. Chapters 10 and 11 of this book offer some ways to stand up against the fascism of the simple.

If there is any literary pitfall that stage-development schemes and empathic inquiry most patently save us from it is fragmentation. Whenever we writers think of ourselves as changing every minute, using words, then going under those words to find deeper words, we can see the patterns in our lives. At that point we stop writing mere sensitive bits and journal entries, one today, one tomorrow, because we see how all that we think and have ever felt can be connected.

Everyone knows that geologists and mathematicians and philosophers nearly shout when at last they can make out the pattern in what they've been looking at. It should be the same for nonfiction writers, too. If we belong to a writers' group, however, some of our fellow members may deplore our looking for a pattern. "It seems so abstract," they may say. Then we need to be ready with an answer: "It's part abstract and part sense impression, because that is the way literature is."

5.

We Have Pushed Off from the Animal Kingdom for Good: Good News for Writers from Neuroscientists

> Once a species has begun to speak, it can no longer do without. Language is not one of those gifts which can be accepted experimentally, on trial. It represses many of our animal instincts. We cannot fall back on them—never! We have pushed off from the animal kingdom for good. The infant that comes into the world equipped with archaic reflexes must cast them off within a few weeks in order to be able to develop normally—into a human being, that is. The frontal lobes of the neocortex have assumed command. Civilization is their product. Language, the medium of tradition, their prerequisite.
>
> —Christa Wolf, *Accident/A Day's News*

The great tools in the middle stage of creative writing of a manuscript—the long stage in which we kindly but thoroughly enlarge or refine our original inspiration—are all tools for trusting our insides more than we trust what any external groups might tell us. Empathic questioning, stage-development philosophy, and, as we'll see in this chapter, recent neuroscience show us how to rejoice in figures of speech and surprising insights never invented in breakout groups and almost always undervalued by breakout groups.

These tools show us how to get rid of the much-whined-about "writer's block." They divide us from the herd. For writer's block, like another artifact called "the inner critic," is caused by internalized group threat, not by lack of ideas from one's own head. It buoys one up to realize that writer's block is a psychological artifact of naysaying, a grunt of the group. All we have to do is not listen to it.

The two main ideas I'd like to borrow from neuroscience for writers to use during the long middle stage of writing a manuscript are, first, that the mind is not programmed, and, second, that the mind performs multilocation reentry, which is a way of saying that whenever a new stimulus comes in from the outside, the mind's circuits race to meet it, and many groups of neurons go back and forth against each other from many sites—all of them participating in the decision of how the new impression is to be categorized and how the very presence of this new impression will change categories (evaluations) previously in place. The mind is thus constantly restructuring itself. In other words, since the mind is not programmed, it makes itself. When it makes new connections it amends itself: it makes itself by performing reentry.

The mind's ability to keep amending itself by performing reentry has a number of implications for writers. First, I see writers as the reporters of the reentry system inside us. That means writers need to be generalists. The more you know about a wide range of subjects, the more material you have to make connections with. The more material you have to work with, the more likely you are to produce fresh, unexpected connections, the kind of connections that make good metaphors.

Reentry also serves the kind of empathic questioning discussed in Chapter 3 because it can galvanize a sluggish mind by revealing deeper meaning. Conversely, empathic questioning can lead us to make conscious connections that might otherwise remain dormant. Stage-development theory, as presented in Chapter 4, relies on reentry, because these new connections in our minds lead to new insights that can propel us to advanced levels of understanding, or higher stages in our development.

When I first began to read books by neuroscientists I started with Antonio Damasio and Gerald Edelman. I began making lists of everything

I found exciting. I will talk about a few of their ideas in this chapter. Of course, like any interested layperson reading for the first time in someone else's field of expertise, I immediately began to organize my thoughts in order to see how Damasio's and Edelman's wisdom, as well as I could discern it, would fit into a theory of truth about people. That's what writers do. We want to add our new perceptions and our new ideological insights into our own potpourri—our conscious mind work.

How we do it—how we understand wise thinking from others, how either roughly or exquisitely we concentrate on their ideas to make sure we have them right before we blend them into our minds—varies according to our own personalities. We have our own personal kind of intelligence, our own personal kind of feelings or Weltanschauung—what Edelman calls "qualia"—and not only does our general set of feelings about things keep changing and changing, but our interpretations of theories we read about keep changing, too. Just about everything connected with the mind is a variable. What's more, scholars of the mind use metaphors to describe how they understand consciousness works—because they haven't got exact, physiological locations or measurements for mental activity. Not yet.

Two points about laypersons reading neuroscience then: first, I would like to urge serious writers not just to read but to *own* a few books by a few scientists. I suggest that everyone buy and own for future reference Edelman's *Bright Air, Brilliant Fire,* and *Descartes' Error* by Antonio Damasio because these books warm a reader with the authors' love of their subjects. The deadbeat expression "for future reference" hides my sanguine belief in owning books by truth seekers so that the reader can change his or her mind when rereading them.

The obvious, much-shouted value of reading primary sources of any kind is that you have it from the horse's mouth. But if you read only one primary source in the field of neurophysiology or neuroscience of any kind, you won't have very *much* from the horse's mouth.

Here is a surprising benison of reading primary sources: they give off the ambiance of love of learning. They help us fight off the comparative lovelessness of paraphrased material. I was a ghastly, indolent scholar when I was young. I read secondary sources even on Plato—a ridiculous form of sloth since Plato's work is so conversational and dramatic, positively enchanting compared to paraphrasings of his work. I spent years reading scholars' comments like "In Book I of *The Republic,* he has Socrates arguing that such and such . . ." The authors of cram books didn't pick up on and transmit Plato's love of the subject, however honorable their précis of the argument.

What I didn't understand was that you *can't* get the pure love of any argument at second hand any more than you can feel much desire at second hand by reading someone's description.

A word about learning a little from professionals. I was sent to live for a number of childhood years with an aunt who was quick to jeer at dilletantism. She constantly said, with evident satisfaction, "A little knowledge is a dangerous thing." I believed her for about forty years. At last I got smart. I arrived at two realizations. First, this aunt was using her posture of intellectual dismay over acquiring bits and pieces of information as an excuse not to learn anything from anybody who had any expertise on a subject other than themselves. Even as a child, I had noticed that her bookshelves were full of memoirs by 1920s and 1930s authors. I would return to her house for the spring breaks from my school, where—restless, ill-tempered, half-crazed at sixteen and seventeen—I had little to do but read. I read all of the memoirs Genevieve had around the house. Some were pleasant distractions; some I thought dull. But even at that age I noticed that none offered any universal theory about anything. The theme of each of those books was "Reader, please note my interesting life. There I was in Yugoslavia (or Germany or Transylvania). Fortunately I spoke the language beautifully." That was more or less the tone of those books. It took me forty years to realize that an old English major can quash her own curiosity about life—about whatever the meaning of life might be—by insisting on being ignorant of the writings of specialists in other fields of knowledge.

Literary people over forty typically adhere to the 1940s and 1950s assumption that any hard or social science is reductive and deterministic, as indeed much of medicine and sociology was in the late 1940s up through the mid-1950s. Others of us are repelled by the jargon-ridden prose style of so many hard scientists and social scientists. Yet some of the best creative nonfiction writers of our time come from medicine, not from literature: In addition to Edelman and Damasio, I think of the physicians William Carlos Williams and Lewis Thomas and Richard Selzer, the biologist Edward O. Wilson, and the psychiatrists Viktor Frankl and Irving D. Yalom. Their personal essay styles are inviting and clear, and I say this although it makes me wistful on behalf of my confreres: they make imaginative connections with as much charm as many of us.

Still, a last word on sketchy knowledge: my knowledge of neuroscience is so small it can't be measured, but I want to add up a few ideas about the mind's workings so that creative nonfiction writers can make use of them. At the same time, however, I earnestly suggest you take aboard my interpretations very skeptically and for the sake of intellectual integrity, read Edelman and Damasio and a few others in the field.

I commend the two neuroscientists just mentioned not just for their accessible, lively ideas, but for both men's love of the problem—the problem of being. That problem—how shall we be in the world—is the problem of nonfiction writers. But discoveries about the neocortex with its six creasy outer layers bring news that is especially good for writers. Everything the eyes see and the ears hear and the other senses pick up is sent in to the millions of neural groupings in our heads. We categorize what comes in not just as "Put that in the redness memory" if the thing we just saw is red, but also we try the new red thing for which *value category* or *categories* it may belong in. And if it doesn't find any previously made categories—then, if we are lucky and have a flexible mind that doesn't get too threatened by changing a category once created in good faith—it maps out some new categories for itself. Next time we see something red we evaluate it differently. We have perception categories, but *also* previously made ideological categories—both kinds of categories always up for amendment. We use the past, and thus we can plan the future, in a way that even the chimpanzee (which is a very smart animal) cannot yet do.

Writers often wonder why we have conflicting responses to a given stimulus. Which one is our *genuine* opinion? we wonder. But if we think of how the mind constantly confers back and forth among its various neural groupings, entering a thought here, entering a thought there, picking up a thought that has been back and forth between recent perception and word from our previous thoughts—the process called *reentry*—then might not a fleeting feeling, the kind so often self-censored, actually be our deepest take on a given situation? The ideas of reentry, the brain's vigorous, various neighborhoods full of mutual firing and the mutual excitement and the strange circuitry of the millions of neuron groupings in the mind, are reassuring. I feel reassured the way astronomers first felt reassured when at last the celestial tools had been improved enough to corroborate what the astronomers had always felt to be true about stars and whole galaxies.

The pure multitude of circuits and connections allows us a dynamic repertoire of many, many genuine feelings about any one sense impression received. We can choose which to give emphasis to. We can choose differently tomorrow.

This conferring from neural grouping to neural grouping in the mind—reentry—is infinitely superior and more promising than mere sensory impression! For example, let us say our eyes are open and our ears are open, our mouth and nose are open, and touch is feathering all over our face—namely, we are taking in an impression.

We are so conscious! The combination of sense impressions we are taking in goes into the cortex. Immediately every impression that we have had in the past comes to meet this new lot to trade notes. A metaphor for reentry: a new reporter speaks, "There's new news, people." But the room (the mind) is full not only of *other* older news, but of philosophies about the old news. The old reporters in there have long ago or recently made their own interpretations on that other news. They come up to meet the new messenger, saying, "All right, let's hear it. And we will weigh in on the new news; we will prop it up against the other news we have of life. And we will prop up our old news in light of your news, too. We are all set to put the whole picture together differently if need be."

I am using only metaphor here. The mind brings up its own various recorded takes on any subject. How the mind makes what might be called a "take" on a subject—that is, how it evaluates experiences that have happened to it sensually, or how it evaluates those experiences that have come about through its own intellection—that is, going back over its previous opinions and categorizations, "changing its mind," so to speak—how it does all that is a miracle of complication. Edelman says in *Bright Air, Brilliant Fire* that the mind loves to get more complicated all the time. Unless it has been damaged or abused, it doesn't want things to be simple. That is, unless its exercise has been cruelly blunted, the mind wants itself—the mind—always to be an active player.

Reentry and Literary Endeavor

Here is Wordsworth using his intuition and literary savvy to talk about what, two centuries later, we are calling reentry.

> The sum of what I have there said is, that the Poet is chiefly distinguished from other men by a great promptness to think and feel without immediate external excitement, and a greater power in expressing such thoughts and feelings as are produced in him in that manner. But these passions and thoughts and feelings are the general passions and thoughts and feelings of men. And with what are they connected? Undoubtedly, with our moral sentiments and animal sensations, and with the causes which excite these; with the operations of the elements, and the appearances of the visible universe; with storm and sunshine, with the revolutions of the seasons, with cold and heat, with loss of friends and kindred, with injuries and resentment, gratitude and hope, with fear and sorrow. These, and the like, are the sensations and the objects which interest them.
>
> I have said that poetry is the spontaneous overflow of powerful feelings: it takes its origin from emotion recollected in tranquility; the emotion is contemplated till, by a species of re-action, the tranquility gradually disappears, and an emotion, kindred to that which was before the subject of contemplation, is gradually produced, and does itself actually exist in the mind. In this mood successful composition generally begins, and in a mood similar to this it is carried on; but the emotion of whatever kind, and in whatever degree, from various causes, is qualified by various pleasures, so that in describing any passions whatsoever, which are voluntarily

> described, the mind will, upon the whole, be in a state of enjoyment.[1]

Journal writers should gratefully take note of Wordsworth's remarks. He enjoys mulling over something as much as catching first sight of it. I think all serious nonfiction writers would be wise to scotch the folk wisdom that downpedals the categorization process, because making new categories is a particularly engaged form of mulling over. What's more, making categories is adventurous and full of feeling, like any philosophical thinking. But there is a caveat: we need to be brave enough to change our categories as fast as light. In psychology such bravery is called "flexibility" or "freshness of spirit" or "open-mindedness." In literature we call it plain "originality."

We have talked mostly about the brain doing the work we call imagination, giving a brief nod to the lower brain functions that keep us alive. We should note that even lower sites, sites in the body, contribute their responses to each new sensory impression to the brain. There is no wall between body and brain. The body, for example, may send up the message that what it's feeling or smelling or seeing is frightening to it. The body may send up the news that it feels inimical. Since both body and its part we call the brain are biological, they do their work by biological means such as population identity. Something new is alien or like. Any novelty might be something we should combine with or perhaps mate with. Perhaps we should eat it up or just kill it. Perhaps we should clear out because we can't kill it. The body has much to say on every sense impression that comes in. Its remarks may be florid or even volcanic, but nothing like so gorgeous as what the imagination comes up with.

A poet whose work is too fussy for my tastes and too intellectual for my intelligence made a remark that I find very exciting. Wallace Stevens said that we should distinguish between mere consciousness—that is, noticing that a bird just flew by and was quite lovely—and *imagination*—or the whole of the reentry process that is at our disposal. Imagination is what ties all else that is going on inside us to our awareness of the bird. What Stevens so admired was that very tying up—the joining up of our memories, our previous values, to this instant's sense impression.

The pressure to put too much stock in sense impression is so forceful that beginning writers who actually long to produce metaphors by processing convictions and philosophies through reentry in their minds are afraid their writing group will find them preachy or strange-hearted. If you are committed to the idea that sense impression is the only source of truth proper for artists then you would be likely to use pejorative language about contemplation, such as "head trip" or "left-brain process." People fond of reentry thinking get called "out of touch with their feelings."

Another (lesser, but related) piece of folk wisdom writers should scotch straight off is the idea that love of nature always comes first and love of art second. It's true that some children appear to fall in love with nature before they fall in love with stories, but we also need to recognize—since we're talking about how the mind changes itself as it functions—that a previously experienced story or painting typically changes how that person sees a perfectly ordinary object of nature—making that person actively feel love, enthusiasm, for some object in nature that he or she might have been merely neutral about.

I have a personal example of this phenomenon to offer: one winter when the snow had melted but the spring was late and wet, I drove in the early morning toward a small town called Princeton, Minnesota, to give a speech. Like anyone else, I took a dim view of the fog, the highway with its scum of sleet, and the smashed grasses in the ditch from the previous growing season.

Suddenly, one bunch of grass in the ditch struck me as quite beautiful. I gave it another look. Why should a bunch of dead, broken grass look so beautiful in late March? At last I realized I was remembering Dürer. Years before, seeing Albrecht Dürer's picture of a bunch of weeds had given me an affiliation with weeds. Today my eyes were seeing only nature, but my mind was alight with the enthusiasm I had once felt for Dürer's weeds. Dürer's weeds transfigured these Highway 65 weeds. That means that my mind was able to overwhelm a dull sense impression with an old neuron category. It was a case of imagination possessing more vigor than sense impression.

Metaphor and Feeling

Taking pleasure from one's mind will never really go out of style, even in the United States, but doing so consciously—on purpose—happens to be out of style just now. Beginning in 1998 I have begun outright urging writing students occasionally to change a sentence that has a subject and a predicate adjective into a metaphor. All language is symbolization at some level, but the use of metaphor exercises the brain differently (more deeply) than does the use of exact adjectives. Metaphor creates stranger connections in those back halls of the neural castle.

Before I launch into the merits of using metaphors, let me first explain predicate adjectives. When the subject of a sentence is described in the predicate, the part of the sentence controlled by the verb, then that part of the sentence is called a *predicate adjective.* The verb is of necessity a form of *to be, to seem,* or *to become.*

One of the style points that Hemingway demonstrated is that predicate adjectives are much more poignant than nominative, stacked adjectives. Hemingway never stacked adjectives. Virginia Woolf never stacked adjectives. Beginning writers, however, especially those working on children's books, tend to stack adjectives. They keep doing it, I expect, because English professors aren't around to nag at them. Here's an example of nominative stacked adjectives versus predicate adjectives.

> *Stacked adjectives in the nominative (subject's) part of the sentence:* The twenty-eight-year-old flaxen-haired girl stood there without speaking.
>
> *How Hemingway would have done it (using predicate adjectival construction):* The girl was twenty years old with flaxen hair. She stood there without speaking.

The predicate adjective construction is a slower-moving, stronger construction than the nominative stacked-adjective construction.

Next let's take the step of creating a metaphor. Remember, we are deliberately allowing the brain to do what it seriously loves to do. It likes to make connections, and it feels deeper emotions when it makes connections than when it creates descriptions, no matter how nice or classy the predicate adjective constructions may be. Here's a comparison:

> *Predicate adjective:* Her fingers were gentle, cool, and delicate.
>
> *Predicate simile:* Her fingers were like snow.

In our best inner work, feeling and thinking are often one and the same thing: they are not separate. When our feelings and our thinking are not extricable, we feel more alive than we do when they're separate. It is an old, grateful, if stale truth that a metaphor suffuses us with sudden feeling; what is rather subtler and less acknowledged is that the metaphor just in itself gives us a philosophical pang as well. I believe this pang occurs because feeling and philosophy are both met in the sword hole of metaphor.

In recent years I have been telling student writers that in addition to keeping journals and taking notes for the works they hope to write, they should keep journals and take notes as a way of developing their own philosophy. Ten years ago I would have felt false about making such a suggestion. Now I know that that's the best piece of advice I have ever given anyone. Each mind wants to have a somewhat unified theory, whatever it can manage. The mind should be willing to change its worldview as fast as a bat can dip or suddenly soar, but at any one time, the mind should have its own way of looking at the world.

Increasing Imaginative Tone

Neuroscience very emphatically suggests that the mind processes not one idea or one emotional response at a time but *many at one time.* We may have several nonconsonant ideas about a given mental event. Earlier in the chapter I mentioned that a merely fleeting opinion on a subject might be our best opinion of the moment. If we look at this likelihood, together with the fact that the fleeting opinion might be very inconsonant with our other thoughts on the subject, we can see how invaluable the fact that the mind chooses to fire on many sites in response to any one stimulus is for an essayist. Our subtlety, our all-around observation of a subject, improves if we regard our several, inconsistent feelings on a subject not as a disgrace but as invaluable mind work. An essayist is helped, not hurt, by saying, "On the other hand, a part of me really winces at that scene I just claimed to admire."

Everywhere in our best-thought through attitudes there are small discrepancies. It's invaluable for an essayist to give such discrepancies credit for possibly being honest communiqués being sent in, straight from the field, so to speak, where the action is, at different sites of the brain. It's invaluable for essayists not to feel threatened that we have a lot of incertitude right within ourselves.

An odd reality check: on the page we have to present things sequentially. Tolstoy wrote sequentially about how Levin felt when taken into a room to meet Anna Karenina. Levin had a number of contradictory feelings about this woman. He felt all these opposing feelings about Anna at the same time because the mind was doing reentry, which happens quite literally as fast as lightning. Tolstoy paid enough attention to his man (Levin) at least to make the list, even if its items were perforce sequential.

I stress the idea of giving some attention to discrepancies in our attitudes and feelings because we need to keep asking ourselves, as we ask ourselves, when doing empathic inquiry, "About this paragraph I just wrote, is that *all* I felt on the subject? It looks a little flat on the page, somehow. Did I feel something else about it, which I haven't put in? Did I, in fact, record only one or two insights out of six or seven?" Sometimes the "something else" was so fleeting that we discounted it. We acted from the conventional wisdom that says that no *fleeting* feeling is a *genuine* feeling.

I can say authoritatively, based on my own experiences with my own mind, that the mind can be be extraordinarily lazy. Perhaps all body parts are lazy. Surely our muscles are. Athletes have to admonish one another or themselves, "Go for the burn." It's possible that even a writer's mind is very unwilling to go for the burn to increase imaginative tone. Our mind is more willing to repeat conventional, oversimplified, partial truths again and again. It will work on conventional projects. It will promote conventional causes. It will write conventional books if we don't call a halt to that way of thinking. Even Orwell, with his mix of self-pity and well-disciplined intellect, confessed that he wrote stupid stuff for years.

At least we know that empathic questioning, either of ourselves by ourselves or of others by others or of us by others, has a way of bucking up our connection-making abilities and broadening the scope of our feelings. Stage-development philosophy says that we all have a good deal more potential for refined, surprising, unconventional thinking than our culture fosters.

I bring this up so that writers can reflect on which gifts of their own backgrounds may have habituated their minds to highly aesthetic goals, to worldly goals, to generalist, ethical goals, or to other goals. Early background doesn't lock you in, but it does give you one or another penchant. Once you become conscious of the effects of your upbringing and environment, you can choose whether or not to resist some of its influences on your thinking and writing. And you can choose to develop yourself in certain ways to emphasize other goals.

Of course, the mind may get encouraged here and slackened there. Mozart's family, for example, stayed in Schiller's or Orwell's stage two: they devoted their lives to music. While Tom Paine was circulating *The Rights of Man* to laborers in England and America, Mozart was composing for strings. Leopold, Mozart's father, worked for the prince-archbishop of Salzburg. Leopold didn't encourage Mozart or the other children to protest the system. His gift to his son was his tireless efforts to *work* the system, for the sake of Mozart's specialist, aesthetical career. His efforts were practical rather than philosophical. Mozart never participated in humanitarian or intellectual life.

Galileo was given an early model for learning to separate himself from the group and to decide what is true without resorting to authority. (See Stage IV of the personal stage-development scheme on page 61 of Chapter 4: what would help a person adjust his or her mind-set so as not to yield to authority?) Galileo Galilei's father, Vincenzo, a musician, had a marvelous scope of mind and intensity and disdain for following authority. He transmitted this penchant to his son, so that young Galileo's mind was freed up from capitulating to authority earlier in life than most people's minds are. Vincenzo Galilei wrote in a manuscript called *Dialogue of Ancient and Modern Music:*

> that they who in proof of any assertion rely simply on the weight of authority, without adducing any argument in support of it, act very absurdly. I, on the contrary, wish to be allowed freely to question and freely to answer you without any sort of adulation, as well becomes those who are in search of truth.[2]

Vincenzo Galilei wrote that passage to his own old music teacher, who had prevented a book of Vincenzo's from being published in Venice in 1578. The old music teacher had opposed Galilei's book because it contained a new theory, and the teacher couldn't abide it.

Very few writers or scientists have a parent who has opposed authority and insisted on searching for the truth no matter where the chips fell. Galileo, who was to be an icon breaker himself, had a great head start from his father.

The essayist and ethicist Scott Russell Sanders points out that James Baldwin had an amazing early advantage as a thinker because his father, a minister, was full of moral rage at the predicament of black Americans. Because his father preached, James Baldwin grew up hearing ideas presented in a magisterial tone. I expect that the Reverend Baldwin never muttered, "I guess so, or maybe that's just me," the way so many adults do when it comes to discussing principle. There was generativity to his father's emotions: that is, the preacher didn't express his opinions as a private man who was involved only in his own life, the way most people do. Baldwin *père* modeled interest in the res publica of people.

So why would having a father like the Reverend Baldwin be such an advantage for a young writer? Scott Russell Sanders tells us that Baldwin had the widest range of diction and syntax that one can find in American literature. Linguists, Sanders says, talk about "register"—the *width of culture* that a writer can draw upon. James Baldwin was able to draw from the width of his father's moral imagination.

Galileo and Baldwin had before them models of people who combined philosophies larger than cogitating and fretting about their own lives. Anyone's mind has *the potential* to focus on larger issues than his or her own, but it is so difficult and unverbalized a goal that millions don't bother. If generativity—the ability to care for anyone or anything outside one's personal life—is not taught verbatim or modeled by lively and loved authority figures, one doesn't learn it. One wouldn't learn even to say *please* or *thank you* if it weren't taught or modeled. Any unnatural behavior has to be taught. Neuroscientists say someone must be actually instructed to focus on a given aspect of life and then to make sensitive connections to other aspects of that person's life. We have to have heard someone say, in so many words, "Your mind has the capability to relate anything coming to it by way of the senses to millions of inner circuits—and what's more whenever it does make such a tie, you will enjoy it." Most human beings don't hear that bracing news. They may never do what Wilbur calls "the very happiest intellection." Mozart didn't want to be a writer or thinker, so he didn't need to call upon the kind of mind work—making connections and having some level of caring for life beyond our own—that creative writers need to call upon. Just so long as we *know* we must try for connections and Sanders's "width of culture," we can work it up, the way one works up any practice.

I am more and more convinced that everyone consciously or unconsciously wants to do inward "reentry" thinking. The vindictiveness in noncontemplative family members shown a philosophically awakened member is usually interpreted as class resentment. The thoughtful person appears to be jumping ship to a greater ship. I no longer think that is the cause of such predictable jeering and sarcasm. Yet why else would loving parents and siblings mete out scorn to the new young thinker? I now think the others feel cross, even wounded because they, too, have the mind of homo sapiens. Their minds, too, want to do agile, conceptual thinking. Their minds are angry because they have been idled back. If the brain makes and amends itself by the very functioning it does, the brain must have the potential to function differently and better at any given moment. C. G. Jung wrote long ago that when the brain has a gift to give, if we don't use it, it turns to poison. The relatives of the joyful new thinker, too unconscious to feel unjustly stuck, give off a sketchy bitterness.

Let's say Jung is right. I suggest, then, that we writers deliberately decide to listen for what might be such a poison in others and in ourselves. Here is an example from my own life.

When I first lived on a farm in rural Minnesota, local young people used to visit my husband and me between Christmas and New Year's Eve. We were the local intellectuals. These college freshmen's parents sometimes came along, too. The parents were quite openly amused and curious about college graduates who didn't even have a "convenient" house. (In western Minnesota "convenient" meant you had plumbing.) I think they partly came to see if it was true that we had to bring up water from the well.

The young college people and their parents would have already had their Christmas doings by the time they came out to our farm for tea. They came to our house to talk about ideas. Some of the parents, oddly enough, peppered the conversations with grating laughs and pointed remarks—"Aren't *we* solving all the world's problems!" and more of the kind. I began to pay attention to their sneering because it came so close to scorn. It purported to be good-natured kidding, but it was sneering. What was this hatred all about? I wondered. For a while I wrote it off as background noise. Then I supposed that people naturally jeer when a conversation departs from small talk.

In the case of the college freshmen and their parents, most of the parents but not the children were stuck in what Schiller would have called "the practical, physical man" stage. They did what Piaget called "concrete" thinking. Their children had climbed a stage and were now into tying disparate concepts into philosophy. The parents were not stupid: they picked up on how enthusiastically their children were drawing up the plans to make their own lives beautiful—Schiller's second stage.

Back then I had not read any stage-development principles—no Piaget, no Loevinger, no Schiller. Later I would come to the conclusion that these parents' *own* minds wanted to be complex. These parents' own minds wanted to do the conceptual thinking their children's minds were doing. These parents picked up on how the children rejoiced in their new lives of making invisible (philosophical) categories. What the parents felt *consciously* was likely this:

1. "We are proud: we got our children to college."
2. "We hope that our children don't 'take up' (a phrase meaning "major in") some impractical subject and end up with an outhouse like these people."

What they felt *unconsciously* was likely: "We are being left out, unfairly. Even the pastor didn't tell us that conceptual thinking made for happiness."

Becoming a Generalist

Creative nonfiction writers need to be generalists, but we are habituated to doing serious thinking only about the issues of literature. If as a beginning writer you decide to become a generalist, you had better defend yourself, somehow, against sneering. We may tell ourselves that people who sneer at other people aren't worth the time of day; nonetheless, being sneered at feels terrible. ("A List of Useful Sentences for Writers in a Tight Spot" in the appendix is designed especially to help student writers ward off joy killers.) The ambiance in some English departments can be cruel. When I was a graduate student we used to say that any English department worth its salt could bring a CIA asset to tears by the end of his first faculty meeting.

For example, since the 1960s and 1970s herd wisdom has guided American essayists to write about themselves meditating alone, either about childhood or looking outward at nature. Those are the common formats for beginning writers. But what if those beginning writers happen to know a bit about engineering? And how wasteful it is that women, in particular, so seldom write about skills they have sharpened with their hands and minds! Loren Eiseley (biologist) and Richard Selzer (surgeon) are lovely essayists in a number of ways, but they are especially blessed in the great virtue of each of them knowing a practice. It's no accident that the hands have many times the number of report-receiving sites in the brain than other body parts have. The more varied one's interests and the more data one has the longer the arc of connections one can make. Some of these interests and data appear impractical or pointless on the surface, yet they seem to exert psychological change.

Thinking about knowing a practice—working with one's hands—led me to a key to the commonly experienced nostalgia not for our own past but for the long past, over 12,000 years ago. I had written off that nostalgia as mere hobbyism before. I had regretted it when it dominated essays I read. But I found myself reading up on preindustrial building techniques. A friend and I were camping in a very remote part of the Superior National Forest of Minnesota. It began to rain. It continued to rain. All the open places in the woods were soon drenched. Soon it would be wet everywhere, even underneath the pines and deciduous trees in full leaf. From widely dispersed areas I took down ten poplar saplings and cut them into eight- and ten-foot lengths. I set up these eight-foot lengths into squares, tied at their corners, until I had a square skeleton of a post-and-beam building made of poplar saplings. Then I tied slightly longer sapling lengths diagonally, because triangles make a structure rigid. Then we staked it down, just for good measure. Over the top of that entire eight-foot by eight-foot by eight-foot skeleton we spread a twenty-by-twenty-five-foot sheet of polypropylene. We drew its huge outer edges far out in all directions and weighted them to the ground. It was so great to watch the water drops smash onto it instead of onto us. Rain kept flowing onto our wonderful, hideous, plastic roof. Then we cut a hole, not quite in the center of our very tall, deeply eaved, eight-by-eight-foot plastic building. We then fed up our fire, because we wanted it going at all times, with its smoke neatly piping out through the eccentric hole.

I foraged deeper into the woods for downed but not rotted birch trees. I cut them into one-inch-thick birch platters with a Swede saw. I hiked these over to our shelter and began drying them on the grate over the fire. When a platter got dry it went into the fire as fuel. The fire stayed hot. Soon we had enough dry wood for a few days, but we kept drying wood whenever we weren't using the fire to cook food. No fable is truer than the ant and grasshopper story. We had been yuppie grasshoppers as campers; now that we were builders we were ants, ants cheerfully gone crazy.

We sat under our spacious, junky, clear-plastic shelter, feeling luxurious. The tent was light, wide; there was room for everything. We listened with satisfaction to the rain slapping down. I was immensely happy. I asked myself at the time, why am I happy? I decided and I still believe that it was because I had practiced a very ancient craft, and not in an interactive folk museum but in the wild, and because we needed to.

Ancientness itself is healing. Once I had a student who had recovered from a childhood of repeated rape by her father. She told me she healed herself by studying knapping. Knapping is the art of chipping off flakes from stone so the core remaining acquires a shape useful for cutting. Anthropology students learn to knap stone as a way to get the feel of Mesolithic life.

Student writers have many such strange experiences, but they are so encouraged to stay ignorant of how the mind works that they are at risk to discount hands-on work. For all we know, hands-on work, like thinking, may be a half-recognized passion even for thinkers, the way philosophy is a dim but genuine passion of laborers.

We need to practice as many different arts—fine arts or primitive arts—as we can, so the mind's circuits can stagger and lurch and catch fire as much as possible. The ancient feelings that our hands send to our brains are not particularly like the emotions we feel as we work on writing. But they bring us closer to other human beings whose work is often different-looking from our own work. Like any biological entity, the brain's structure shows uncountable effects of evolution. Its experience has repeatedly adjusted what happens where.

The Love of Thinking

An important point about the mind is its determination to love the subjects it thinks about—and to love the process of thinking. That is the *philo* of *philosophy*. We can see from the following poem that D. H. Lawrence prefers to *think about* the love life of elephants, as opposed to researching their behavior in some pre-Attenborough resources on elephants. Lawrence's mind deliberately sets out to make a poem that happily (a) exhibits his own moral and sensual tastes (which show everywhere in the poem) and (b) stands as a kind of monument to good humor. The best way to look at pieces of literature like "The Elephant Is Slow to Mate" is to see them as conscious experiments in lovefulness. The trick to this genre (so to speak) is trusting your mind's reentry system.

If that sounds bizarre, remember that Wilbur mentioned the mind's "*happiest* intellection," not its neutral intellection.

THE ELEPHANT IS SLOW TO MATE

The elephant, the huge old beast,
    is slow to mate;
he finds a female, they show no haste
    they wait.

for the sympathy in their vast shy hearts
    slowly, slowly to rouse
as they loiter along the river-beds
    and drink and browse

and dash in panic through the brake
    of forest with the herd,
and sleep in massive silence, and wake
    together, without a word.

So slowly the great hot elephant hearts
    grow full of desire,
and the great beasts mate in secret at last,
    hiding their fire.

Oldest they are and the wisest of beasts
    so they know at last
how to wait for the loneliest of feasts
    for the full repast.

They do not snatch, they do not tear;
    their massive blood
moves as the moon-tides, near, more near,
    till they touch in flood.[3]

What Lawrence is doing in this charming poem is deliberately trusting his mind's ability to make madcap connections. The joy of this poem comes from the poet indulging in what Wilbur called the mind's "happiest intellection." Beginning writers need to give themselves permission to do this kind of work.

We should read the 1990s neuroscientists because they may be right—that when the mind decides to contemplate a subject, choosing its subject partly from habit, partly from free will, partly from life experiences that have come our way, and the mind chooses to go right on contemplating that subject even though doing so can bring no possible profit to one's portfolio—it means that the mind is so glad to be contemplating that subject that it immediately gets wittier and acquires more solemn language.

The mind gets so pleased that its cup runneth over: it may even attribute to others' philosophies that are a little more beautiful than they are realistic. After all, Lawrence's elephants may not mate slowly just because of lack of greed. They must shift great mass just to move one foot. If I weighed 24,000 pounds I'd mate slowly, too. But Lawrence knew how to let his imagination amble along with disinterested love.

As I've mentioned before, a common fault in current literature is its lovelessness. We writers may as well pick up whatever tools of affection we can find. It helps to avoid reading the creative work or textbooks turned out by loveless people. Student writers should read as few loveless critics as they can.

Let's suppose you say to a fellow student writer, "Since I am a writer and each day has twenty-four hours, no more, I am going to read Edward O. Wilson and Gerald Edelman instead of Foucault and de Man."

A loyal colleague might warn you: "Your plan begs for dilettantism, frankly. There's no way you can quickly get any real grasp on complicated subjects like biology or neuroscience."

I think the right answer is: "You are right. It does beg for dilettantism. And, of course, I won't get anything like what you could call a *grasp* on either field. For one thing, neuroscientists themselves haven't got a *grasp* on the brain yet. . . . On the other hand, I like it that our minds—the minds in all of us—want a unified theory of everything. I am going to read up on it."

A conventional question: if we writers do study the current developments concerning MRI or other revelations about the brain, won't we spoil our feelings of amazement? Feelings of awe are very dear to our species. Let's give awe a second look, however. We can divide awe up into at least two quite separate feelings—one is fear in the presence of scary unexplained phenomena. (The brilliant opening shots of *2001* show us our ancestors cowering.) A second component of awe is admiration for strong effects achieved by someone other than ourselves, sometimes by gods (rogue waves, electric storms).

When people inform themselves about electric storms or neural activity, the more information they get, the greater part of their "awe" is transmuted to admiration and interest, the fear having become the lesser part. Here's Damasio on the subject:

> Finally it is important to realize that defining emotion and feeling as concrete, cognitively and neurally, does not diminish their loveliness or horror, or their status in poetry or music. Understanding how we see or speak does not debase what is seen or spoken, what is painted or woven into a theatrical line. Understanding the biological mechanisms behind emotions and feelings is perfectly compatible with a romantic view of their value to human beings.[4]

I want to reprint a short essay about playfulness in trusting the metaphor-making mind, Ted Kooser's "King: Dog of the North." In this work Kooser tells us about the occasion that made him first trust his literary mind.

KING: A DOG OF THE NORTH

> When I was a freshman in college, when I was beginning to take myself seriously as a poet, I came down with pneumonia following a drunken tobogganing party. I was very ill, hospitalized for ten days and out of my head with fever for the first week. The walls and ceiling of my room took on a strange, softly undulating life that terrified me. Once I saw glossy wet fur growing out of the grain of the wooden door. I later recalled having well-wishing visitors—friends and relatives—who in fact had never been to see me.
>
> As my fever fluctuated, I experienced brief periods of clarity, and would lie with my sweaty bedding twisted about me,

reading a book that someone had left by the bed. It was the only reading material in the room, a boy's novel about a German shepherd named King. Time and again, King came to the rescue of his blundering master. I knew that it was a book my intellectual college friends and teachers would sneer at, but my illness had reduced me to childishness, and as a child I fell for this simple, engrossing story. I was twenty years old, but because I was sick I had regressed to half that age. I was completely dependent upon the loving care of adults—my parents, my doctor and nurses. Near the end of my hospital stay, when my sweetheart of four years came to my hospital room to tell me that she had found another boyfriend, I let her go without an argument, having been beaten back into a bemused, passive, prepubescent state.

The story of the noble dog, King, sustained me against the billowy craziness upon which my bed floated and bobbed like a raft. His story was richly detailed and absorbing. He made his way through snowdrifts; up and down the sheer faces of mountains; through flooded, ice-choked streams. King's adventures were breathtaking, marvelous, and like the faithful dog he was he was always within calling range when his master needed him.

When my temperature finally went down and stayed down, I began looking about the room for the book, but it was nowhere to be found. My nurses told me that I'd been given no books because I'd been much too ill to read. When my parents came to visit I asked them what had happened to it and they said they couldn't recall ever seeing such a book. No one could account for the missing King.

But the book was vividly impressed upon my memory. I could still feel it in my hands and see its print in front of my eyes. It had to be there somewhere. I described it in detail: it had no dust jacket and was bound in red cloth frayed by wear; the binding was slightly sticky after holding it for a while; it was a little over an inch thick and had a comfortable, serious-feeling heft to it; the pages were of good pre-war rag paper and had deckled edges; it had the good, glue-and-ink smell of a book; the spine was stamped with the title in gold foil: *King: A Dog of the North.*

There were, of course, many such books in print at the time, the dog story being a staple of juvenile reading, and I had possibly read one or two of them when I'd been younger. But what I came to believe is that in my delirium I wrote, printed, bound and published *King: A Dog of the North.* I made it all up. Just as King, the dog, was always there when his master fell into the arms of a bear, *King*, the book, had snatched me from the jaws of pneumonia.

I have been a writer ever since. Oh, I'd written some poems before I got pneumonia, but it took pneumonia to make me serious about writing. The creation of *King: A Dog of the North*, a solid accomplishment of the imagination, may have given me the confidence to try my hand at letting my imagination carry me forward, toward other stories, and poems, and essays like this one. And whatever success I've had as a writer I may owe in some part to that magnificent silver-haired German shepherd who vanished into the frozen wasteland once he had sent me back to health. Writing late at night, sometimes I imagine his great paws padding through the snow.[5]

6.
Literary Fixes

This chapter takes up a few craft issues in nonfiction writing. Other authors have handled them wonderfully. We all need all the help we can get. We need to hear one another's diverse opinions about questions of craft.

Of the myriad how-to-write and how-not-to-write resources, I suggest that essayists *own* three. If you have these (two books and one essay) at hand you will have a generous treasury on language, style, and tone that you can return to again and again until their advisories are written in your mind.

- "Politics and the English Language," by George Orwell (originally published in *Horizon* in 1946, and much anthologized ever since). This is still the definitive essay on how the use of fresh or dead language is related to how beautiful a piece of writing is and how much meaning a work has. Orwell's is still one of the most technically exact and generous essays about writing.

- *Writing Well,* by Donald Hall. In several editions (1973 to 1988) Hall identifies a huge number of beginners' natural technical mistakes—and provides cures for each. Hall's work can save you what might otherwise add up to years of wondering why your writing hasn't so much flavor or brightness as you wish it had.

- *The First Five Pages,* by Noah Lukeman (Fireside Books, Simon and Schuster, 2000). A personable, funny, sensible-minded discussion of dozens and dozens of specific points of style for fiction as well as nonfiction writing. Lukeman also pays attention to key issues in presenting manuscripts to agents and publishers. This is the perfect all-terrain book for nonfiction writers since Lukeman specifically relates problems about feeling and tone to language issues.

All three of these authors are focused on how we keep our spirit clear and not gassy when we write essays. Dylan Thomas was no doubt right in saying that a lot of the time we make "our sullen art in the still hours of the night for lovers who pay no heed (or wages) to our craft."[1] He tells us that the lovers have their arms round each other, round the "griefs of the ages," he says, so we may not get them to heed our creative nonfiction. Still—to whichever human beings do pause in their ordinary life long enough to read our essays—we want to offer literary *craft,* not hapless rambling.

The main idea of this chapter is that literature should drive *inward.* If the manuscript seems a little too sociological, we want to move it inward from mere sociology to, say, both sociological and psychological content. If your manuscript seems stuck in extroverted physical description, then you may want to make that physical exposition—of nature or a town or a room—symbolic or suggestive of the inner feelings of the people in that landscape, in that town, or in that room. The twelve fixes outlined in this chapter are tools writers can use to drive their observations to subtler, more personal levels.

It is important to remember that literary fixes are only literary fixes. They are appropriate only to the third of the three stages of writing a piece of work.

Driving the Exposition Inward

Exposition is the description of places or people, usually done early on in a piece of writing, and providing a setting for essays as well as works of fiction. There are basically two ways to write exposition. The first way is to describe the person or the place, using adjectives in a straightforward manner. Two people famous for this kind of exposition are W. Somerset Maugham and D. H. Lawrence. Maugham had a realist's interest in describing exactly what a person's face looks like or what a person's getup looks like or what the weather was like at four in the morning when that person happened to be leaning over the scarred rail of a second-rate ship. I don't know of anyone who surpasses Maugham in this. D. H. Lawrence gives a wealth of adjectival detail too, but he chooses it for symbol at least as much as for extrovert interest.

In a second kind of exposition, difficult to do, as soon as possible the writer drops in abstractions that lead inside the characters. The faster we see inside people, the faster we get the drift of what the places, the people, the props mean to human personality. Natalia Ginzburg is an expert at this. Here she is using her art in a short passage that purports to be simply a description of the Abruzzi mountain range in Italy.

> There are only two seasons in the Abruzzi: summer and winter. The spring is snowy and windy like the winter, and the autumn is hot and clear like the summer. Summer starts in June and ends in November. The long days of sunshine on the low, parched hills, the yellow dust in the streets and the babies' dysentery come to an end, and winter begins. People stop living in the streets: the barefoot children disappear from the church steps. . . . Many bricklayers come from that area, and some of the houses were elegantly built; they were like small villas with terraces and little columns, and when you entered them you would be astonished to find large dark kitchens with hams hanging from the ceilings, and vast, dirty, empty rooms. In the kitchen a fire would be burning, and there were various kinds of fire: there were great fires of oak logs, fires of branches and leaves, fires of twigs picked up one by one in the street. It was easier to tell the rich from the poor by looking at the fires they burnt than by looking at the houses or at the people themselves, or at their clothes and shoes which were all more or less the same.[2]

The text starts in a matter-of-fact sort of way but quickly brings in mysterious, inward kinds of considerations, cordially bringing the reader into the thinking through her exposition. Ginzburg says, "You would be astonished to find large dark kitchens with hams hanging from the ceilings." The fine touch of this description of a place is that having described what the rooms looked like, with their dirt and poverty, she remarks, "It was easier to tell the rich from the poor by looking at the fires they burnt than by looking at the houses or at the people themselves, or at their clothes and shoes which were all more or less the same." Now the essay resounds. Some people are poor, some people are rich. Ginzburg's passage draws on a large repertoire of intense adjectives: *parched, astonished, vast, dirty.* They brace up the style. Ginzburg has surprise content as well as language: She gives us the unusual—it's not the clothes that distinguish the poor but their fires. Instantly I know she had it right and was speaking for those of us who are less precise.

In my own country experience: we were at my brother-in-law Jim's farmhouse to play whist one evening. It was near the end of corn picking. Jim was a rich farmer. There was a knock. It was a poor farmer. The two men talked at the door in low voices so the poor man wouldn't be embarrassed by the rich man's wife overhearing. The poor man had come to ask if Jim was going to use that pile of corncobs piled up against Jim's machinery building. Cobs make a fast, hot, workable fuel. Tending such a fire is very labor-intensive, so better-off people burn less troublesome fuel. A rich farmer like Jim would not burn corncobs for fuel if you paid him, but the poor farmer would be delighted to fill his beat-up pickup bed with cobs. He had his wife out there in the dark ready to help. For an hour we could hear the thuds of cob-loading and the occasional talk of the couple working outside. We were making our own sounds, too—shuffling, laughing, vowing vengeance in the next hand—but we were aware of those people outside. I was glad when they drove away.

It's a good idea for creative nonfiction writers to read poetry because poets drive exposition inward so much faster than most fiction writers and nonfiction writers do—they have so little space.

No law says that an author *must* drive the exposition inward, though. Some nature poetry, for example, describes only the outside looks of things; the writer uses adjectives and an accurate eye, mines a journal, getting it right about what it was like by such and such a snowy lake or on the John Muir Trail or near a brown well at Riyadh. There's nothing wrong with such writing. We call it "nature writing" because its tempo is the easy tempo of somebody observing things outside himself or herself that have feeling but no particular profound *meaning* for the person making the observation.

More serious poets or nonfiction writers may keep the usual notebooks full of nature observations, but they don't value nature observations for their own sake. They want to cast light on the troublesome or passionate things of the human mind. This poem by Scott King is quoted in its entirety so we can see how very fast a writer can move inward right down through the physical aspects of the place setting.

AT THE SHORE OF SNOWBANK LAKE

Search in your heart
for the sun that has left
—Yannis Ritsos

This would be a good place to look for the bones of poets,
the ones who had no paper, who knew what it was like
to speak through holes in the wind,
a good place to listen to the wind filling up the silence,
clamoring over the deadfalls of a brutal century.
I stand here and only watch as seagulls
gather up remnants of shattered light off the waves
watch the sun crumbling at the horizon, knowing soon
the moon will come and place its hands in this lake
in order to rinse the blood from its bandages.
I was born with a war in my eyes, so it is easy
to imagine ashes dissolved in this lake's clear water
like sugar or the taste of glaciers, easy to imagine
the long sound of rocks being ground to sand.
This is a strange place, however peaceful, however isolate,
where trees freeze upright in winter unable to bend
to the sun, a strange place where the stars have labored
thousands of years to wear these grooves in the rock, here, where
the one road ends and begins in water.

I look at all the yellowed leaves steeping in puddles,
I watch the pale eyelids of the dozing lichen.
I notice the spider webs that buttress the ruins of autumn,
the strewn desolation of the forest's floor.
I study the bleached and rusting claws of crayfish.
I catch myself living in the moment's decay.
Now five or six snowflakes come down from the clear sky
and I realize I have no gods to invoke, nothing but
this solitude, a single loon calling
somewhere between the sun and a tiny minnow of moon,
somewhere between all the stars and drowning,
as though it had carved a whistle out of my bones.[3]

To make clear what's meant by "going inward as quickly as we can" with exposition, not settling for writing only "outer" observations, here is a version of Scott King's poem in which the words and phrases that drive the writing inward have been deleted, leaving only the surface observations of nature.

I stand here and only watch as seagulls
gather up remnants of shattered light off the waves
watch the sun crumbling at the horizon, knowing soon
the moon will come and place its hands in this lake. . . .
This is a strange place, however peaceful, however isolate,
where trees freeze upright in winter unable to bend
to the sun, a strange place where the stars have labored
thousands of years to wear these grooves in the rock, here, where
the one road ends and begins in water.
I look at all the yellowed leaves steeping in puddles,
I watch the pale eyelids of the dozing lichen.
I notice the spider webs that buttress the ruins of autumn,
the strewn desolation of the forest's floor.
I study the bleached and rusting claws of crayfish.
I catch myself living in the moment's decay.
Now five or six snowflakes come down from the clear sky. . . .
nothing but
this solitude, a single loon calling

somewhere between the sun and a tiny minnow of moon,
somewhere between all the stars . . .

The poem still has its beautifully observed remarks about a peaceful, lonely place. Where King says, "I catch myself living in the moment's decay" there's pathos. But how light the feelings are compared to those in the lines that were taken out! King actually went inward with the very first line of his poem: "This would be a good place to look for the bones of poets." That's fast work, but he plummets even faster:

the ones who had no paper . . .
a good place to listen to the wind filling up the silence,
clamoring over the deadfalls of a brutal century.

Deadfalls, originally "dead furrows," is a term used in plowing. In the middle of the field where two center rows of plowing have thrown earth away, one to the left, one to the right, leaving a positive trench—which makes for rough work later. King uses this image for its realism and its deadness. He isn't five lines into this poem before he is telling us that people want to write who have no paper and that we live in a brutal century. And then, a little later, when he says that he knows that "the moon will come and place its hands in this lake," the line would be only beautiful (a stage two value of Schiller's and Orwell's) if King hadn't added, "in order to rinse the blood from its bandages." Now we know that he is talking about people being cruel to other people. The next line is really a classical *telling, not showing* sort of line. It is a little sententious, but it works perfectly: "I was born with a war in my eyes." If he had said, "I was born in a time of constant wars," that wouldn't be so interesting. When he says the war is *in his eyes* we know that when he looks at other things with those same eyes he will always see the war back in behind them. It's psychologically acute and beautifully put, I think. Imagine when we think of the ashes of gypsies and Jehovah's Witnesses and Jews in Germany—to hear this line in the central United States: "So it is easy / to imagine ashes dissolved in the lake's clear water." John Donne would say, yes, that's right, all ashes are your ashes.

A poem is structured very much like an essay. Its metaphors don't keep it from its essaylike thought. Vague love of nature and primitive religions cannot spackle over this kind of thinking. Serious authors may celebrate nature or celebrate ritual, but they can't mollify their griefs in either genre.

King's subject and the dramatic quality of his writing remind me of Arnold's "Dover Beach." Matthew Arnold makes a perfectly satisfying seaside-nature writer until he tells us that none of the old, comfortable unified systems work, and, as Sophocles long ago noticed, no providential god is looking out for us. Therefore it's doubly lonely out here at night, looking at the edge of the sea. Of course, the sea is quite wonderful. But *people* do such terrible things to each other. The human race is such a disaster, Arnold says, that if we are in love with anybody, we should cling to him or her, because public Homo sapiens behavior is about "stupid armies clashing in the night."

Once we learn the literary trick of inviting several different memories to come up to meet whatever physical scene we're looking at, then a child's enjoyment of natural realism is over for us. Whenever we see a lake or look at the moon we are vulnerable to thinking of hands and we might think of blood. We might imagine people's ashes at the bottom of the lake, and it might occur to us that we live in a brutal century. This is a literary version of *loss of innocence*. It means we'll write better prose or poems, but it's likely we'll never again be blithe or provincial.

Scott King is a fairly new poet who, as we've seen, happens to do very well this process of driving the exposition inward, inviting his brain to do what the neuroscientists call "reentry"—letting imagination join our consciousness.

How shall we do that? At the edge of a lake our mere consciousness cries, "Here's the lake; it's beautiful (or it isn't beautiful)." Then we can ask ourselves very pointedly, "Yes, and what else is going on?" What else is going on is all the things in our imagination that we really care about, and not being wooden heads, can't escape them. Asking ourselves, "And what else is going on?" is what Wallace Stevens would call being sure you work not just with consciousness but with imagination.

Here are four perfect examples of exposition that might have lain supine on the text surface as "realism" except that, in each case, the author wrested up from inside himself a very strange metaphor. All four examples are from James Salter, one of the most enchanting makers of metaphor in English.

> ∞ She was too tired to make love. It had been left on the dance floor. Or else she did, halfheartedly, and like two bodies from an undiscovered crime they lay, half-covered in the early light, in absolute silence except for the first, scattered sound of birds.[4]

I expect hundreds of authors have described people being too tired to make love. Such passages are typically done in a casual, half-disrespecting vein. But James Salter never diminishes his characters. Even though he writes about physical love a good deal, he manages to avoid superciliousness. Here the surprise comes from the crime metaphor. We feel the author being imaginative and funny, not offhand. Lying like "two bodies from an undiscovered crime, . . . half-covered in the early light" is both nice and funny. The "scattered" sound of birds is an awfully nice parallel for those two, the man and the woman, themselves "scattered." Anyone who's ever experienced bad sex is glad of Salter's getting it right without writing scornfully.

> ∞ From the house, Louise was watching with occasional glances, impatient, half-resigned, like a woman whose husband is intent on some ruinous, quixotic labor.[5]

I am grateful for the Louise passage because it's one of only two passages I've ever read in American literature in which a housewife is resigned to some inanity of her husband, but the author doesn't blame it on her as if *she* were a joy killer, someone too dull to see what an ingenious man is really about.

An exquisite touch is the author's use of an intensifying simile. The abstract word *labor* adds dignity to any scene. If Salter had said that the woman gave her husband "occasional glances, impatient, half-resigned, like a woman whose husband was doing one more pointless weekend project in the garden," the subject itself would be different: the subject would have been her irritation. Salter's subject is bigger—major: the husband will ruin them financially, and he doesn't have a good grasp on reality, but the word *labor* is dignified. Not all labor is worth doing, but labor has its own honor, all the more honor if it is "quixotic labor." The original meaning of Don Quixote's labor, please know, was "honorable labor," not feckless make-work.

> The rock, when he touched it, was like the side of a deep, sunken wreck.[6]

> It had been a large villa but there had been a decline in its status, like the palaces taken over by troops in a revolution. It contained a number of ill-defined apartments. The walls were bare, the plaster faded.[7]

The power of the images in these two quotes lies in their likening ordinary structures—mountainside rock and villa, respectively—to structures of more momentous feeling than rocks and villas usually evoke.

Raising the Tone

Now that we've come closer to finishing our manuscript, it's time to check over the tone. Some of the following points about tone may be surprising. Others are the usual, useful remarks made by thousands of teachers of creative writing.

Start with small tone fixes. Run through the manuscript and take out, wherever you find them, expressions like "kind of a" followed by a noun. Leave the noun itself. If you wrote, "He was some kind of a crook," the sentence will read better as "He was a crook"—unless you are deliberately echoing the midwestern use of "some kind of a Communist" or the Marine drill instructor's "some kind of a fairy." You want to make a stronger commitment to what you're saying. If the man was a crook, go for it. Say so.

Remove every use of *seemingly*, because *seemingly* deintensifies what you have just said. If someone is "seemingly rude," you probably mean to say that he or she is rude. You had better stand by the idea that the person is rude, and say so. *Seemingly* is chickenhearted.

I would remove British Toryisms that make manuscripts seem thoughtful but in fact really flatten them. Some examples are "as it were" and "perhaps" and "a bit" and "in the event," each of them as spineless as blancmange. Decide how strongly you feel about something and then say it, instead of half saying it and half taking it back. If you're going to half take something back because you aren't sure about it, you might want to do this: put your point in confident, clean prose, and then add, like a genial essayist: "On the other hand that's not always true." One of your opinions may come from one site in the brain; the other might hail from somewhere else in your brain, as was discussed in Chapter 5.

A second means of scouring off wormy style is to add more pure information to the manuscript. Creative nonfiction writers sometimes fear doing any research lest it spoil their spontaneity, even though readers really like to learn some information. So instead of writing, "God knows how many people died in the cause of what's-it," either get onto a Web site and find out the death toll, or find the e-mail address of someone who knows. "Over three million soldiers and one million civilians died in that particular cause" is a thousand times more telling than exclaiming, "Who knows how many millions of people died."

When we start writing, we pay too little attention to how intrigued people are by specific information, not to mention how grateful they are if that information is correct. There are no psychological studies to suggest that ignorance or inaccuracy improve the imagination. In fact, as anthropologists and sociologists have pointed out in various ways, the more we *know*, the less we go round and round in rituals. Rituals satisfy those who like them but they are a psychological artifact of *celebration*, not of fresh thinking.

The appendix of this book includes a handout called "A Format for Writing Essays." This formal layout is actually freeing. It suggests several ways for writers to be both informative and opinionated, no matter what your subject. One of its points is that if people other than you have been thinking about the material you've been thinking about, and they have offered thoughts or useful data, it is comradely to mention them. If other cultures have produced contrasting opinions about your subject, it is pleasant and it's informative to point to those opinions.

I see no reason not to bring to an end the present habit of creative writers' being vague and unscholarly about who is saying what on their subjects. Civilization is partly about noticing and appreciating what other people are doing.

Changing Statement to Theater (Showing, not Telling)

Changing statement to theater means giving readers the scene by telling a story or short anecdote to illustrate a thought. Narratives are the meat and potatoes of creative nonfiction. (Of course, narrative is the very backbone of fiction.) Story isn't absolutely necessary in nonfiction, but we miss it horribly when there isn't any. Those old hardtack essays of Francis Bacon's, for example, which lack even a single example, are uncollegial. Who does Bacon think he is, sounding off without providing examples? Dickens was best at presenting things theatrically instead of discussing things, although he did a great deal of both, and both with a head of steam. Dickens shows ingenuity in how he combines *unlike issues* in a given scene; we essayists, too, are best when we combine unlike issues. We place a reference to one kind of memory next to some mention of another kind of memory. We shove together references to unlike events in history, as Scott King does in his poem discussed earlier in this chapter. Dickens combines unlike worlds beautifully in *Great Expectations.* Pip, the classic self-centered egoist, who makes up to the rich and condescends to the poor, has arrived at Wemmick's house. Wemmick has put the "aged P" (aged parent) by the fire and is spoon-feeding him. At one point Wemmick interrupts his business conversation with Pip to ask if Pip will please do the aged P's sausage for him while Wemmick attends to some other small task. We get first-class self-centeredness in Pip and first-class kindness in Wemmick together.

Some writers may ask the question, "How should I change what now stands as acceptable direct comment into theater?" or, as they say in the usual fiction-writing manuals, "How should I stop *telling* and how can I *show*?" I think the easiest way to effect this literary fixing is to look over each of your general comments one by one. Say you have written this sentence: "People capable of poisonous wrath are also capable of simple kindnesses." Say you have just written an essay on that theme. You can empathically ask yourself: "What incident first made me feel so warmly on the subject?" Let's say you got attracted to the idea through the wisdom of Ray Carver's "A Small, Good Thing." In Carver's story, a baker was outraged that a family never got around to picking up the cake he'd baked especially for their child. The baker couldn't know that the child had died that week. At last he does know. He invites the family members to take chairs in his bakery. He gives them rolls and coffee. He speaks to them compassionately, but it is in the drawing up of the chairs and his urging them to take food that his kindness is shown.

Another great example of a piece that explores an idea as theater (story) when the idea could have been covered with just psychological comment is W. H. Auden's famous "Musée des beaux arts" about Brueghel's painting *Icarus.* The painting shows Icarus falling into the sea because his wax wings have melted. A ship has not changed course to save Icarus because the ship had, Auden said, "somewhere to get to." Children, dogs, and horses carry on business as usual in the foreground of the painting. An essayist might say, "Basically, when something of passionate concern is happening for one person, such as his own death, others in the neighborhood may not be interested." That is telling. Auden is a show-er. He is often conversational:

> how everything turns away
> Quite leisurely from the disaster . . .
> and the expensive ship that must have seen
> Something amazing, a boy falling out of the sky,
> Had somewhere to get to and sailed on.[8]

Combating Lying and Cowardice

Checking Self-Aggrandizement

A problem of our communication age is that we know words for intense crises, terrible tragedies, wonderful ecstasies, tremendous glamour, and so forth, a good deal of which may not be any part of our own lives. Our lives might be quite simple and in the low-key range of feeling. For example, I myself have never seen a genocide. I have not even been introduced to anyone who *wants* to kill other people by the tens of thousands. If our life has run in a safe and middling course, in a reasonable climate, we had better not pretend that we have experienced all sorts of violent things we don't know anything about.

Maybe we should be *very* hard on ourselves, and say, "No, I have not had such and such an experience. I may have tragic feelings on behalf of the people who *have* had that experience, but commiseration is not the same as personal knowledge." If one is born in New Jersey and lives one's life in New Jersey, occasionally in New York, and does some summering in Maine or New Hampshire, that is not the same thing as being born in East Timor or in Rwanda and not getting the opportunity to live long enough to summer anywhere.

We can make Chekhov our model: most of his work shows the depths in the most tepid, inland waters. That nonglamorizing quality of his accounts for some of his exquisitely vivid scenes.

In the final stage of preparing a book or essay it helps to read the text aloud. Then you can hear any false feelings that remain in the work. Your voice might tell you, "That sounds hollow. I think I was being gassy here."

A tangential benefit to reading a manuscript aloud is that you have another chance to change your mind about the honesty of something you've said. As you hear it you can say, "Oh, I felt that so strongly when I wrote it, but now that I hear my voice saying it, exactly the opposite seems to be the truth." This kind of revelation is a gift of step 4 of the empathic inquiry technique described in Chapter 3. I consider this phenomenon to be also an artifact of reentry (Chapter 5). Amending the conversation is easy for creative nonfiction writing, since we are in constant conversation with the reader anyway. We essayists can actually say that such and such appears to be passionately true, and on the other hand—at the same time—another inner voice calls out exactly the opposite. We can name what that opposite is. In other words, we can take the reader with us through our deliberations.

A last word about self-aggrandizement in creative nonfiction. Because we live in a nonjudgmental, vapid culture, people commonly tell writers, "You are too hard on yourself." We had better look askance at that remark when it comes to literary fixing. Much writing is sloppy and casual, poorly thought through, full of classic beginners' mistakes; likely most of us are *not hard enough* on ourselves.

Checking for and Distinguishing between Surprising Insights and Conventional Insights

It is easier to write in a narrative, conversational, nonconventional way if you check over your manuscript for conventional opinions you may be mindlessly passing along. Sometimes nonfiction authors feel that they must show acquaintance with the conventional opinions on a given subject—but giving them play time is a good plan only if you mean to refute them or sturdily admit that they are tiresome but right. Otherwise, watch out that you don't get stuck in the lukewarm sargasso of usual ideas. Usual ideas spread here or there like flu. They do harm. Conventional opinions can spoil your ears. Their constant drumming deafens you to symbol.

An essential difference between experienced and beginning writers is the amount of *surprise* they give us—not just surprise in language but surprising insight, that is, surprising connections made in the brain. One way to write fresh prose is to look at any shopworn observation you have put down and say to yourself, "But what else do I think about that?" It's no good scolding yourself for having used a shopworn expression. Shame does not make us write better. Shame only makes us feel irredeemable, and then we don't write at all. We float away from the page completely. Instead, ask yourself, "And where am I on that subject really, myself?"

The first time in my life I ever said anything surprising, what I said was a lot less attractive than what everybody else was saying on the subject. I was living in Iowa City at the time. My dinner guests were eight people from the Iowa Writing Workshop. Of the several foreign writers attending that year, one student (not a dinner guest) was very much in style. Everyone was praising him. Everyone said how wonderful he was, particularly since he wrote so beautifully about the peasantry of his country. (He did.) So this young writer had tremendous cachet with the head of the workshop, Paul Engle, and the poet, Marguerite Young, then a visiting eminence and a witty presence, and the other foreign students and miscellaneous other members of the workshop. They spoke of how magical his writing was, and so forth. I listened to all that dinner-table praise as I made the rounds offering seconds, dessert, coffee. I fell into a Nietzschean *ressentiment* because I had cooked the meal and provided a lot of liquor, which these literati were lapping up in their 1950s way. The adulation went on and on and on. I thought suddenly, I've been listening to this fellow being praised all fall, and you know what? There is something precious about his work. . . . I am not so crazy about his work. . . . Besides, anyone can write about peasantry. What's *hard* to write about is the middle classes. Suddenly I heard my voice singing out over the group saying, "Yes, but he gives me a pain in the ass."

There was a silence. Then Mary Engle, a very original loose cannon of a person, changed my career life. She gave a howl. She shouted, "That is the most wonderful remark! Thank you very much." Oh, then, I thought, it is all right to add the truth that half sours an earlier truth? The writer was wonderful and *also* a pain in the ass? No one had said it because people want to be attractive, not grouchy.

I suggest that when you find yourself repeating conventional opinions in a manuscript, ask yourself, "Well, is there some sense in which I really don't agree with this opinion at all?" If the new, or amended, opinion sounds grouchy, tell yourself, "What if Toni Morrison or William Hazlitt or Adrienne Rich worried about sounding grouchy?"

Let me add a last word about sounding grouchy where others are affable. Memoirs tend to be loyal to the family. But if in the memoir something comes up that future generations need to know in order to be spared the same old suffering of past generations, we have to decide whether we write to spare those future generations or if we write to stay affably loyal to our mother's half brother who raped four of the kids when they were little. I suggest everyone read Richard Hoffman's essay, "What's Love Got to Do with It?"[9] which points to the issue of soft-soaping felony so that the author will appear to be a loving person. Hoffman has also written a book on the subject of whether to write attractive, forgiving literature about pederasts: *Half the House*. Hoffman, an experienced fiction and essay writer, says straight out: name felons. They need to be in prison.

A blessing of creative nonfiction, this genial, formless form, is that an author can outright confess how embarrassing it is to stand up for something that everyone else finds ridiculous. We have to remember that somewhere out there in the readership are people like us; they will be grateful for our surprising opinion, because that's been their opinion all along. They have been longing for that rapist to be imprisoned.

Removing Self-References

Self-references are remarks that are about you, not about your subject. Self-referencing pulls the reader out of manuscript time, thereby vastly slowing the pace. In the remark, "I remember how in 1980 such and such happened," "I remember" is self-referencing. In the sentence, "In 1980 such and such happened," there is no self-referencing, and the pace picks up. Your reader stays focused on such and such, which happened in 1980.

Two considerations regarding self-referencing: one is that by putting yourself in the text all the time saying, "I remember . . . ," or "I will never forget how . . . ," you may be blocking not only readers but also *a part of your own psyche* from staying concentrated on the thing that happened, because you are thinking of yourself. Too large a part of you may be dwelling on how *you* were there, and oh, you were feeling this and you were feeling that. Back off, emotionally speaking, the better to see all the differentiation and fine points of the scene you're describing. If you actually remove, quite mechanically, those mechanical phrases "I felt" or "I could hardly believe" or "I remember," you might get a lightning improvement in focus.

"I remember" is the most common form of self-referencing and the second least interesting. Memoirs naturally tend to be cursed with "I remember." Sometimes it appears as "I will never forget how . . ." The worst curse of all is "I *don't* remember." Beginning writers are obsessed with where they are or were themselves. Let's say you write, "I remember living with my sister all those years on Scheissenstrasse," and then you add, "I don't remember whether she and I shared meals or not." Well, if you don't remember, don't write down that you don't remember. Either skip mention of the meals, or, even better, call up your sister if you two are still speaking and find out if she shared meals with you. In other words, "I remember," "I don't remember," and "I will never forget" are too self-centered. You may keep the self-centered *material*—that's all we writers have to work with!—but don't keep the self-centered *language*. Self-referencing feels, in fact, like a limp type of what Virginia Woolf called "author intrusion."

A psychological, inward way to quit self-referencing is to remind yourself to trust the material itself. The parts of your life that move you, embedded with their particulars as they are, are of universal interest. No matter how peculiar your particular situation seems to be as it rises up before your memory, others will see in your material something of meaning to them. They will be gratified that you wrote about your experience. We readers are right with you, nearly recalling it as our own. Trust us to be touched by your past.

One of the most extraordinary validations of good literature I ever experienced was in the School of Nursing office at the University of Minnesota half a century ago. I was a very junior clerk typist. My immediate superior was the administrative secretary, an intelligent, serious-hearted woman named Margaret Peterson. Margaret Peterson told me at lunch one day that what was good about Tolstoy and the reason she liked his work was that it was universal and that *we all have those feelings he talks about.* I looked at Margaret Peterson. She was thirty-two, spending her working life as an executive secretary in a lively enough office, but it was just an office, and it was in the United States, in 1951, all so different from Count Tolstoy's world. I thought of sixteen-year-old Petya longing to go to war, and how he was killed after *one minute* of action in *War and Peace*. I thought of the love affairs of Natasha and of Count Bolkonsky and of the vagaries of Pierre. Margaret Peterson read about Pierre's interest in Freemasonry, his capture by the French, and she felt inside herself everything Tolstoy presents in the novel. Why, then, shouldn't we all trust that when we write anything we feel, others who may not at first glance seem to be of like temperament or experience will be touched by what we write?

I've since learned something else that I didn't know when I made my endless multiple carbons for Margaret. American literature needs to be written by people like Margaret Peterson.

If you get rid of self-referencing, your manuscript acquires formality. Formality serves to intensify material. Here's an example: "I will never forget how, in August of 1914, the heat lay all over Europe and our ears filled with rumors of war" is not nearly so intense as "In August of 1914 the heat lay all over Europe, and our ears filled with rumors of war." Formality does *not* make the writing cold and distant; it makes it possible for people to *jump into the scene faster.*

Notice how formality blesses our experience of the intensity of music. The director comes out to direct. No sound, no anchor chat to the audience. The conductor bows to us with the respect of an artist about to serve us and art itself, then turns around with his or her back to the audience, and raises arms or baton. The message of this ritual stirs deeply in the audience member's mind: "I am capable of receiving intense art suddenly. I don't need to have some dumb radio continuity written into it. I don't need to be told, 'Well, hi, folks, here we are, it's evening in the Ordway Theatre, and pretty soon we'll be warming you up with some Mozart. Our own [hometown director's name] will be working the crowd tonight. And of course, Mozart's probably somebody a lot of you have heard about.'" Formal silence says that if Mozart did something beautiful you will get it, and the Mozart piece performed will be the more beautiful if there is total silence beforehand. So I suggest the same framing, some formality, in our creative nonfiction writing.

Removing All Fiction—All Conflation of Events and Hybrid Characters—from Nonfiction

The issue with lying in creative nonfiction writing is that the trust between the author and the reader comes of the writer telling the truth and only the truth. If the author is telling lies, the reader can't use this work of nonfiction as history to learn from. The reader cannot base any psychological insights on the work. The reader can't count on it as evidence of how human beings behave.

There will be enough lies in what we writers say, since it's almost impossible for us to remember anything accurately. If we remember a thing accurately once, we may well not remember it accurately next time, because the process of memory being what it is, in the meantime we have reevaluated the thing and therefore are at risk of forgetting whatever old data don't agree with our new evaluation.

Chapter 12, "Some Issues of Aesthetics and Ethics of Writing Literature," carries a discussion of the deliberate fudging of facts in nonfiction writing, including some reference to literary scandals that arose when authors were caught in the act of not telling the truth and outright lying.

Pushing Off from Mindless Male Realism and Mindless Female Realism

I've included "Pushing Off from Mindless Male Realism and Mindless Female Realism" in this book only as a safeguard, in the same way you would pass out as many parachutes as you could to a group of people whom you saw climbing into a shabby-looking aircraft.

The major work of getting rid of mindless male realism and mindless female realism in a manuscript is usually done earlier on in the writing process, during the *middle* stage of the work. It is in the middle stage of our writing that we question ourselves psychologically: "What is it we really want to talk about here? Do we really want to be talking so sociologically? Do we really want to be talking in psychological clichés, or do we want to etc., etc.?" Still, some mindless realism may have escaped our attention. While we are doing our literary fixes, we can make a last check for this problem.

Mindless *male* realism typically involves males making needlessly stalwart comments on superficial subjects; or instead of responding to females, not talking to them, but talking past them; or saying nothing because mindless males don't do communication. These are the clichés for representing un-grown-up American males.

The mindless *female* cliché, as it shows up in writing, is people contemplating a piece of fruit, seeing how the light on it has the same colors, if it's a plum, as the light of the windows of Notre Dame. Mindless female realists start with one emotion, saying, "I felt such and such," then glide to another emotion that seems more delicate, and then interrupt that with a sense impression that is more spacious, such as seeing the piece of fruit as like a cathedral window. They work themselves up.

In other words, all we have to do is check our manuscript to make sure we aren't following a code of behavior of expecting males to be gritty—to grind out cigarettes on stones and to be noncommunicative—and expecting females to be always eating luminously, feeling much about little, and suffocating thought with grandiloquence.

Both types of mindless realism are tremendously unfair to both sexes, but this kind of writing is promoted and furthered by manuals that some people read when they decide they want to write popular literature.

Unfortunately, there are a good many Hemingway imitators practicing the mindless male realism style. They are not imitating Hemingway's content. They are picking up on some stylistic artifacts. I implore you to check through a manuscript and get rid of all Hemingway imitations, especially the run-on sentences in which unrelated comments are connected with *and.* This style was very affecting when Hemingway first did it. Given that everyone, particularly young males, has been imitating that practice for three-quarters of a century, it's time we gave it up.

Virginia Woolf introduced the Truly Poised, Messy Sentence. She did it because she was so interested in showing inner reality—how people's feelings and impressions flit back and forth from one thing to another, and how each thing they flit over drops a flare over the next one. In the novel *Mrs. Dalloway* we stagger along with the inner thoughts of Peter Walsh or Septimus or Clarissa Dalloway and the others. I am afraid that Virginia Woolf set us a dippy style model, a literary equivalent of smells and bells in Anglican churches. Woolf never did bad *thinking,* but she allowed herself a good deal of tricky craftsmanship in *Mrs. Dalloway*—even in her morally brilliant *Three Guineas* and in *A Room of One's Own.* We need to decide when a style is overdone and then not copy it anymore.

Checking for the Skinflint Syndrome and Enhancing Your Manuscript as a Gift to the Reader

Roger Angell at *The New Yorker* once instructed me about *nondirectives*—that is, giving readers so little information that they can't imagine the scene for themselves. If the particulars recorded are too sparse, readers don't get the sense that the writer was really there. Perhaps the writer really knows no more about the experience being described than any of us do.

Even at fourteen, when I first read *The Red Badge of Courage* by Stephen Crane, I found the novel short on particulars. Years later I learned that Crane had never witnessed or experienced the Civil War. Paul Fussell's writing about being a lieutenant of infantry in World War II is far superior because not only is the author generous in what he confesses about himself—he is not a braggart—but he is generous in describing beautifully certain things that we never would think of unless we had been there. One night Fussell's unit got lost in the middle of a forest, a common military experience. At last the men simply hunkered down and went to sleep where they were. When they woke they discovered that some of the obstacles they'd been tripping over the night before were young, dead German soldiers who had lain there so long their faces were green and white as marble. Nothing I've read of World War II would have led me to write that remark. Fussell writes nonskinflint literature. (Note: Describing the corpses as green-and-white-mottled like marble is more profound than saying that they were "beginning to rot.")

Once we are in the final stage of our writing project, we can check for fullness of scene. We can ask ourselves, "If I didn't know what I know, and were reading this manuscript, would I be able to see the scene that I'm now seeing as I reread this paragraph?"

My family and I lived in the countryside of western Minnesota. I liked to go down to the well to get water. The old iron hand pump would bang as you pumped. The handle took exactly four pumpings before its leathers were primed enough to draw up water. Then that delicious, magical water surged up from underground and into the bucket hanging over the nub.

One very dry summer, lots of bees hovered around me while I was pumping. At last I realized they were wildly thirsty. I returned to the house and brought back a number of facecloths and rags, dipped them into the cold water, and spread them sopping on the meadow grass near the pump. Bees instantly landed all over them. They nestled and growled over those rags and facecloths. Presumably they were drinking water with their tiny bee-nose straws. No one trying to imagine farm life without running water could know about the bees.

As you go through the manuscript for the last time, it's a good idea to make a serious effort to recall peculiar details that no one could fake.

Asking, for a Last Time, What Is Still Missing from This Manuscript?

This question sometimes brings to mind a new gush of ideas. This is your last chance to include some of those. But you might find that you wish you'd written your whole essay differently. A psychiatrist once told me, "Life is long, and whatever you can't do in this minute you can do in the next moment." If you think of so many things that you wish you could add to the manuscript that it looks as though you need to rewrite it, you might tell yourself, "Look, this manuscript is what I can do for now. For now, at least, this is *it.* I will write other books in future. There will be time, but I had better start taking notes on those other books."

Small Language Fixes That Help Remove Humbug

Most of the work we do in the long middle part of our work on a manuscript is psychological work we do for *ourselves.* But now that we have gotten to literary fixing, we *are* concerned with the reader as well as ourselves.

Small language fixes can be divided into those that have a psychological effect on us and those that have a psychological effect on the reader. Most beginners don't realize that some of the fixing they do on a manuscript, even in the last stage of their work on it, will be clarifying the content for oneself as well as for readers.

I am not going to take up all the classical fixes one does for readers. Orwell, Hall, Lukeman (see page 100 in this chapter), and many others offer thorough discussions of these kinds of corrections. Since literature is a product of the human psyche, some small language fixes are universal. Marcus Aurelius needed to be clear and give particular examples. Loren Eiseley needed to be clear and give particular examples. Dava Sobel needs to be clear and give particular examples. If brevity ever was the soul of wit it still is. If cordiality toward the reader was ever of any value it still is.

A quick list of eternally valuable mechanical fixes: getting rid of the passive voice completely; getting rid of sets of prepositional phrases in a sentence (some beginning writers sometimes have five or six prepositional phrases in a sentence, such as "I had a sense of feeling of guilt" instead of "I felt guilty"); getting rid of run-on sentences; getting rid of comma hooking or comma splicing—that is, sticking two complete clauses together with a comma instead of a semicolon, a colon, or a period.

Those fixes pick up the pace to heighten interest for the reader. Now we will look at some textural fixes that give the writer a last chance to discern humbug in the manuscript, to spot and eliminate sentence structure that cools the tone—waters down the author's feeling—when you (the author) don't really want to come on cool and watered; and finally, a last chance to take out of the writing any cheap posturing (use of rhetorical questions).

Mellifluous Sentences and Humbug

One difficulty for people who write easily and fluidly, and who have what is so unremittingly called "their own voice," is that their voice does sound good. They write with ever increasing confidence. They have frightened their peer groups into revering the way they ply their own voice. These writers like to hear their own voice.

Once you learn to write a rhythmic, long sentence with some commas and some dependent clauses, and that sentence seems to enrich itself as it glides forward, you need to make sure you haven't simply gassed on. The long, mellifluous sentence that breasts along over its comma breaks is wonderful for revealing physical details because it adds detail after detail after detail so that the reader can see and feel more. This construction is not so good for observing human feeling, although that is the very way it is most commonly used.

Here is an example of a mellifluous passage which does *not* bring in false feeling, written by James Salter and taken from his book *Solo Faces.*

> There was less traffic now, nurses driving homeward, Japanese, bearded blacks, their faces bathed by dawn like true believers. It was 7:00.[10]

This passage needs its rhythmic and beautiful images and pauses to work up to full drama with "true believers," the sudden turn inward. This is vintage James Salter.

A way to get rid of spurious, mellifluous passages is to imagine that you must describe whatever it is you are describing to two people: one is a resolute and aged professor, and the other is a young working person of great intelligence. The professor will want brisk, elegant language because he or she is accustomed to using and hearing such language in conversations—used to taking the trouble to find the right word for what wants saying. The young working person will be impatient with anything that looks like phony talk. The more and harder the physical work you do in life, the more you love literature if you can get hold of literature that isn't social climbing, or more to the point, affected. Therefore, imagine that this professor and this very intelligent working person are your audience. Try for clean, ordinary speech, as if you were talking to both of them, mixed with just a little beautiful language and slightly unusual vocabulary. A perfect example of someone who writes like that all the time, who never writes gas, and who frequently uses current slang or everyday references, is the essayist Edward Hoagland. In his nifty "The Courage of Turtles," he says that the turtle is a creature with "the governor" turned way down. Anyone with a lot of miserable experience with push lawn mowers knows about governors. They set motor speed up or down. If someone tells you that a turtle is a creature in whom evolution has left a very low governor setting, you realize this man is telling you the truth.

A further point: The professor whom you are pretending to be talking to may have been hanging around academic halls for decades. He or she is probably starved for actual knowledge of everyday life. He or she may avidly watch *This Old House.* No one loves the everyday hands-on nitty-gritty of life more than people who have been deprived of it. Those are the people who undertake the most bizarre projects with their Skilsaws and routers.

And conversely: people whose work is physical labor love language when it is used without lying or pretense. They are also touchy about language, however: all too often it is used to lock them out of book culture. I would like to expand on this issue of lying or posing to less educated audiences. This practice is carried on so unconsciously that writers lie and pose probably by the thousands *without knowing they are doing it.*

In the late 1970s I worked with other "humanists," as we were called, on the American Farm Project, a project ingeniously put together by the National Farmers Union and the National Endowment for the Humanities. The idea was to introduce young farm people to the liberal arts. As we trotted our seminars around the central and western states where the National Farmers Union was a presence, we asked, wherever possible, some liberal-arts professors at local colleges to talk to our groups. Some of these professors helped people further their respect for and their own belief in land stewardship and other rural ideals. But some of the professors who had been collegial and warm in our own planning sessions seemed oddly stiff in front of the farmers. They commandeered the young farmers' attention and then talked down to them. At first I couldn't account for their tone. At last I realized that these particular speakers, themselves from working families, had persevered and won their life's dream: to live the life of an intellectual. Somewhere inside themselves was a living fear of being dumped back into hardworking, no-philosophical-conversations life. The presence of our farmers probably ignited the fear. They got tiffy. They mounted some elegant, incomprehensible technical terms from their own disciplines—history, English, philosophy. The audience picked up on that unconscious hostility, as people classically can pick up on hostility the speaker is unconscious of.

Unerringly the farmers discerned that social-climbing coolness. Just as unerringly, the farmers discerned the love of ideas in others of the professors, and were quick to take down their remarks as talismen, not just talk.

Therefore, once we've gotten to the last handling of a manuscript, it is a good idea to check for fancy tone possibly emanating from unpleasant psychological smoke. One can watch for it, once one is aware of the problem. Any author has a right to be a social climber, but it's a good language fix to get all signs of it out of a manuscript.

Starting Sentences with Dependent Clauses

This suggestion about the proper place for dependent clauses sounds finicky. If you think only in terms of *style*, then it is indeed fussy to quibble over whether or not a sentence should start with a dependent clause. But let's look at the *psychological effect* of the construction: the purely sensible, management-style tone of dependent-clause openings steadies and levels feeling. That is why the practice of starting sentences with dependent clauses is dear to people in executive meetings; they want all feeling in the room to be as steady and level as possible. Leveled-down feeling is dear to insurance companies and to the writers of military communiqués—it serves to kill immediacy of feeling so that those of us who must keep our cool can get along with one another and go on planning our honest or unpleasant or outright dishonest work together. This style of writing suits those who hand out horrific news but want hearers or readers to stay biddable.

If you say, for example, "Because of his great reticence on this issue, I decided to say nothing," you come across as more low-key than if you had said, "I decided not to say anything because of his reticence." When you start with the main clause you are showing more commitment to what you are saying. You show yourself to be frank. That is because the main clause of any sentence is its spine.

I have never seen this particular suggestion made to creative-nonfiction writers, perhaps because the sane-and-balanced-sounding dependent-clause opener is all around us. As Wittgenstein pointed out, ocean fish make no judgments on the salinity of seawater.

Rhetorical Questions as a Way of Controlling the Reader with Implied Scorn

A rhetorical question is the most evasive and scornful device of our language. It is a question you ask to which you already seem to have an answer. The question is asked not to get an answer but to control the reader's feelings *without revealing your own.* The tone established by a rhetorical question is both so hostile and so patronizing that the reader feels cowed and scarcely able to respond.

For example: "Who would ever want to drive a car like that?" The author is not asking who would drive such a car. The author is saying that nobody worth his salt would want to own such a car. By implication anyone who owns this kind of car is neither becoming nor admirable.

Families who habitually practice bad communication skills among themselves or who are unhappy with one another but don't dare say so out loud often use rhetorical questions. Bullying kids are fond of rhetorical questions. Literary idealists shriek rather than think when they cry, "If it keeps going like this, where will it ever stop?" The first rhetorical question that American human beings learn is "So what?"

Even though controlling the reader with scorn is a device of sermons and of speeches, rhetorical questions are such a cheap shot I think writers of literature should delete all of them.

Getting Rid of *We*, *Everybody*, and *All*

I learned this lesson from Emilie Buchwald, the publisher of Milkweed Editions. I had somehow reached the age of sixty-two without ever hearing that one of the curses, from the point of view of an experienced editor like Buchwald, is that writers try to increase emphasis of what they have written by saying "we" and "everybody" and "all" and "always." If a writer says, "We are a species that is cruel, and so forth," that's one thing. If a writer says, "We Americans have a problem with greed," or, "We are given to starting wars," the statement includes in those *we*s the hundreds of thousands of U.S. citizens who are not greedy and the hundreds of thousands of Americans who have protested our various repulsive wars since 1945.

In fact, the author himself or herself usually opposes whatever it is that that very author says "we" or "all of us" are constantly doing. It is a case of "we" and "they." *They* do some bad things that *we* don't do. We may do some bad things that they don't do. Name the guilty parties. Be specific.

Some use of the all-inclusive "we"—tossing the guilty and the nonguilty together—comes from the common 1960s misreading of Jungian psychology. One of C. G. Jung's most helpful insights had to do with *projection*. That is, you project a fault of yours onto "them," accusing them of it, while it's still inside *you*—something is really wrong with you. You say things like, "They are cowardly and greedy, a horrible people," when cowardliness and greed may well be problems of *yours*: your own unconscious is serving you in a satisfying if untruthful way by designating cowardliness or greed as properties of an enemy who is separate from and outside yourself. It became very stylish in the 1960s for intellectuals to be vigilant about "not projecting." It went too far, however. People started claiming responsibility for everything that was going on around them, as if everyone were equally culpable. If you were driving by a gas station and saw a robbery going on, as a trendy nonprojector you would say, "Well, we Americans have a proclivity for robbing gas stations; we are such thieves by nature," when in fact what you needed to be saying was, "Oh, look, they [someone who is not I] are robbing that gas station. I will never rob one all my life. I haven't robbed one so far, and I think I'll call the police."

In other words, let's be sensible. If you find that you're writing a huge, collective *we* in order to appear modest, then your modesty is humbug. If you are using a huge collective *we* because you simply haven't figured out exactly who *is* doing the wrong thing, then stop writing for the moment and go to the library or get onto a good search engine and find out who is responsible. Create at least four groupings—perpetrators, victims, the indifferent, and the uninformed. Consider it your duty to discover and name the wrongdoers for the following reasons: Those whom you want to accuse know who is wrong and who is right on the issue. As long as they see you including both themselves (the patently guilty ones) and you (the innocent) in a general "we" statement, they know you are not pointing fingers. You're only wringing your hands. They grin. They know they are perfectly safe from you.

7.

Seven General Issues in Teaching Creative Writing

This chapter will discuss seven general principles of teaching creative writing that might be useful to all kinds of writing students and to all kinds of writing teachers. (Chapters 8–11 focus on teaching writing to particular populations—elementary school children, middle and high school students, college and M.F.A. students, and the uses of weekend, weeklong, and summer conferences.)

Writing Literature *Can* Be Taught

Unfortunately, a great many creative-writing teachers secretly or half-secretly or outright belligerently believe that writing *cannot* be taught. Even at writers' festivals and in large conferences these writing teachers sometimes announce that writing cannot be taught. Their tone sounds like that of a foreign diplomat showing up at the White House in striped trousers the day after his country has bombed our naval harbor to tell us that he regrets the action taken yesterday. He sounds solemn, sententious, trustworthy.

Experienced English teachers and authors who believe that creative writing cannot really be taught are sincere, however. The problem is they don't know how to teach creative writing. It's a question of getting access to modern methodology. We must fervently hope that medical schools don't let young people who have taken one course in biology and one course in chemistry teach first-year or second-year medical students. But in our profession, not just on the level of a summer retreat or Elderhostel program but in graduate schools, creative-writing courses are being taught by people who haven't learned ways to exercise control over their own work.

Still, some creative-writing teachers answer a "calling" by teaching, as do teachers in any trade. Others teach creative writing only to pay for their own studies. Some teach creative writing because you don't need any particular know-how to do it. Some teach creative writing because they notice, with gratified feelings, the new movement surging across the United States: people are pouring into writing classes in order to think about life and become a new breed of informal philosophers.

A person who stutters does not stutter when singing a song out loud, even though he or she stutters over the same lyrics if asked to *say* those words without music. Why is that? We can't be sure yet, but a rational assumption would be that speaking words and singing words are accomplished at different sites of the brain. Similarly, creative writing comes from a different setting in the mind from where practical, realistic talk comes from. That's why some of what we teachers do to pull together an impressive lecture so often doesn't make for impressive nonfiction or essay. Good creative writing can't be outlined ahead of time. Good creative writing has little to do with whatever we mean by "common sense." Early criticism kills it utterly. "Works of art are of an infinite loneliness and with nothing to be so little appreciated as with criticism. Only love can grasp and hold and fairly judge them," Rilke said.

To teach writing we have to teach people how to access, give credence to, and take comfort from the less-used places in their brain. We have to teach the brain to jump from one less habitual, less banal circuitry to another less habitual, less banal circuitry. By way of illustration, here is part of a poem by Denise Levertov on the subject of changing one's mind about spoilsport assumptions such as "creative writing cannot be taught."

All humankind
women and men,
hungry,
hungry beyond the hunger
for food, for justice,
pick themselves up and stumble on
for this: to transcend barriers, longing
for absolutions each of each by each,
luxurious unlearning
of lies and fears,
for joy, that *throws down the reins*
on the neck of
    the divine animal
who carries us through the world.[1]

Creative writing can be taught because our species has the potential for taking joy in writing. Students who all of their lives thought they had no imagination of the literary sort often look radiant when shown that they have. They look as if they had unlearned an old lie or fear.

Elementary school and high school creative-writing teachers regularly assume that, unless deflected, any child can write imaginatively. They are required by their job descriptions to assume that everybody *should* write imaginatively—that is, deeply, truthfully, and with humor and with such wisdom as they've accumulated so far, inside themselves.

Let us assume, for the sake of helping people older than elementary school kids, that people have a number of influences in their life that make it hard for them to do the inward record keeping that our species wants to do. People also have a number of influences that *will* help them do that inward record keeping. Let us further assume that in our job of helping others write we will keep our eye on the goal of inward record keeping and urge each writing student to do the hard work such record keeping requires.

I used to sing in the church choir of Thaxted, Essex, England. Long before my time that choir had been directed by the great girls' school choirmaster and composer Gustav Holst. Holst used to repeat to this village choir a wonderful remark usually attributed to G. K. Chesterton: "If a thing's worth doing, it's worth doing badly." He used that comment with respect to learning to sing Palestrina. When I joined the Thaxted choir, they were still singing Palestrina. Palestrina has the different parts—trebles, altos, tenors, and basses—making entrances in "O bone Jesu" at very different times—often while other singers are in the middle of holding notes. So if you don't sing with discipline, entering the music "spot on," as the English say, the choir sounds like village cats in the springtime. Holst used to tell that choir that they weren't making a very good sound. But then he always added, "If it's worth doing, it's worth doing badly, including Palestrina."

We might repeat that axiom to writing students when their efforts are not up to their best because they are lazy or they have lost heart. Writers lose heart easily and often. Writing is many times harder than singing. We can tell writing students, "That's all right. You did very badly this time: join the club." Everyone has to learn that they inevitably will do *some* bad work at some time.

That maxim applies to all enterprise. In farming they say you can't really get past being just a beginning farmhand until you've committed all three of these particular stupid, common beginners' mistakes: the first one is leaving a part of your tractor or equipment somewhere out in the field. At dusk when you can hardly see and you are so tired you totter, they send you out walking along the furrows to find what you dropped. The second one occurs when you are pulling a tractor with a hopper after it so the hopper will dump the corncobs onto a belt, and the belt will elevate the cobs to the top of a growing gold pyramid of corn. But you park the tractor wrong, and the elevator starts to lift the tractor itself rather than the hopper, and it tips the tractor over. The third one happens when you are cultivating. You get sleepy and thus carve up hundreds of feet of corn instead of cultivating the ground between the rows of corn.

Most beginning writers think that if they had any real talent, they would be writing well from the first. They have to learn that they will fail in a number of ways for a considerable time.

Some writers suffer from the *hotshot* problem. Every so often a navy flight instructor finds himself or herself teaching someone who seems to understand air and the aerodynamics of aircraft intuitively. This talented trainee learns everything peacefully. What is a humbling struggle for his or her classmates is a joyride for this student. The instructor tells such a pilot that he or she is a "hotshot," and the instructor is waiting, frankly, for a near disaster so that the hotshot pilot will drop his or her perfect confidence, and with it the comfortable two-class philosophy—me just naturally good, others pathetic.

The hotshot philosophy of creative writing lies so deeply rooted in Americans it sometimes takes all a writing teacher can do to get rid of it. Hotshots think that anyone meant to be a writer will get it the first time. I have had few beginning writing students who weren't half-blinded by that idea. They have to learn that the holy work of making literature is in revision. Even middle-aged and older people sometimes bring me a brand-new poem they wrote *instead of the revision of yesterday's work I assigned them.* They say, "I just *got* this poem! It just came to me! I just got it!" They put a value on "just getting" a first draft. The sooner a writing student can stop wanting to be "special" or to "just get" something, the sooner he or she can start to learn.

Protecting Student Writers from the U.S.A. Junk Culture

The most damaging cant appearing in teaching manuals or making the rounds of English departments is the notion that the teacher must "respect a student's goals for a given piece of writing."

A student's first goals tend to be artifacts of the conventional American culture of the moment. Most writing students are far too self-deprecatory to respect whatever lives inside themselves. They are likely to assure us teachers that they want to "write a very sexy, very violent book that will sell," or that they want to "write a romance that readers will find satisfying as escape literature."

Some writing students may be correct about their goals. They really do want to write a sexy or violent book. (See the discussion in Chapter 3.) They can't think of anything else to write about. They sincerely want to make a lot of money writing escape literature.

Others of our students, however, hazard remarks about wanting to do hack sex or hack violence writing because they don't want to sound any more principled than Americans are supposed to sound.

Since we are just teachers, not prophets, our only democratic and pedagogically hopeful stance is to assume that behind every self-defined bottom feeder is an unconscious, potentially sentient person.

Say that a writing student firmly states that she has this totally neat idea for mortaring together some really hostile, but volcanic sex with some sadism involving vitriol and a bunch of little rural Quaker kids, and it all takes place on a ground-polluted old arsenal site. She has fifty pages of it already. The guy in the story thinks he is impotent but he really isn't. His girlfriend has a lot of faith in him. It'll work out some way. Anyhow, they are a neat couple and the heroine talks him into arranging for an accident at the home place so that he can inherit from his parents faster.

The only way to teach someone with a plot like that is to assume that she might develop a second writing goal from material inside herself.

This student has paid careful attention to the most widespread, most tasteless predilections of the American reading public and means to pander to them cheerfully.

We say, "All right—good, that's part of it, and what *else* would you like to write?" She replies, "Well, I don't know." So we might say, "Well, say that ninety percent of it is that you would like to do a market-driven piece of work. Would there be five percent or four percent or three percent of you that would like to try something else, too? Talk about things from your own life, for example?" "I don't know," the writer says, and adds, "So what?"

At this point we can move fast: "OK—let's do two exercises. Write up your life, for starters, three thousand words by tomorrow. Make sure you bring it up to your present age. Then I will give you an exercise based on that piece of writing."

Some people quite quickly learn enough self-love from such an autobiographical assignment to get the point of literature. A caveat: we absolutely must read and respond to that autobiographical writing fully and quickly. If we don't, the writer sinks into even more horrible cynicism.

A shockingly large part of our job as writing teachers is to save students from the junk culture. More and more people sign up for writing classes for the very reason that they do want to escape from the junk culture. M.F.A. candidates are willing to compete in massive droves for jobs that don't exist now (teaching creative writing) and may never exist because they want to avoid the psychological habitats of 1990s and 2000s big-money corporations. They want to do work they themselves can respect. Self-respect is fraught in the mean, lean corporate setting, where a company may trim off its middle-level executives for the sake of doling out higher income to the upper-level people or to the stockholders. Corporations will fire not the recent recruits but long-term employees with seniority, in order to save money. This gravelly practice lowers everyone's spirits. It lowers the level of work being done by the group—a further discouraging phenomenon just in itself. Doing good work over the years is not valued. The policy says, "We have no particular loyalty to you. You and everybody right up to the people near the top are just creatures of our profit motive."

People who cannot bear to work in or who have failed in such a setting are showing up in M.F.A. programs. Their expectations are unclearly stated to us teachers. For one thing, if they want to get into an M.F.A. program they have to say that they are very, very interested in writing literature. If they won't say that, they won't get in. For this reason, we are not getting straightforward statements on what all of these prospective students' motivations may be.

Still, I admire their hatred of a debased life and their bravery in taking up a profession as chancy as creative writing. Wanting to write not with the idea necessarily of becoming an author—not necessarily with the idea of becoming even a teacher of writing—but with the idea of living a meaningful, reflective life: that is a very superior motivation. I feel glad of the presence of such people in our various programs.

A last word on our mission to help people save themselves from the American junk culture: junk cultures are not new. William Wordsworth in "Preface to the Second Edition of the *Lyrical Ballads*," berates English culture:

> For a multitude of causes, unknown to former times, are now acting with a combined force to blunt the discriminating powers of the mind, and unfitting it for all voluntary exertion, to reduce it to a state of almost savage torpor. The most effective of these causes are the great national events which are daily taking place, and the increasing accumulation of men in

> cities, where the uniformity of their occupations produces a craving for extraordinary incident, which the rapid communication of intelligence hourly gratifies. To this tendency of life and manners the literature and theatrical exhibitions of the country have conformed themselves. The invaluable works of our elder writers, I had almost said the works of Shakespeare and Milton, are driven into neglect by frantic novels, sickly and stupid German Tragedies, and deluges of idle and extravagant stories in verse—When I think upon this degrading thirst after outrageous stimulation, I am almost ashamed to have spoken of the feeble effort with which I have endeavored to counteract it.[2]

A classic problem of our species is our having two opposing instincts at the same time. The first is to be civilized and sensitive—to be willing not to settle for fast, easy answers for things, to be willing to look at the whole of life instead of at only one's own province. That elegant instinct is always rippled and tipped by the second instinct, which is simply to go along, to take care of oneself and one's family, and never mind all the rest.

I love Wordsworth for two ideas in the quoted paragraph—first for saying that we are often reduced to a state of "almost savage torpor," and, second, for saying in the end that he is ashamed of himself for the feeble efforts he has made to counteract the common instinct toward "outrageous stimulation." The contemporary "outrageous stimulation" that Wordsworth deplored was what he calls the "sickly and stupid German Tragedies" and "extravagant stories in verse," the sit-trags and sit-coms of his time. In our time the "outrageous stimulation" shows up in salacious novels full of cruelty and oddly generalized, half-felt sex. Wordsworth, like Schiller, and to some extent like Shaftesbury,* was a precursor of the idea of reentry in the brain. Wordsworth had a taste for the way the brain is constantly casting over and resetting its notions: it likes to take a fresh measurement.

So if our job is to save writers from the junk culture, one way to do

*Anthony Ashley Cooper, 3rd Earl of Shaftesbury.

so is to help writers stay with their own most intense philosophical feelings. These feelings may change from moment to moment, but at any one time a writer needs to identify and honor whatever feeling is most intense. Literature thrives best on an intense idea, even if it must be abandoned in favor of another.

As will be discussed slightly in Chapter 8, on teaching elementary-school children to write, the pressure of the junk culture is always promoting steady fun. Teachers often say, "I want the kids to have fun with their writing." They ignore the psychological need of kids to express whatever part of them wants to be serious. Anne Frank said that she got sick of "the endless round of jokes."

We writing teachers can help writers of all ages both to be humorous and to be dead serious but we should not abet them in smudging their own brains with kidding.

A teacher is a mildly directive person, but only in the sense of intervening on behalf of a writer's *higher* instincts, helping the writer to do a check on his or her simpler, or lower, instincts.

What's a "simpler instinct" or a "lower instinct"? One simple and lower instinct is to kid about serious things. Another lower instinct is to write lyrically but not truthfully about life—as if lyricism were what makes literature valuable.

We all wrestle with a very ancient, simple survival instinct—to be neutral most of the time. Blandness is a survival tool of growing value in this frightening era. People want to be bland in order not to think about the scariness of the world. Somerset Maugham said, very amusingly, but a good many years ago, that if a person spent all his time thinking about the folly of human beings, he would live in "a state of constant ire." That sentiment was true then, no doubt, but things are worse now because the folly has now achieved critical mass. On the other hand, if one lives in a constant state of being lyrical and simply writing some kind of a specialty art—like literature that's divided away from life—then one lives in a constant state of silliness. On average, we'd prefer pretending the news is better than it is. Such a pretense lets us enjoy literature as if it were separate from life. But writers who practice this mode of art do so at the sacrifice of the personality. Why does it take a Denise Levertov to think up something so ecstatic as "the divine animal who carries us through the world"? She can do it because she allows herself to be mad at some "old lies." She doesn't try to be lyrical about them.

A writing teacher, then, can to some degree help writers intervene with and check their own simple instinct to be bland.

Squashing any culture-induced habit—blandness being of course only one of many—is the more difficult because the U.S.A. junk culture doesn't suggest that we *can* get control over ourselves. The culture says, you can't help how you feel. In fact, you earn this Bud—and any other blessing—not for "all you do," but for not doing much of anything. Getting hold of yourself psychologically is *not* a priority of our culture.

Therefore, writers need to pull themselves *out* of the culture, just as serious professionals in other fields do. Serious professionals have to say to themselves, "All right, we're not doing this emotion right now: we can get back to it later." Americans from all kinds of undisciplined or chaotic families expect it of themselves to be very professional on the job—in the nursing profession, for example. A nurse himself or herself does not expect to give a patient less attention because the nurse "is having a bad day." The nurse needs to be able to think aloud at the beginning of the day, "All right, today my personal life is a disaster, but I'm going off to work, and at work I serve my patients."

Writers, too, could say, "All right, I'm having certain bad feelings, but they do not have to get into the writing today." When teachers can teach that one tool—the expectation of being professional—it helps writers out of the psychological slough.

Some aspects of the U.S.A. junk culture are easy to spot. One is a jocular tone. Someone who has just read aloud to a class might say, "Well, what I was experiencing there was envy as much as anything else." That "as much as anything else" has a cynical, offhand cast to it. It is not earnest, and it's not professional. Here is the opposite. Joanne Ward, in a summer 1999 class, wrote: "I was astounded at how calm and unselfish I felt." That is an earnest, and intense, and therefore literary statement.

Post-teenage junk language seems to infest women's nonfiction language more than men's. Teen words are "wimpy," "ploppy," "scootching over" (instead of moving your buttocks), "squishing," "scrunching" (which means cramping). All such language lowers the tone. Worse, however, it lies like spoor in the ear of the writer. What is in a writer's inner ear can spoil *future* prose, not only today's piece of prose.

A cure for teen language is reading all drafts aloud *slowly*. The ear will serve us provided we read aloud *very slowly*. If we read quickly, we are modeling to ourselves lack of confidence, since people speak quickly who have less confidence than people who speak slowly. It helps to practice Winston Churchill's sonority, as though what you are saying is of inestimable value and as though the times in which we live are real times and we are faced with real issues.

Curing Writers of the Bad Habit of Perseverating

Sometimes either a youthful student or an adult student will write up the same autobiographical incident or related incidents over and over. The writer goes from writing teacher to writing teacher, from this weeklong writing retreat to the next weeklong writing retreat, writing up the same (usually unhappy) occasions over and over.

Social workers call it "perseverating" when someone gets stuck in some past bad experience. They break up perseverating by getting you, the client, to describe the whole thing thoroughly. They question you intricately, so that every corner of the story gets kind light cast on it. The therapist then agrees, "That really was an awful, awful experience. Horrible." Then the therapist ever so slowly, ever so gradually, suggests that it is over now. You have done well to have gotten back up on your hind legs again: now move into the rest of your life. The therapist thinks of the old bad occasion as a *snarl* to be raveled and then left to rot on its own.

Because I teach older people and middle-aged people to write, I have had to think about perseverating. I have tried various exercises. The best thing I know of so far is to hear out the entire story once. Often perseverators quite understandably don't, or won't, tell a writing teacher the whole snarl of their story at once. A perseverator sometimes behaves like an alcoholic, cannily gauging the amount of the delicious, prohibited substance—drink for the drinkers, mention of the old snarl for the perseverator—this many ounces now, and I get to scarf down more later, or, for the perseverator, just a hint or two to this teacher or writing class now: I can tell more and more and more later.

I've found it is best not to let students write about the same event in more than three pieces of writing, the first one being whatever essay it first showed up in. If it shows up in a second paper, I ask for the whole story at once. Whether or not the writer is willing to write it all up once and for all, I try to discourage the appearance of the same old snarl of personality in a fourth work by that person.

However frightful the victimization that writer received at presumably someone else's hands, that writer has had other experiences in his or her life. Those other life experiences need to have attention paid to them. Other of that writer's life stories want telling. Therefore I have found it best openly, tyrannically, not to allow any further clinging to the old bad snarl.

I know this sounds directive, and it certainly sounds like "not respecting the student's goals," but even in the brief time of a week-long writing retreat this proscription sometimes frees a perseverator to look at the other rich landscapes of his or her life.

Convincing Writers that *Surprise* Is the Inevitable Eternal Principle of Literature

Surprise is just about everything, if the writing is to be beautiful. Both the insight and the phrases should be fresh with each author.

Poor literature does not surprise us. We begin reading, and in a second we see where the author is going. The author duly goes there, and we feel testy because we had wanted something original but instead got something conventional.

I am sorry that surprise is necessary to good literature. It would make more pleasant teaching if we could say to our students, "Anything you say is valuable." But the fact is, in the end, one must say something original. When writers complain of this standard it sometimes helps to remind them that in medicine we want every young doctor to have learned anatomy. It is not permissible for a doctor to be ignorant. Every discipline has some stressful, inescapable difficulty to it.

Literature has low enough standards. But we can avoid writing the worst literature if we make ourselves ask ourselves, every two or three sentences we write, "Is that what *I* really think?"

Surprise simply means saying something deeper on some subject than you thought you were going to. Some beginning writers achieve surprise as if by accident. They write something surprising by accident without realizing how original their writing is. The job of the teacher, then, is to say, "By the way, that was a wonderful surprising expression you used there. May I read that aloud to the group?" "It was?" the student says numbly. "I didn't think anything of it." We can answer that, in turn, by saying, "Well, there's lots wrong with being old and tough and experienced in literature, but there's lots right about it, too. One thing we learn, the more and longer we read, is that it's marvelous when anyone uses a phrase or tells a truth that we haven't heard before. And we are grateful for it. So I'd like to read your surprising passage to the group."

Then this student, with a glad, stupid expression on his or her face, goes back into his or her mind and thinks, "I must have better stuff in there than I thought I had because that lot came up without my noticing. From now on, I will be open to any other little creatures emerging from the wainscot of my imagination. I will do everything I can to encourage my mind to be more original. Apparently, I *can* be original."

On surprise, I would like to return to a scene I briefly mentioned previously, involving a writing student named Joanne Ward. In her story, a woman was called to the hospital because her husband was having a heart attack. She was still married to him, but they had parted ways over his various adulteries. A doctor stood next to the husband's bed. The doctor was taking up all the space so that the wife couldn't get near. The doctor was the woman with whom he was having his current affair. The scene, then: the wife and the patient's mistress are standing about this man who is dying or in danger of dying.

The author now has the wife say that she was "astounded at how calm and how unselfish" she felt. What Joanne Ward accomplished with that phrase was not only the earnest formality for which I praised this phrase earlier but also something that Hemingway was famous for: putting ordinary adjectives near each other that we are not used to seeing together. Ward put together the adjectives *astounded* and *calm* and *unselfish*. What's more, her *thought* was surprising too. We expect the wife to report how galling it was. Nothing of the kind! That is a perfect case of the surprise possible when an author doesn't resort to a stencil. The underlying psychological dynamic is that writers must absolutely, sooner or later, keep their material clear of any writers' group. Even inside ourselves, what's more, we mustn't follow our most habitual path if anything catches the corner of our eye.

It is very difficult. We are in groups much of the time. When we start a sentence we're likely to keep on with it because the group expects us to keep going in the way we began. One writes unconsciously for the group.

The little mind theory we may know, such as that the mind has not one but several opinions at once (Chapter 5), lets us confidently put two ideas together that seem contradictory, provided each of the two feels true. Once writers realize how to listen for those apparent dissonances, they get a taste for the oddball exactitude of writing this way. From then on they will choke on conventional phrases.

For example, "Well, he's very beautiful, and I am attracted to him, and I notice that he has an unpleasant, bullying look about him as well. When a young man like that holds forth in a room, the older men glaze. Of course they are partly envious—how could they not be?—but they also know he is no good. They want to show him up for the con man he is, but the old men can't do it because the young man will read them as pathetically envious. He might even grin." This is only a rough sample of an author's following four pairs of dissonances.

Practicing Professional Reticence

Creative-writing classes are so friendly and full of conversations about personal life that a writing teacher may forget that personal sharing by the teacher can actually harm students. Student writers' concentration needs to be on *their* work. Self-oriented writing teachers actually thwart their students' development as artists in a surprising way.

Most of our students are Americans. In our culture people do not often contemplate one another deeply. Many of our students have never been asked a question about their inner feelings by anyone they know. They have literally never had that experience. So our job as the writing teacher is to fulfill that need. That means that we should do no reminiscing about our own work. If we are so vain that we must allude to our work, then we should at least mention only our failures. And we certainly should leave off the bleating so common in English departments: that is, complaining that *we have our own work to do*. Student writers have a hard enough time making a mental image of their own work: this image dissolves at its edges if they must make an image of the teacher's work. And here is a more banal reason for not being self-indulgent: students pay on average a thousand dollars or more per course. For a thousand dollars they deserve a teacher who won't whine about his or her own griefs, just as hospice patients deserve to have nurses and doctors and lab technicians focused on *their* situation, not on the staff members' problems at home.

Being Aware of Bullying

Bullies do their bullying only *some* of the time, but they do it wherever they are. You would think that writing teachers would be beyond wanting to bully anyone. But just as robbers aren't always in a good position to rob a bank and therefore must stoop to robbing women's shelters, bullies do their part-time bullying wherever they can—teaching writing classes, if that is where they are.

Unfortunately, beginning writers ask for bullying. They give their souls into their work. They are very vulnerable. They believe what teachers tell them. They shouldn't, but they do. They honor our (teachers') seniority. Our judgments are probably worth a tenth of what students give us credit for. If we have the least weakness of ego or the least career-climbing corruption or the least inability to reject flattery from people around us, we are at risk to bully. When we are tired we might even do a little bullying without noticing.

Being an ancient, primitive pleasure, bullying lights up some low place in the brain, like an orange, acrid fire. The better parts of the mind get blindsided. It is curious how we get a retro streak every so often. Sweet old Anglicans who seldom miss Evensong and who sing the hymns on tune and get the treble entrances right sometimes pinch something from a donations box fast as a cat, without really ever having planned it. Apparently the impulse just comes upon them. The hand goes out, and there you are. In some like way, bullying can leap up in a writing teacher, especially in individual conference. Here's a true case of lightning bullying: a teacher who has been routinely kind and thoughtful to all students, whatever their level of skills or acumen, suddenly says, "Did you *intend* these poems for your own pleasure?" The student feels that the correct answer is yes, so she says, "Yes, I guess I did." He says, "Good thing, because they really won't ever come to anything."

The teacher has flipped into prophesying—a mode that is to teachers what lifting a club was to Paleolithic man. But jejune writers *ask* us to prophesy. We can always say, "I'm only a teacher. I'm not a prophet. I can't possibly know." The student asks a common question: "Do I have any future as a writer?" We can say, "That question cannot be answered. We can't tell yet. It all depends on what kind of work you do, what kind of access you get to your insides; what kind of instruction you get, how much leisure you have so that you have time to work on writing."

The most common kind of classroom bullying is the sensible-sounding put-down. The hour has gone dully by. The discussions have gotten cloying. The "sharing" has been unrelievedly high-minded. The talk has been of passions, principles, deaths, births, the stuff of poetry and essays. Suddenly the rankled teacher cries, "All right, but it's time for a reality check." "Let's do a reality check" is a phrase that produces one and only one result: it hurts the feelings of whoever spoke just before the teacher said it.

Some classroom bullying is built right into the structure, as has already been mentioned. A flagrant example is the agreement in group work that a student whose manuscript is being workshopped will not speak (this harmful practice is discussed elsewhere).

Making the Classroom One of the Great Places on Earth

It is a simple act of will to regard a warmed room with sixteen or twenty people trying to help one another become artists as a great place on earth. Anyone can do it. A writing class should be a mix of the formality that helps one respect one's own innermost nature, and that promotes a sensitive sociability.

Here are a few suggestions for how to make a classroom one of the great places on earth.

First, there should be some level of formality. I learned the uses of formality from musicians. Duluth, the town of my childhood and youth, was the summer setting for yearly classes by a master concert pianist named Frank Mannheimer. I had an aunt who was a friend of Frank's. She often visited his master classes, and she brought me along when I was about fourteen or fifteen.

I had thought of Duluth, a city on the corner of Lake Superior, as a beautiful, conventional, somewhat mindless place full of heartbreaking physical beauty. Mists in the summer mornings made the harbor foghorn grunt every few minutes. In winters the city's redbrick buildings stood up brave and raw over the iced bay. I did not know that exquisite performance on the piano was being taught by Frank Mannheimer.

Frank's class taught me manners. Frank bowed a little to each person, the way we think of Japanese bowing. Frank looked carefully into each person's eyes and thanked each one for coming. My aunt and I took seats in the back. The students were going to sit around in an informal circle within fifteen feet of the piano.

Frank stood up before everyone to explain what we would hear that evening—we would begin with what Joey was working on. Joey played the first movement of a sonata. Frank said to all of us, "Well, you can see the problem is in the phrasing only. Let's see, someone else is working on difficult phrasing. Yes, Judy, you're working on the Debussy. Would you come up and play the such and such a passage?" Then Frank discussed a few principles of phrasing.

Clearly, class attention was paid to the work and intentions of a few composers, not to the performers. The performers were there only to learn how to do exquisite service to these live or dead composers.

I was struck by the combination of courtesy and formality. The formality, the silence between comments, the lack of small talk, let us concentrate on the work. I felt transformed.

A few years later I lived in rural, western Minnesota. Our little town inveigled the St. Paul Chamber Orchestra to come play for us.

Several of us sat cross-legged on the gym floor to hear their practice. When the violinists found their A my body dropped temperature. I had never heard strings players in my town and might never again. That evening the orchestra played for us. What was most striking, sociologically speaking, was that there was total silence between musical sounds. When the arms and baton went up, the gym was still. Very little happens in a small town without garrulous conviviality, welcoming remarks, harmless jokes by way of introduction—what on radio is called "continuity." Radio and TV have to have continuity, because a station or channel can't be silent. Announcers tell us, "You've just been listening to this, and now you're going to listen to this." There, in our ordinary gym, famous musicians sat in utter silence. They had their note. Now they waited, instruments already under their chins. Their silence said, "Use this time to break away from the patter of other human beings. Now you're free to attend to something dense. In fact, each of us can triple our own specific gravity."

Eventually, even the most wandering sort of mind will put two or three somehow related experiences together, focus on the combined aureole of the memories, and base some willful decision on it. From the Mannheimer class experience and the St. Paul Chamber Orchestra's visit to Madison, Minnesota, I decided a teacher had better deliberately give formality to the creative-writing classroom.

My first shot at this was a freshman composition class I taught at Hamline University in the fall of 1985. Until then Hamline had offered me only upper-level classes full of advanced English students. Now the chair of the English department diffidently asked me to take a section of freshmen. I was pleased. I like teaching seventeen- and eighteen-year-old people.

Four months earlier I had sat outdoors with thousands of parents and gowned students, listening to the wind gasping in the speakers, taking shade from the ancient huge trees of Massachusetts. The graduation formality seemed positively glamorous. Derek Bok told the class of 1985 that he hoped they would transform their undeniable privilege not into mere self-advancement but into service to the entire world. His tone and scope stuck with me all summer.

Now it was a Monday in September. I walked into my classroom. My fourteen students were slouched in various positions in their chairs. I pitied them because they were only practical. If you are tired and are only a practical person, you slouch.

I had gotten behind the desk. I asked them if this was their first class ever in college. I wanted to know if any of them had had a class during the first period. (This was the second period.) They all said yes, this was their first college class.

I stood up and went around the group. Starting at the right side of the room I shook hands with each one. I more or less repeated to each what the Harvard president had told seniors four months earlier.

"Well, welcome to the company of educated men and women."

The first handshakes I got were like getting hold of a dead mouse. The faces were all grins. Some of the young people bothered to stop chewing gum as I spoke to them and some didn't. The first students didn't even straighten up in their seats when I made them shake hands. And behind me, I could feel people circling their right ear with one finger.

As I got to the fifth and sixth person, however, the handshakes seemed to be firming up a little. Two boys even got to their feet. They practically tottered with self-doubt but they got up there. By the thirteenth and fourteenth student the handshakes were firm and all smirking and giggling had ended. I was still saying the same thing over and over, "Welcome to the company of educated men and women." A pathetic offering really, a sententious phrase pinched from someone else, and maybe everyone since John Harvard had been grinding out the same remark.

Still, formality is a weapon against smirking, and therefore it is a defense against cultural deprivation. We have to learn it or we won't recognize places of moment when we're in them. I longed for these young people to put up a wall of formality in their brains—to guard their dignity against their own inclination to hoot at everything. It's impossible to write creative nonfiction if life is a hoot and nothing but a hoot.

8.

Teaching Elementary School Children to Write

Very great elementary school writing teachers work with children now. I talk to them in groups and as individuals. I am constantly impressed with their ingenuity and with their generosity. Their mission is to help each child become more like himself or herself. Nothing could be more honorable. The only reason I have the side to offer any wisdom to such devoted teachers is that these suggestions emanate from certain principles of psychological growth.

Ways to Use the Appendix When Working with Children

The appendix contains writing exercises that on first glance will appear to be entirely for adults. All one has to do to make some of them—not all, of course—work for children, is adjust the language and change the examples given, if any. Three of the writing exercises work absolutely wonderfully with children. The first of these is "Writing without Clichés about a Beautiful Place," but one should remove the directions about clichés.

Children should not be taught any techniques of writing. Every technique we teach them, other than how to use their hands to write words on a page and to use computers to put words into print, distracts them from their *content.* We have to remember that American children don't grow up like nineteenth-century children: they are subjected to twentieth-century and twenty-first-century life. That is, lots of pressure is exerted on them from nearly every corner of their environment—from their day care, from their parents even, and certainly from their schools and from the other children on the playground—to be how-to wizards, but not confident, original thinkers on their own. It is hard work to protect a child's holy insides from our culture. One of the best ways to accomplish this is to let them devote a lot of attention to subjects that they are experts about.

The "Beautiful Place" exercise, when explained in language that's appropriate for the elementary school teacher and the children, is fun because every child has some opinion about what's a beautiful place. A note here: children should not be allowed to write about anything they see on television—not because I think everything they see on television is bad, but because television is so engrossing and stimulating to their senses that they don't back away from all those stimuli, and move into confident reflections arising in their own minds. Children scarcely credit as real experience the things that happen to them outside television. We writing teachers have to do all we can to stem the flooding of children's intelligence centers with junk.

Exercise 4, "Paying Respectful Attention to Background Settings," is ideal. Obviously the particular example I gave in the appendix is not ideal for children, but children do know the backgrounds of things, and they enjoy recounting small points of expertise. For one thing, their minds pick up small details much, much faster than ours do. Dr. Spock once said that a child is fascinated by a speck of dust and will stoop over in what looks like the most uncomfortable position, especially to try to pick up that speck of dust between his fingers. It should delight children, then, to write about the background settings of their own lives or the background settings of stories that they've heard. A teacher can set children loose on the background setting of "The Three Little Pigs." What would the background be? Obviously it would be near some sort of forest where the wolf lives, and perhaps the outer suburbs where the pig was building either a straw, twig, or brick house. Children, even more than timid adults, like to be asked questions about peripheral matters. If you've worked with grown people who have no confidence in their own minds, you may have noticed that they love to be asked something simple. They feel threatened by the actual crux of a story, such as, "What is the point of Alexander the Great cutting through the Gordian Knot?" But they *do* want to be asked if a sword can be sharpened up enough to cut through a tangle of rope.

Exercise 14, "An Irritating Person Exercise," is ideal for children because by the time they are four, five, six, and seven years old and are sitting in schoolrooms, they've had lots of chances to be irritated by adults in authority. They will have something to say about their parents. They may have something to say about older siblings and other people they know. I would tell them to give whomever they write about a different name from the real name. Tell them to write about Ms. Stensky, instead of writing about someone called Mama or Mom. Tell them to write about Mr. Borgese, instead of writing about their dad. Be sure not to use traditional American English names. Try to use names of minority groups when making "John Doe" suggestions for names. One way that minority groups get unconsciously, mildly discounted is that their names don't ever show up in lesson examples. So if you know some names like Ha Pol or some other Southeast Asian names, use those in preference to John Doe or Mary Brown. This is a move toward normalizing those usually thought of only sociologically as "diverse."

When children do the "Irritating Person" exercise they need every encouragement—that is, as the teacher you need to comment on how clearly you were able to visualize the person. You might also exercise, with that child, steps 3 and 4 of the empathy inquiry—those in which you as the teacher reflect back a little to show that you've taken in what the other person said. If this seems precious, bear in mind that some children may never have been listened to by anyone except you, the teacher. And if you are the second-grade teacher, that child may not have been listened to much in the first grade, because the first-grade teacher might have been desperately busy just trying to teach the child to read. And this second-grader may well not get listened to in grades three through twelve. So figure that over the course of a child's education, paying attention to a child's writing is thoroughly worth doing.

You may be the one island a child can step upon in a sea of either disrespect or simply lack of interest in what's going on in that child's mind.

Some of the material in the appendix is very useful for children's small groups. All teachers like to break up their classes into small groups. We don't know if children really like working in groups or not. They seem to like it. Others, of course, are so heavily socialized by the time they leave day care and get to school that they know how to pretend that they like activities that are inevitable (like being put into small groups), whether they really do or not. In any case, it's fun for a child to sit around a little table with other kids and talk about projects together. It's fun to do things with your friends. Children delight in that. But it is extraordinarily harmful for children to submit their writing to one another for peer comment. The practice of peer review is as damaging to small children as it is to much older adults.

Exercises 8 and 10 and the Usage Sheets, however, are good for using with children's small groups. I'm assuming that we want to put the children in a small group so they can talk things over together. They can talk their way through the "Essay Pot" exercise together. Actually, each small group can have index cards on which they write some subject that they want the group to talk about. After the group members have discussed the topic, they can share with the whole class, time allowing.

If I were a small child, say in grade three or four, I would put down on my "Essay Pot" index card "white bears or polar bears" because I liked them back then, when I was eight or nine, and I still like them. I would want to hear other people's comments on them. If somebody else objected to polar bears on the basis that they are predators, I would want to defend the polar bears, whom I think of as cozy animals—even though a single clawing from those many-inch claws of theirs would be lethal.

Exercise 10, "Attending to Other—Specifically Attending to Relatives, Nonhuman Creatures, or Plants," obviously needs to have its title rewritten for children, but this exercise is something that children can, with humor as well as realism, do together. For example, let's say that your building has a tremendous number of cockroaches. It may also have rats. Likely the rats won't make it above the level of either the super's or the first-floor apartments, but they're there. Children always seem to know about such things. The life purpose of cockroaches—a consideration of what a cockroach would consider a delicious environment—or the life purpose of rats—the wishful thinking of rats—might make a good subject for urban kids in the "Attending to Other" exercise. Practicing seeing things from the cockroach's point of view is an empathic exercise. It appeals to children's natural humor, their love of the particular, their love of whimsy. Let me give an example: a cockroach would rejoice if you dropped some fried fish, spilled some milk, and broke an egg, and then in wiping it all up, missed whatever rolled or slid underneath the stove. If the linoleum is loose in your apartment, some food might get underneath a corner of the linoleum that has curled up. You can't get it out, not for love or money. That kind of thing is heaven for a cockroach, just as a rotten goose egg was heaven for E. B. White's Templeton. Children would get a kick out of looking at disgusting stuff from the cockroach's point of view. As for children who live in other environments, they may choose to think about other animals. They may choose dogs, cats, parakeets—whatever the animals of their life are. An important point: When you suggest examples (like my cockroach above) for the "Attending to Other" exercise, be sure to choose examples that are familiar to children in all walks of life. Children of both privileged and unprivileged backgrounds need the confidence to write about what they know about. Children need utter equality in their small groups.

The Usage Sheets themselves make very good material for small groups of older (sixth- through ninth-grade) students to rewrite in amusing ways. Small children, of course, don't know the principles of usage. (We don't teach much usage to anybody!) But by the time children are in the sixth and seventh grades, they will have learned some usage rules. There is no reason that they should be left out of the *writing* of such sheets. You will see that I provide ridiculous examples for plurals and plural possessives—listing neo-Tudor doghouses and so forth on one or two of those sheets. Help children to use their humor to rewrite the Usage Sheets. If they can do this exercise in small groups, it will give them the lovely experience of working cooperatively with others, thinking of crazy stuff, and using their humor without reference to anything they have seen on television. At the same time, they will not be exposing their own creative efforts to the other children.

Two items in the appendix are useful for teaching children the psychology that will help them protect their innermost selves and grow and discern the difference between scholarship and creativity. One of those is "A List of Useful Sentences for Writers in a Tight Spot," which is designed to help writers defend themselves from intrusions by others. The list as it appears in the appendix is designed for adults. You would need to rewrite it slightly or at least go over it with the children to make it useful to them. Children have many uses, however, for this communication skill.

A lot of inappropriate and intrusive things are said to children, even though these things are said by parents or people in authority with the best motives—such as saving the child from danger. When children hear such remarks, however, it helps if they can say something back to protect themselves. Have a look at "A List of Useful Sentences for Writers in a Tight Spot," and see if any of them strike you as being close to something that would be useful for children to know. One thing children will do, if they learn self-protective sentences, is try them out on *you.* You must be sure to let those sentences have their effect. Be sure to laugh and congratulate them on using these tools. Having this protection will not diminish the children's respect for you, their teacher. If you react with good humor, the children will see that you have a sense of humor, which to them means a grown-up *should* have a sense of humor, and they will see that you take their point. Bear in mind—I keep reiterating this because it is so easy to forget—that some children may never have been around an adult who "took their point" about anything. Certainly many of them have never been able to stand up to an adult and object or erect a tiny safe and prideful barrier against something that adult said.

The five-step empathic inquiry technique offered in Chapter 3 should be taught to children in terms that are useful for them. There is no reason that children can't learn to listen to one another. If one says something that the other doesn't understand, then the second child can learn how to ask a question politely, without sounding begrudging or angry. Often, you'll notice, uneducated adults—and I expect this includes children—when they don't understand something someone has just said feel so threatened that instead of asking the speaker to explain it they are likely to say rudely—"I don't know what you're talking about"—in a begrudging or hostile tone. Children can practice simply, coolly, neutrally saying, "I didn't get what you just said; run it past me again." This skill has to be taught.

One of the most original suggestions in the appendix of this book (Appendix IV: Formats and Strategies) is the "Vertical Line Way of Taking Notes." It is discussed in Chapter 4. I don't know how early one can start this process with children, but one can suggest it in talk if not in actual writing. That is, a human being, as is exemplified in the "Vertical Line Way of Taking Notes," needs to do two psychological things at once. First, that person is paying close attention to someone else's writing. Second, the person is paying attention to his or her reaction to what is being said. It is valuable for that person to become *conscious* of the fact that he or she is carrying out these two quite distinct psychological processes at the same time.

The example given on the "Vertical Line Way" page is listening to the story of "The Three Little Pigs." The left-hand side of one's notes should have to do with what that story is about, but the right-hand side represents the *second* psychological process the reader is involved in—namely, forming and honoring one's own private response.

I don't think that we should press children about this, but we can frame the questions we ask in small groups and classrooms or in the large group of the whole classroom, around those two questions, asked separately: "What was that story about?" and "And where were *you* with that story?" It isn't productive to ask children yes-or-no questions such as "Did you like the story?" You can ask the children questions about the man who sold straw: what kind of man might he be? Children can even "attend to the man" in the way suggested in the "Attending to Other" exercise. We could guess why he is taking a wheelbarrow full of straw along the road. Why would he sell some of it to a pig? Or we could "attend to other," with the "other" being the wolf: Children might consider: is that wolf a mother wolf or a father wolf? I think these kinds of questions show children, first, to pay attention to what they're hearing, and, second, that what they think about it, what thoughts it excites in them, are worth thinking about. Besides, what we are doing in the classroom is asking beginners to enjoy a conversation about a piece of literature.

No Children's Writing Should Ever Be Subjected to Peer Review

There is no more controversial issue in the teaching of writing than the vexed question of peer reviewing. Peer reviewing is so heavily established as a habit in the United States that it appears to be authoritative, like a science. I suggest we break the habit right away because the practice does damage.

It appears to be a sociable, friendly process. Group work appears to show children how to be kind. They are taught to say something nice before they say something mean about someone else's work. When they say something mean it's supposed to be a "constructive suggestion." All of these factors lie across the top of the surface of this issue.

What is my complaint, then? It is that peers cannot recognize what is deep and good in a child's writing, and if the writing is original in vocabulary, the other children grow cold. Most of them can't even recognize good or bad grammar, never mind the spirit of a piece of writing. They should not be expected to recognize what's going on for a child through a written piece, nor should they be allowed to make comments on what's going on for a child. The implication of writing for peer review is that one must write something that will get past all those peers. That in itself leads writers to be superficial.

If the schoolroom is to be a "safe place" in which children can learn to write, they should not be put into small groups for any kind of review of one another's work.

We should not go along with the business-as-usual concept of American life. Given the state of American culture, following the norm is not desirable for children right now. Most children are oversocialized and *undersymbolized*—that is, they don't get enough chance to use words to describe the things that are going on inside their minds, and they have too much chance to learn cloying expressions such as "I really liked the way you did such and such, but I was wondering if it would be more effective if you did thus and such." Invariably, peer critiquing bends the members of the group toward very sociable topics, whereas much that children need to write about, in our lonely culture, is not sociable.

We have to acknowledge television as a mind-damaging experience for people. It is mind-damaging in a number of ways. First it is loud and noisy and coarse. It is too simple. It ruins one's ears for delicate sound. Its stories, of course, are violent. All the stories shown on television are constantly interrupted by advertisements, thus destroying children's attention span.

Therefore, the task in working with twenty-first-century children partly involves undoing the mind damage caused by television watching. Children need to be taught to rejoice in some half-flown idea they thought up. They need an adult to acknowledge any half a metaphor they bring out. That attention can consist of simply repeating the metaphor with obvious pleasure. Actual words of praise needn't be offered. Young writers need encouragement to bring to mind a scene that's no longer before them. Every time a child narrates something on paper, that child is undoing some of the alpha-level learning that goes on in front of television sets.

Unfortunately, American children don't start on a level playing field. If they have been allowed to watch a lot of television and have not been read to aloud, they are already, by age five, stalled in imaginative growth. Adult mentoring is one way to help children catch up. Adult-mentor comment on their *writing* is a particularly effective way for students to catch up.

There are further reasons that it is bad to set children to peer-reviewing. First, children don't know the feelings involved in writing. They have their *own* feeling to do. Second, if one child has written something surprising and original, the other children may decide it's weird, especially if one of their ringleaders speaks first and says, "Wow, weird." An earmark of primitive societies is that anyone who shows up as an individual gets pounced on. (Pouncing classically means meting out public humiliation.) Children maintain some primitive attributes even in adolescence, so an adult mentor must protect (a) minority voices and (b) any *original* voices from any judgment by juvenile group members. Third, peer reviewing socially encourages children to lie. They may exclaim, "Boy, I really liked that," when in fact a piece of writing left them cold.

Some sociology helps here. In his vivid, readable book called *Group Psychology and Political Theory*,[1] C. Fred Alford discusses many psychological outcomes specific to group-centered life. His most stunning point is that all animals run in groups, and early mankind uniformly ran in groups: that is, primitive man did not stand apart from his grouping. He would have been scared stiff to try it.

Alford describes how cruelly the modern-day Wolini people ostracized any tribe members of divergent opinion.[2] Suicide was common. The group rejected innovative agricultural solutions because an individual tribe member, not the leader, thought it up. The group ostracized the one who offered the solution. He ran away, thus making it possible for Alford to talk to him and study the Wolini. The Wolini, Alford shows us, destroyed themselves because they couldn't abandon primitive groupthink for what Socrates would have called the kind of reflection that makes life worth living. Civilization is what makes it possible for individuals to think apart from the group. Alford's story ties in wonderfully with Stephen J. Gould's remarks about how it is the individual breaking from the group continuum who is likely to bring about sudden disequilibrium of values, that may be followed by changes in decision making, which will, in turn, jerk a species into a new, life-enhancing direction.

If kids are to preserve their individual intelligence, we should never let the group weigh in on their writing.

Validating the Serious as Well as the Fun-Loving Spirits of Children

Some mistaken practices in pedagogy are natural reactions to earlier malpractice. Throughout the nineteenth century and much of the twentieth, schoolteachers were likely to be joy killers—they were people who disciplined us for not practicing penmanship just so or for misspelling or for laughing aloud in class or for not folding our hands on our desks. In reaction, first the "progressive" schools, then other private schools, and finally the public schools, began in the 1930s to encourage individual personality and especially *fun* in elementary classrooms. Quite right too.

The irony is that American children have been watching kidding and practical jokes on television for fifty years. They are a long way past the days when children learned somber hand skills and violin playing in the cultivated living rooms of their elders. These days they are tossed into fun day-care groupings at less than age one. They are bused to fun, interactive museum demonstrations. At home they master fun computer games at an early age. They are choking with fun. Schools of education, which are in the habit of promoting fun-loving teaching approaches, especially to the teaching of creative writing, need to pull up rein and consider whether or not a better task for education might be saving the children's own serious nature, not barreling them into still more and more superficial fun.

We had better do the oddly psychological work of giving children "permission" to be serious. TV conditions them (a) to keep smiles on their faces and (b) to entertain only the simplest insights. Little TV programming, whether designed for children or for adults, shows people happily learning math or science or creative writing. What arts children are exposed to are almost uniformly smiley and playful—as though the arts were all play. Teachers have even been ordered to make writing "fun" for kids. Teachers approach me after talks I've given to the National Council of Teachers of English (NCTE) and say, "I always encourage the kids to have fun with their writing." In the nineteenth century, when life, at least for laborers and farmhands, was doubtless not much fun, perhaps "having fun with one's writing" was a good idea. It would have encouraged expressiveness and humor and given relief from oppressive church doctrine. But now that American children spend so much of their time having fun, we writing teachers might do better to help them to explore the serious sites in their minds.

A solution: teach children the satisfaction of being reporters of interesting news. The news will be inner news, perhaps, but it is news, and a child can be interested in being clear, getting it right.

Rule number one for teaching creative writing to children is opposite to rule number one for trial lawyers: ask the child a lot of questions you *don't* know the answer to. Then the child becomes the authority on his or her own story—the expert on the writing content. People who feel respected as experts tend to respect their own *serious* nature more and more. They understand that they can always kid around when they want to, but they don't *have* to.

Susan O'Hanian, one of the most interesting educators of the 1990s, goes further about fostering seriousness in children: she suggests that we invite children into the world of making moral decisions—of having moral opinions of their own. I recommend her book *Who's in Charge?: A Teacher Speaks Her Mind.*[3]

I have many fears about what happens to children when they go home from school. The better the school environment, the more psychologically healthy and invigorating it is, the greater the contrast must be for some of the children when they get home. Much of what we teach children about spontaneity and trusting authority would not be safe for children with coarse or outright brutal caretakers.

Some of our schoolchildren haven't any homes. Increasing numbers of children show up at school unwashed, not warmly dressed, and generally not cared for. I have only a few beginning suggestions for what we can do for these children. I had not even known that there were such children until a first-grade teacher in Grand Rapids, Minnesota, a midsized community in the northern part of my state, told me that first-graders come to school without having been woken up or given breakfast by a parent. The children come to school without mittens, despite the brutal Minnesota winter climate. The first-grade and second-grade teachers keep boxes of mittens especially for these children. They keep scarves and caps, and they don't let the children go out to play at recess without putting on warm clothes.

It is very likely that we should be doing something parallel to that to protect such children's *minds.* The first thought that comes to my mind is that each child should have a portfolio. Many writing teachers have already created portfolios for their children. If a child has a home, then that child takes comparatively casual pleasure in his or her portfolio at school. If a child is homeless, or if his or her home life is compromised, however, that private portfolio (kept safe by the teacher) may be the only outward proof the child has that his or her inner life is real and valuable.

Offering Some Comment for Every Piece of Creative Writing a Child Does

As will be discussed in Chapter 12, Some Issues of the Aesthetics and Ethics of Writing Literature, one of the crimes of the United States is that there are too many children in the classroom and not enough teachers. One of the outcomes of crowding in schools is that writing teachers can't comment as much as they would like on children's papers. It sometimes follows that teachers simply don't assign papers because they won't be able to comment on them anyway. Writing teachers can't live a decent life of their own if they comment properly on all the children's papers in a classroom of forty-five students. Our response to this situation should be a protest to the United States Congress for allowing these conditions to continue.

In the meantime, however, we must do patchwork. I suggest that we as teachers make sure to write at least a one-sentence comment on every child's paper we receive. Writing one sentence takes about half a minute. A sentence is very different from a drawn smiley face. Reading the paper takes one minute, let's say, or two minutes. You can make that sentence seem more beautiful if you underline it (don't highlight it because highlighting is conventional and, in a bizarre way, intrusive—that is, it paves through the writing that is already there). It is infinitely better to underline certain words or phrases or expressions or even bracket a paragraph of the child's writing that you find especially charming or useful, and then underline a word or two of your one-sentence comment, too.

Teachers also have to mark students' grammar and usage errors because children need to learn the logic of the English sentence. If we give each child's paper two minutes, then, for reading—one minute for usage and one minute for comment—I think we will have done as well as we can for the students in a crowded classroom. It is important never to give a usage comment without including a content comment because we have to undo the message being broadcast throughout America—that how-to techniques are more important than the essential content of things.

A final point to remember when commenting on children's writing is that most of the pressure exerted on children, even by the best teachers, is to be *socialized.* Children are always invited to look at the bright side of things, and to say things that can be said to a *group.* They are conditioned to write papers that can be read aloud to a *group,* in general to be acceptable to a *group.* Try to make your comments, which needn't be more than one sentence, encourage that child's private philosophy and not that child's group-adjustment skills. Socialization has to take place, but my particular interest as a writing teacher is to support the invisible insides of people, even of very little people.

Giving a Child Two Opportunities to Answer a Question

During discussions involving the whole class it's so hard for children to think aloud quickly. I therefore suggest that teachers *come back to any child who muffs a question,* giving him or her a second chance to speak.

Say we have asked the student once. The student starts floundering. At this point, instead of gliding over to someone who is wildly waving a hand, I think it's important to say, "Wait, Arlene, I want to come back to you. Figure out where you are on this, and I'll be back to you in a minute." Then be sure to make a note to yourself on your desk, recording that you *did* ask her, so you will remember to keep your promise and go back to Arlene. Even if she wishes you would *not* get back to her, you promised to, and she grows cognitively if she gets the idea that promises are to be kept. For teachers who may not yet have had time to read present-day philosophy, it's encouraging to know that Ludwig Wittgenstein and John Rawls both set great store by keeping promises. Promises are a major, not a trivial, issue in teaching.

Let's say that now the discussion has gone around the class some. Students are discussing the Mother Wolf getting killed by the third little pig when all she was doing was trying to bring home the bacon. Now it is OK to ask Arlene, "Did you want to come in on this or not?" And if you act very relaxed Arlene will feel as if she has permission to say, "No, I don't." And then you can say, "OK," and quickly, briskly, go on to someone else. This student hasn't contributed to the discussion, but she has learned something. Because she was given two chances, she is likely to raise her hand later on about something else. For her you have removed one horrible now-or-never aspect of class discussions.

Asking children, or even older students, a question twice is unpopular with teachers. Teachers quite appropriately have their own agendas, one of which is to provide their students a lively, not deadly, classroom experience. The atmosphere is not so lively if questions and answers don't flit quickly around the room. Yet if we ask students only once, their minds come to the conclusion: "I failed my one chance." They may decide that only fast thinkers count. These slow thinkers need to know that they might miss at occasion number one but that they have an opportunity to redeem themselves at occasion number two. I suggest that teachers get up their courage and place less emphasis on having a quick-paced classroom.

A second suggestion is a subset of the first. When a child has just spoken I think it's important to allow a small pause, not to jump in with a response immediately. Let the child's answer stand for half a second before acknowledging it. Let that child's remarks have their moment, so to speak. The child will gain confidence, feeling that his or her remark made you, the adult, pause to think. This approach also models respectful behavior for other children who, however socialized they may appear on a superficial level, tend to be inattentive to one another on a deep level. Your pause after Child A speaks gives Children B through Z a chance to let A's words go into their ears. You are modeling adults' learning something from children, saying, in effect, "OK, I'm taking this in: it is worthy of my attention, and you are getting through to me."

Teaching Children, as Well as Ourselves, the Psychological Skills that Protect a Person's Personality from Group Bullying or from Unfair Pressure by People in Authority

I discussed earlier how certain items in the appendix, namely "A List of Useful Sentences for Writers in a Tight Spot," and the empathic inquiry technique offered in Chapter 3 might be used. Throughout the last twenty years, children have been offered interesting psychological savvy—problem-solving formats and in a few cases even Kohlberg's moral development stage theory—and no doubt other psychological aids I've never heard of. To these I would like to add the concept of children learning certain responses by heart (both the responses for addressing unfair situations ["A List of Useful Sentences for Writers in a Tight Spot"] and the empathy format) so that they can defend themselves automatically and need not panic at any sudden movement. They will have a little equipment to help them.

The equipment is simple enough. It reminds me of the marvelous old story of the fox and the cat. One day the fox and the cat met by the edge of the woods. They greeted each other cordially. The fox had with him his gunnysack full of tricks. The cat said, "Well, you've got a whole bag of tricks, haven't you? What would you do if a dog came along?" The fox said, "Oh, I've got dozens of things I'd do if a dog came along, Why, what would *you* do?" The cat said, "I only know one thing to do. I'd run up a tree." The fox said, "Oh, I've got ten tricks better than that." He began to undo the thongs at the top of his bag. Just then a dog leapt at them. The cat automatically went up a tree, and the fox, still struggling with the ties, was caught by the dog and bitten. Not all the psychology we teach people need be subtle. Some of it can be quite simple.

Asking Children to Memorize One Hundred Stories by the Age of Eighteen

There are many reasons that you should ask children to memorize stories and learn to tell them aloud without notes. First of all, storytellers use language. If they memorize *great* stories—great fairy tales, folktales, not just family anecdotes—the tellers will be using classical language. They will hear their voice saying great words. They will hear their own voice describing creatures *very unlike themselves*, such as the nanny goat who has ten little kids. Schoolchildren will never be nanny goats who have ten little kids, and they will never meet a wolf who whitens his paw with chalk, but when they hear themselves *talking* about a wolf who whitens his paw with chalk in order to deceive the nanny goat, they are experiencing firsthand something *very other.* They are practicing the groundwork of learning empathy. If they do this at a very young age, they will be filling their minds with at least some classical feelings and classical humor before the U.S.A. junk culture overflows the banks of their mind and floods away their own personal taste.

Telling stories about animals and strange places like the Black Forest or the great Sultanate of Delphi or the unbounded grassy steppes of Russia gives children practice in loving life outside the American tribe. If the story has the word *steppes* in it it's important to keep the word *steppes.* It is important not to translate such words back into current provincial usage, thereby losing the wonder and the tone. Children love strangeness if they're not afraid of it, and they are not afraid of it when they get to say the strange words in their own voice. When they tell stories of unlike creatures and unlike places they are free-heartedly exercising curiosity about otherness—about things that will never be like what they know. This is a major way for children to experience the much touted "diversity."

When you are telling a story from memory that is not from your own life, you don't feel any pressure to sneer. You need not talk it down. In fact, you *can't* talk it down. You don't need to doubt your own confidence or make self-deprecating comments. ("Well, that's what I thought then but maybe that's just me.") Some family storytellers sell out their own spirit over and over. Scott Russell Sanders feels utterly serious about *respecting,* not deprecating, very young children's feelings. He warns adults not to sell out their own youthful feelings: "Don't condescend to your younger self. Your feelings back then have authority. Condescension to your younger self is bogus. Whatever you were as a child you had a full heart. Do not mock your old younger self."[4] You *can't* sell out a memorized story from literature because the rule of the game is that you remember it respectfully. And because it is somebody else's story, it is not threatening to you. In fact, children get awfully good at telling other children stories, even in a formal setting.

Telling stories predisposes kids to seeing the *invisible present,* which we call "the past." It predisposes kids to enjoy history.

Memorizing stories is also a lesson in what Jungians call "containment"—keeping the essence intact—that is, a story shouldn't be "framed" any more than can be helped. A storyteller might have to explain that *steppe* means million-mile prairie, but he or she should keep such peripheral talk minimal. No first-rate story should have any low-key framing retrofitted to it. It shouldn't have stupefying comments by a teacher such as "Oh, and as we think about the three bears, children, does that remind you about anything from our field trip?" There should be no attempt to make surface connections. A piece of good literature stands alone. The three bears discovered that Goldilocks, in her wisdom, had invaded their house and used their equipment, and they scared her out of there. That's the story. It has to stay clean to keep the humor. While you're telling it you, whether child or adult, vanish into it.

Abused children get special pleasure from a classical story being kept intact: story is their second life, in which they do not have to think about what Dad or Mom is likely to do this coming weekend when they can't stay safe in the school. The mind learns to honor this category, story. A child's mind learns to keep walls around each story so long as that kid needs walls.

Memorizing a hundred stories and telling them models courtesy at a level that exceeds the courtesy levels that are exhibited in most modern American children's families. In stories people are a little formal. The little pig said, "Please, Man, may I have some of your straw so I can build a house?" For many children this is the first use of the word *please*, and the pig addresses the man as "Man" in a poised, formal way.

And, finally, if children can tell stories they can entertain their peers. By telling a story a child is entertaining a group of people for about five minutes or ten minutes. Being able to amuse or engage peers while being protected by the teacher removes some of a student's trepidation about speaking aloud.

Memorizing stories has an odd side effect: it teaches children to love others even if they have such undeveloped self-esteem that they scarcely love themselves; that is, the storyteller feels for the wolf and pig, bears, cat, or fox. A literary gift to the field of psychology: loving these others can model loving yourself. The conventional wisdom is that you have to love yourself before you can love others. Right enough, but an ingenious quality of literature is that you can first love *characters* in stories, giving you some practice in caring for anyone or anything—or yourself.

Let's imagine a woman named Emily who has never exercised love of self or love of others. She is an American whose teachers have never told her how to imagine something she has not physically seen. She has not seen the ocean. She also has not seen her own heart. Her *only* deficiency may be that she hasn't got the knack of loving what she has not seen.

Well, I will be her creative-writing teacher.

The lesson takes place in a department store. I am keeping up with Emily. She is briskly pushing a shopping cart toward the far aisle where all the goods are marked down three-quarters. I try to tell Emily a story in which a young merchant marine officer was so terrified by a gigantic green sea coming right across the bows that he gave a bad order. He sent a seaman aft on an errand and the man went overside.

"You see," I say to Emily, "the sea was so swift that it seemed to have no motion at all! It was emerald and gleaming like igneous rock—a horrible magma filled with awful, impersonal force. What's worse," I add—trying hard now to get Emily's attention, "you see afterward, he was afraid he'd make the same horrible mistake again. He could still see—months and months later—that horrible sea in his mind's eye."

"So?" Emily finally says, her eyes casting left and right down the aisles we are passing. "Some people are just cowards. Period."

"But if you could imagine yourself in that first mate's position," I say. "If you could imagine the sea . . . you'd see it's more than just being a coward. . . ."

She says, "It's only a story anyway," going past the dishcloths, the mouse seed, the Styrofoam. "I'm not the type," she adds.

She *is* the type, though. Everyone is the type. Everyone's imagination can be cultivated to visualize and feel some circumstance far different from one's own experience (like the sea). Everyone can be trained not to write off other people's characters with some abstract comment like "some people are cowards, period." Everyone can learn to see complications, such as the terror in the merchant mariner. All we teachers have to do is *expect* Emily to develop her mental taste. How can we do it? We make *her* tell a scary sea story.

Another use of story is that it presents *the ideal case.*

One of the faults of decision-making groups is that people often forget to ask whether the project they are going round and round about is really any good. We are expected just to go along with what seems to be the consensus. It is very important for young people (and middle-aged and old people) to learn the moral, sometimes spiritual work of making up one's mind about whether something is glorious or gross. Once we develop a taste for evaluating, we won't absentmindedly wander into what John Kenneth Galbraith called "accommodation of evil"—that is, going along with some dreadful plan without noticing what we've agreed to.

Knowing a story or two militates against that. Here is a classic example of the eighteenth-century fairy-tale genre. A father and mother of substance have two promising sons and one stupid son. This last boy is idle and unpromising. The parents get the two elder boys beautifully outfitted to win the princess. All systems are go. The boys get good mounts, good trail food, good clothes for courting royalty. Along the way to see the princess, these boys are indifferent to strangers' needs because their parents have also kitted them out with self-importance and feelings of entitlement.

The elder sons fail, of course, since fairy tales present the ideal case. At last the youngest son is to try for the princess. His mother gives him a scant lunch; his father gives him no horse. This boy helps animals, people, and even trees along the road. He will succeed with the princess. He has a signal ability to empathize with others' needs—no matter how different from his own. When the apple tree cries, "Help! Shake me! I am too borne down!" the boy helps, although he will never have the apple tree's particular problem himself. (Our Emily in the supermarket, or the boy's older brothers, would have said, "Some trees just naturally bear too much fruit. Period.")

What do we know about this foolish boy?

1. He went through a transformation. He looked like a fool, but he had a more complex psyche than his brothers had.
2. He lived scorned by the peer group—and he did not try to act like the others in order to be popular. He was outside the system.
3. He was capable of imaginative sacrifice.
4. He was able to take counsel from people and things unlike himself.
5. Nothing he did seemed particularly sensible.

This last aspect—his not behaving particularly sensibly—is important. The natural inclination of people in in-groups is to check out what sounds sensible and to weed out anything approaching the bizarre. In the beginning of Pearl Buck's story "The Old Demon," the old woman listened to a report of the invasion of her homeland, China. She said, "I don't believe in these Japanese." An invasion did not sound sensible to her. She was making a mental image only of what her eyes actually beheld—the landscape of her home valley with its river. What she needed to be doing was making a mental image of thousands of invading foreign soldiers instead.

Stories as "the ideal case" also lead us to engage in a moral exercise called learning to despise evil. In story, we do not "feel comfortable with" Snow White's stepmother: we know straight out she is serious scum. In story we are not "comfortable with" *any* of the bad guys. Present-day life is oddly prone to condoning evil, even though it is more useful to recognize evil than to deny it.

Older children—but adults especially—need to know about the mother in D. H. Lawrence's story "The Rocking Horse Winner." It is useful to know that if a woman is so obsessed about money that her heart has gone cold and angry, it will be impossible for her children to make her happy. Children cannot parent the parent. It is useful to despise the mother in that story. Besides, children find it inspiring, even freeing, to despise evil. In *Little Women* Amy said, "I shall marry for money." How ugly of her! I thought. I certainly will never do that! I felt charmed by the challenge.

Aristotle's suggestion that we should love what is lovable and despise what is despicable lives on in the inner landscape of us all—preserved better in stories than anywhere else.

Stories give the gift of mixed courtesy and playfulness. It is courteous to tell someone a tale, a yarn, an anecdote. It is playful because we know the story isn't literally true; for instance, "This is a true story, I know—because my grandmother had it from her grandmother and her grandmother got it from hers, and she got it from the stork on the roof." There is courtesy and delight in such a lie. The soul hates practicality; it cheers up the moment someone does something extra, which is of no immediate use, such as telling a story from memory.

We underestimate the grief caused by the hours of daily rudeness between human beings. Tension causes rudeness—particularly where people are not trained to watch for it. Our old people return from getting their pension checks, trembling with indignation at the rudeness shown them by clerks. Teachers are appalled by the rudeness of children, right in class. Social workers are thrown off guard at the rudeness they experience in working with perfectly unexceptional, privileged families.

Story poses an ideal opposite. Story tells us there was once a princess who could not stop weeping. It tells us there was once a duckling so ugly its siblings tormented it. Story assumes we are capable of sympathy and outrage at injustice. The assumption that we feel sympathy or outrage is a courteous gift from teller to listener. It is the very opposite of the rudeness and banality we—and children—experience daily.

Story—reading and telling—gives us a reprieve from our peers for a time. Such a reprieve, such solitude, nourishes anyone's spirit. Yet it sounds off-base to be promoting solitude in children's lives. It may sound off-base to say, "I'd like my child to get away from her friends a little more." Still, if we adults know adult stories like Shirley Jackson's "The Lottery," we understand the value of solitude.

"The Lottery" is not only about an imagined culture of classical scapegoating. The villagers stone someone to death every spring, in every village. That is the event of the story. The theme is that any established grouping of people can scarcely stop an evil practice once it gets going. Peers in the group use evasive language together, with one another, language with a studied low-key practicality to its tone, thus hiding the evil they do. Mr. Summers said, "All right, folks, let's finish quickly," as if the townspeople were cleaning up after a church fête. He meant for them to hurry up and throw their stones at the scapegoat. The author's tone is very sensible: "In this village where there were only about three hundred people, the whole lottery took less than two hours so it could begin at ten o'clock in the morning and still be through in time to allow the villagers to *get home for noon dinner.*" That would be the noon dinner to be enjoyed after stoning someone to death. Jackson is writing about how adults normalize group cruelty to children.

Stories help children identify any finer feelings that may be budding out in their minds. The human mind recognizes a feeling only when it knows *words* for it—which means that you have heard someone else talk about it or you have been exposed to a story about it.

If our life is made up only of someone handing us a wrench when we ask for it, or finding merchandise at half price, or hoping it won't rain for a certain occasion, or any other merely practical, natural issues, we may never celebrate invisible blessings. We may never celebrate friendship or love of nature. We may be neutral for ninety-five years, except for physical pain, fear of death, and startling sense impressions. We may never develop the habit of *celebrating* certain fine feelings.

Two "fine feelings" which good story preserves for us are love of beauty and love of friends, as in *Charlotte's Web.* There is a third fine feeling, which is so delicate and so easily scorned that by the time they are fourteen most children deliberately kill it just so they won't be humiliated by revealing it before peers. It is *the desire to do right by helpless victims.* (It sounds absurd even in the writing.) This easily mocked feeling is the essence of children's love of "Beauty and the Beast." All of the characters in any story generally live autonomously inside a child's mind. One small child may be all three—Beauty's father, the cruel minion to every bad worldly value you can think of, and Beauty herself—who tries to love where love is difficult, and also the Beast, symbolizing the higher nature of humankind that looks ugly to ordinary folk. The Beast is the secret good inside us—unseen or disvalued by parents, friends, lovers, and society in general. Only *we* know how good this Beast is, there at the very center of our finer feeling. No one understands this dilemma more intuitively than children do.

No one is particularly happy in a meaningless life. If children memorize and tell stories in school, they can remind themselves of how they would like to change the world. They may have to push shopping carts down the aisles or be the checkout at the end. They may do such work for hours and days and years, but if they learn to see the sea in their mind's eye because of story, they will be able to imagine and then mull over other invisible realities. Feeling that life is meaningful is oddly related to having a developed imagination. If you can see in your mind one thing that your eyes have never seen, you can give design to your own life.

9.

Helping People in Middle and High School Learn to Write

Adolescents and Monoculture

Adolescence is about newly discovered wit, idol smashing—smashing bad idols and some good ones with them—parent bashing, joining the herd, and developing idealism and cynicism side by side.

Some adolescents invent their own monoculture like a pop-up tent; they zip themselves into it and learn only *its* skills and mores. The monoculture has its coaches, to most adolescents nearly shamans. A few adolescents' monocultures may involve literature, but most consist of football, basketball, rock, Web site links of too many kinds to list, becoming an artist, street crime, and extraordinary love of nature. The shamans of these monocultures are, respectively, coaches, stars, computer tech-support people (often known only electronically, on-line, even if they work in a nonvirtual supply store), art teachers, youth orchestra directors, gang leaders, and outdoor leadership people.

Adolescents wend their way around potholes as often as they totter into them. Sometimes the monoculture is *being saved.* Then the shaman is the school social worker, the psychotherapist, sometimes a clergyperson, or a peace-studies leader. Being saved is a growing culture among young people. Usually the parents don't recognize how much it envelops the young people, but the parents disdain its outward signs.

I recently stood in a south-looking window, high up in a Manhattan apartment. It was late dusk. Most of the city was lit up—it stretched off as magical as ever between its rivers (I say "as ever" because New Yorkers themselves never stop being fascinated by their own cityscape.) Behind me old friends talked quietly. The son of one of them had been introduced to us the day before. He was a mannerly fellow, shaking hands, smiling. He was seeing a psychiatrist twice a week. We looked at him as if he were a very nice boy full of potential, presently seeing a psychiatrist just as another adolescent might wear a cast while a bone mended. As I looked at him a second time, I got this very different impression: he had dismounted and raised his visor to greet us because he was a nice person, but he was not defined by woundedness: he was a knight of his monoculture—the monoculture of getting saved.

At dusk I looked southward at thousands of lighted city windows. I may have been looking at tens of thousands of homes in which young people were taking all their mind's nourishment from a coach or a sculptor or violin teacher or a gang boss or a somewhere-bound leader or a psychologist.

I bring this up because we English teachers need to see adolescent writers not only in the way we are told to—as wildly changing, cognitively churning people with polar mood swings—but also as people who may be steadied on some ideal course we don't see. When you fly over the west Atlantic you sometimes see far below a sailboat heeled well over, out in the middle of dark gray sea and whitecaps. Half the reality is what it looks like—a small vessel in travail on rough seas, maybe swamping, maybe making it—but the other half is that the crew are right on course and making knots as planned. That boat's crew know their exact longitude and latitude because of the Global Positioning System.

Any monoculture means trouble in the long run, as any decent farmer or environmentalist knows. For instance, southwestern Minnesota is officially already a desert because its once diverse species of plants and animals have been reduced to so few. Adolescents should not risk their inner life by listening to the edicts of only one culture, but thousands of them do it. Whatever their monoculture coach can teach them they learn. (That can be a good deal, too. Coaches teach you how to be excellent at the same time as you exert yourself unselfishly for the team, an admirable balance. Coaches teach you to be efficient even when you are scared.) Sports coaches never teach you how to have a different outlook on life from that of your peers. Strings teachers teach you not to let yourself do less than your best. They can save you from the junk culture of being laid back and "having fun with" the violin. But strings teachers never teach you to give a damn one way or the other about United States domestic and foreign policies. Psychotherapists and psychiatrists, with notable exceptions of existential psychoanalysts like Viktor Frankl and moral therapists like Tom Kitwood, teach you to attend to your own life. If all your guidance is from coaches, strings teachers, or psychological professionals, then you learn the skills of Schiller's and Orwell's stage two—how to get beautiful performance into your life plan. *But you do not learn governance* from those teachers.

For two reasons we English teachers should keep an eye on writers who are enveloped by a monoculture: first, we need to discern what the students' monoculture is, if they have one, and respectfully make their creative-writing manuscripts a safe place for them to talk about it. Second, we should watch for signs that while these students are still taking sustenance from the monoculture, they are starting to listen at other doors as well. Creative-writing assignments should be safe places for their uneasy explorations.

I pay close attention to what social workers who specialize in group dynamics do with adolescents. Their work is nearly one hundred percent designed to help adolescents who are failing. English teachers have a different task. We must help writers not adapt to ordinary life but to escape into originality. We have to look for individual genius.

Using the Appendix of This Book with Adolescent People

Writing Exercises 1 and 4 through 10 can be used to help teenage students honor their expertise in their own lives. As with young children, we must not allow teenagers to write anything that refers to something they have watched on television. They need to see their *own* lives as the real treasury, not whatever they see hurtling at them from a screen.

We teachers have to make them *conscious* of this issue. It can't be left to their parents.

I suggest Exercises 1 and 4 as a good beginning, because they are about *place,* the easiest subject for people of any age to write about. Love of place, love of nostalgic feelings, and patriotic feelings are the easiest feelings to write about. Most people are so comfortable with whatever their place, nostalgia, or patriotic feelings are that they write about them over and over, all their lives, making more or less the same observations. Exercises 2 and 3 for writing about place are designed to help adult writers leave off the usual exclamations about what is in front of them and take a deeper look. I don't quite like these exercises for adolescent writers, because adolescents shouldn't be doing any more self-censoring than they can help.

In any case, no matter which exercises you use, it is infinitely better to assign exercises to writers than not to. If we do not assign material requiring some fresh thought, students get stuck summoning up the same vague memories in their minds. One of the greatest differences between stuck writers and expressive writers is that when a stuck writer originally from Point Reyes Station hears the name "Point Reyes Station" he or she skids to a landing in the same old memories and taxis round and round the mind's old tarmac of nostalgia.

Our job is to show stuck writers how to say, "*Last* year I noticed this about life. . . . I felt such and such. . . . *This* year it is entirely different." Exercises often help writers go at their work with playfulness, instead of devoted gloom.

Exercises 5 through 7 and 9 through 10 lend themselves to students writing about aspects of life adolescent people know a lot about, no matter what their background. Number 11, like "An Essay Pot," Exercise 8, can be used in small-group work—talking.

Adolescents, like children and some but not the majority of adults, like to get into small groups. They need the thinking tools provided in Exercises 8 and 10 to help them learn about writing *without subjecting their own writing to group perusal.*

Usage Sheets 1 through 3 can be copied and returned along with students' papers as needed. Small groups could also rewrite some of the Usage Sheet examples on a rainy day. As with elementary school children, encourage your adolescent students to come up with zany examples. I personally distinguish between fantasy and imagination. I consider fantasy to be anti-intelligence, but adolescents should be allowed to indulge in junk culture occasionally, right in school. Rewriting the Usage Sheets is a perfect way of doing so, no harm done, provided you make sure the rules of usage are correct. The high point of any "Essay Pot" exercise or rewriting of the Usage Sheets is the last twenty minutes of the period when the small groups read their work aloud to the whole group. The loudest, most confident students will wire up the class to hooting and clapping or jeering. Good thing no one's serious writing is the grist for this particular mill.

The Abbreviations sheet in the appendix explains itself. One might ask adolescents to add to it, especially from the large collection of Web site abbreviations students no doubt are familiar with. I know only AOL abbreviations from 1997—lol (laughing out loud), wtg (way to go), IMO (in my opinion), among the respectable ones. If students offer more modern abbreviations and these could be used for marginal comment, I would thank the students, add them to the Abbreviations sheet, and distribute copies to everyone the next day. (Why the next day? To show how any good idea the students offer gets snapped up quickly. Young people like good results *fast.*)

The "Vertical-Line Theory of Taking Notes" on books and on life is also described and discussed in Chapter 6. Appendix IV carries an example. For convenience, here is the rationale for "vertical-line note taking."

All notes should be written on full-sized pieces of paper rather than on scraps or index cards. This is not just so that you can do the Vertical-Line Method, which requires a full or sizable piece of paper, but also so that you have unfragmented consciousness of the notes you take. Otherwise the book there in front of you—on which you're taking notes, let us say—is handsome-looking with its binding and print, but your notes on their bits and tags of paper, perhaps with spiral-ring hole-tearings on the left-hand side, are ugly, and you don't respect your thoughts. 8½-by-11 paper is the right size. Draw a line down the center of a sheet. In the left-hand column you are noting the author's main points and perhaps some points about the author's style as you read the text.

On the right of the line you are jotting down your own responses or spin-offs to the text. Sometimes a text reminds us of something else, that something else being important but off-task.

The example of this in the Appendix, page 332, is "The Three Little Pigs." I've used the example of "The Three Little Pigs" in lecturing to social workers and psychologists in order to show how hidden in perfectly ordinary stories are moral points of view that we miss unless we're looking for them.

"The Three Little Pigs" is a story in which the author has no interest in mercy, kindness, fairness, or in what it feels like to a wolf to be boiled alive. "The Three Little Pigs" follows only a plot, that being the practical problem of having a house that will resist critical stress from huffing and puffing. Well, so what?

Psychologists, especially Jungian psychologists, often blithely dance about in the metaphors of a story that they are using to illustrate some preset notion of their own. They may not realize that there's heartlessness demonstrated in the story, because they are thinking about some other theme. Whenever heartlessness is *present but not mentioned*, it is normalized. We don't need any more normalized heartlessness in our culture than we already have. Let me give an example.

Jungians have made public presentations of "The Handless Maiden" as if it had to do with a woman's spiritual journey—as if it is a story about a *victim* instead of a story about a *predator*. "The Handless Maiden," in Jungian interpretation, is the story of a young girl's spiritual growth. The father cuts off his daughter's hands because he has made a deal with the devil. The Jungian interpreter glides past the part of the story that deals with a male parent mutilating a female child. What the interpreter brings up is a lot of excitement about the young, handless maiden's "spiritual journey" afterward. As if that mutilation, with the extraordinary and yet normalized sadism in it, counts for nothing.

Back to "The Three Little Pigs": let's say the wolf was a mother wolf who had to go down the chimney to get meat for her children. This rouses some extratextural feelings that we should *keep*, parallel to but not confused with our scholarly reading of the text. Our feelings can be reported on the right side of any page of notes we're taking, so that we don't lose them.

Therefore, on the right-hand side of this 8½-by-11 piece of paper, you are jotting down your own responses. The right-hand side notes can be your own thoughts or even merely will-o'-the-wisp associations brightened by the text. You are practicing that kind of *self-respect* that tells us our own ideas are valuable. Our feelings *are* valuable. In fact, sometimes our feelings as we read are finer than the easy shots of an author whose text we've been asked to study.

Let me suggest what too often happens with students' note taking on reading assigned them. They use 3-by-5 or 4-by-6 cards if they've been told to do so. This means that they are keeping separate ideas in separate places. That is excellent for organization but horrible for keeping our philosophy conscious and connected. Index cards have no fluid drape to them. To preserve our connectedness, we need to see a pageful of phrases or sentences. We are willing to pay scholarly attention to the author's ideas, but we also want our own agreements or dissent to take up some decent space.

Classically, adolescents are not in much of a position to disagree with any prevailing authority. They are like future whistle-blowers who haven't been hired yet, never mind fired. But their minds are roiling with the spume and turmoil of dissent. Even if their turmoil sounds like ordinary parent-bashing, somewhere in some of their minds there is rebellion against the ideas of the herd.

If an adolescent's ideas are half-crazed, writing assignments sometimes ease wrath. Writing assignments can ease the frustration of having so little power to change things. The "vertical-line note taking" exercise provides an outlet for finer stuff than you might suspect. What's more important, if a person at fourteen years old starts taking double-column notes with a vertical line between them, recording personal notes on the right-hand side of the page, by the time he or she is twenty-two years old that person will have a potpourri of his or her own informal philosophy.

And vertical-line note taking preserves our own sense of humor. Let's say we are reading some serious author and the ambiance of the text shrieks at us: "Take me seriously! Oh, take me dead seriously!" Well, we needn't. On the right-hand side of the vertical line we could write, "This is portentous stuff." On the right-hand side of the vertical line we can say, "This author is a royal pain." And even if we're not sure just at the moment of reading, and haven't time to stop to think about it, later we might analyze what precisely we meant by "royal pain." If we hadn't taken down the note in the first place, we might later forget our indignation completely.

Taking miscellaneous notes while we read also shows us how some of our ideas are *small.* They are sincerely felt pieces of thinking, and they are valuable, but they're small. They aren't worthy of a whole essay, but we can use them as side remarks.

Adolescent writers can learn to organize ideas by content rather than by paragraph sequence by using "A Format for Writing an Essay" in Appendix IV. It carries its own justification.

Middle or high school English teachers probably ought to ask their writers, in small groups, to add to or amend "A List of Useful Sentences for Writers in a Tight Spot." You might suggest that they start by making all the gross suggestions that come to mind. Experience has taught me that kids with chutzpah who are dying to substitute "Up yours, too" for sentences 1, 2, 3, and 7 won't do any real thinking until they have made their awful witticisms.

No Peer Reviewing of Manuscripts

Chapters 2 and 3 strongly argue against peer critiquing in any circumstances. But, unfortunately, peer grouping has a great hold in elementary, middle, and high schools, and with college writing teachers.

First, group work is what the establishment tells teachers to do. Second, it is easy. All you have to do is train students to settle for a little sociable thinking: that is, students who have come up through middle school with experience in small-group work or peer reviewing have a full kit of bland remarks that sound emotionally mature, for example, "I found the group gave me some really helpful suggestions."

How can any teacher resist such a balanced, intelligent, and properly civilized-sounding comment—especially since that kind of comment is so touted by conventional educators?

What we had better do instead is remember that Virginia Woolf or Wolfgang Mozart could have made little use of peer critiquing. In reaction, we mustn't let our lip curl and say superciliously, "But how many Woolfs and Mozarts have we got around here?" (I am sorry to say that some writing teachers do make just that remark.) Since we don't know which of our young people *is* the future Woolf or Mozart, we need to use only those teaching processes that honor people's innermost self. Even the peer group or small group that purportedly helps "at least with clarity" might be harmful, because that goal, mere clarity, gets focus attached to it that sometimes belongs elsewhere. Adolescents are influenced so much by groups that we must be very sensitive to what kind of undernourishment they are getting from any groups we put them in.

If we are putting adolescent writing students into small groups because the whole class is too big, then we are trying to remedy a culturally abusive situation. Classes should not be so large that teachers have to jeopardize their students' learning experience. (See "Teaching Spoiled Not by Instructors but by Government or University Policies" in Chapter 1 and the discussions in Chapter 8 and Chapter 12.)

The argument against subjecting writing students' work to peer review was so thoroughly gone into in Chapter 3 that I will add here only that the evils of peer review *are* more harmful to children and adolescents than to older people.

No Teaching of Literary Techniques

There should be no teaching of literary techniques to high schoolers. We live in a world of how-to conversations and technological toys. The *how* question is the prevailing question of pop culture. The writing teacher needs to balance that huge pressure by stressing the *content* in literature. We shouldn't give way on this.

Specifically, we should not assign the end-of-unit study questions in anthologies to people under the age of twenty or so. For one thing, those tricky, manipulative questions spoil one's reading pleasure. The questions offered for discussion and writing are about literary manipulation—what did the author do in order to influence you, the reader?—as if writing were an enterprise of tricksters, not an art practiced by people who love to tell stories and mull over life. There is no need to teach a young child how to skin a rabbit when what the child loves is the Easter bunny.

It is easy to say, "I think that we should not be teaching our students to become technocrats," if one needn't make a living in a high-school English department. Most high schools are committed to the idea that technological skills, or to phrase that more kindly, *craft*, is what writing is about.

I hope that more and more English teachers will stand up and be counted on the need to emphasize content. Young people are experiencing some boredom with the ignobility of literature. Even a half-century ago, young people who grew up loving to read suffered a shock when they discovered that English courses involved this groveling business of looking at what *methods* an author used.

Aldo Alvarez,[1] an English professor at Indiana University, discussed what he calls "craft fascism" on an on-line message board called "Integrity and Art in Fiction" on America Online Writers' Club, February 14, 1997.

> My own analysis of the concept [craft fascism] led me to stand behind this idea: the discourse of standardized craft damages the integrity of the subject and the integrity of the artist because it places them as secondary—as slaves—to the fulfillment of the abstract craft idea. In the process of stunting or fitting a subject into the discourse, the subject's distorted to fulfill the priorities of the discourse (causality, linearity, centrality, etc.). This also places the artist in the position of being someone whose status involves the issue of reproducing the craft rather than engaging with it as an individual: he or she becomes a machine that reproduces the standards of "goodness" outside of him/herself. In both ways, this kind of conception of craft as the end of writing institutionalizes oppression of the subject and the artists to the discourse the craft dictates as good and salable writing.
>
> The end product is neither reflective of the subject or the artist, but reflective of the cultural codes invested in the craft. Translation: craft fascism serves to uphold itself in the name

of cultural and economic prejudices. It's psychologically and politically disempowering.

A surprising reason for not teaching literary craft techniques to adolescents is that we have so little time, hour for hour, to help them out of their accidie. Spiritual boredom in adolescents is so prevalent that we English teachers, especially writing teachers, should see if we can take it on.

Boredom is a much more dynamic and pervasive feeling than most people recognize. In the beginning of *A Rumor of War,* P. J. Caputo confessed how boring life was for a young man growing up in Westchester, Illinois. The family conversations were not reflective or humorous. The suburbs were boring, and gradually the suburbs were chewing away at the fields where pheasants still flew, and at the woods Caputo hunted. He felt less and less as if he could do anything that felt honorable and ancient. This put him "at risk" to go to war.

The Marine Corps had set up a stand on the campus of Loyola University, where Caputo was a student. He wandered past one day. He saw the picture of a young Marine officer wearing a sword and a dress blue uniform. Fast as a gleam, he signed up for officers' training.

How can one explain that? Let's try some possibilities. Just as giggling and fooling around is part of teenage life and teenagers theoretically love it, perhaps having a rather sober sense of noble purpose in life is also a teenage interest. Perhaps teenagers love noble purpose, too. The suburbanites of Illinois or parents living anywhere else might be totally oblivious of noble purpose. But we are creative-writing teachers: we are in the best position to encourage any young person's classical feelings. (School social workers are in a good position, too, but not everyone comes to their attention.) Since English is still taught to nearly everybody in middle school and high school, we writing teachers have the best chance to lift kids above boring and ignoble thought.

To throw away potentially rewarding conversations in favor of analyzing craft seems awfully wasteful to me.

No Asking for Rough Drafts of Creative Writing

Why should we *not* ask to see rough drafts of adolescent students' creative-writing projects? Answer: a piece of creative writing can't be planned ahead. It comes into being as one writes it. (See Chapter 3 for a discussion of how this dynamic works.)

Most beginning writers don't know that writing literature is a process. They have internalized the general folk wisdom that writers are born, not made; they think you can plan a story ahead of time. They are sure you can outline ahead of time. Of course, they are right: you can, to your detriment, thus limit the growth and shape that would otherwise evolve in the course of the writing. If you are a student, it is pointless to show a teacher a rough draft of creative work: your own mind may already have sidled past the material of the rough draft long before the teacher returns it with suggestions. What's more, having the teacher get into the act just after you have made a first draft of something is a poor idea: a writer needs his or her own voice to get louder and louder. What I am calling the writer's "own voice" has to come up from underneath: it has to get through all sorts of culture blots that have leaked into all of our minds. A writer's voice has enough to do without dealing in the teacher.

There is one wonderful use for rough drafts, however—which doubles as a good project for high school small-group activity as well. I have urged all my students, but especially young people, to make a list of wonderful and horrible values—that is, wonderful and horrible behaviors of human beings. (See Exercise 5 under "Easy Exercises.") Here is a way, without taking very much teacher time, to honor students' ideas and establish a way of giving students feedback on substance. If the teacher photocopies all of the students' values, before returning a little praise or questioning of one or another of each student's list, then the teacher has a compendium of all the good and bad qualities listed by the group. If you combine the good ones on a given day, perhaps the bad ones on another day, without identifying which author made which contribution, you can then distribute these lists to small groups to develop into either illustrative anecdotes or discussion pieces.

After small-group discussions and reports to the whole class, students sometimes want to elaborate (privately) on the rough list of their own values. I can think of few more useful assignments than encouraging young people to dwell further, make themselves a home, rather privately, in their own particular ideas.

A caution: if you ask students for a list of deeply felt good and bad qualities, it is extremely important that you read them all and make a substantive comment on at least two or three of the qualities listed. If we don't respond to a few specific points, the student may feel that he or she was asked to reveal serious thoughts, in trust, but that the thoughts went to a psychological shredder.

Never Failing to Comment on the Core Content of Students' Papers

Commenting on students' papers was discussed in Chapter 8, with respect to children's writing. If students' inward work is ignored by negligent teachers, those students feel betrayed. Next, they slippy-slope down into the usual intellectual indolence of our culture. The general U.S.A. junk culture always lies ready to receive cross-hearted writers who feel their most delicate insights or sensitive philosophies got blown off.

All writers, but the young more acutely than adults, take nonresponse as treachery. If it happens over and over, they feel that they then have permission to pass along scanty intellectual service to others. Nonresponse—indifference—becomes the norm. For this reason the creative-writing teacher needs to make a little personal comment on each student's paper. The comment on Easy Exercise 5, the listing of wonderful and horrible behaviors, can be nearly anything. I sometimes scribble or type, "I loved your ideas four, five, seven, eight, and nine. I have to trust you on ten because I don't know anything about that—I've never gone there. I think your whole list looks very promising. You can bear it in mind as you write other things in this course."

Teaching Adolescent Writers to Continue Memorizing Stories, if They Started in Elementary School, and to Add Poems

Young people use oblique communications with each other,* and will continue to do so. But if they know some crisp, surprising language by heart, that crisp, surprising language will be *theirs*. They can pull it up later when they are ready to take pleasure in it. People are set free when they hear their own voice speak beautifully. (For the reasoning behind this, see "Asking Children to Memorize One Hundred Stories by the Age of Eighteen," in Chapter 8.)

An Ethics Code for Teachers of Adolescents

Please see "The Robertson-Bly Ethics Code for Teaching Creative Writing to Middle and High School Students" in the appendix.

*As in friendly but noncommunicative remarks like "I'm like what's that all about."

10.

Helping College Students and M.F.A. Candidates to Write

Teaching college and M.F.A. candidates to write is less vexing when we know some modern dynamics that help people *change* faster. Change of heart—change of our own hearts, that is—is the true occasion in literature.

Our first aim is to learn whatever helps bring ourselves and our students to that kind of change of heart we call inspiration.

Leaving Behind the Natural but Useless Attitudes Common to Any Enclave of Creative Writers

Nowhere does Schiller's schrewd description of leaving one's life of merely natural spontaneity and natural practicality in favor of deliberately shaping for oneself a life of principles and doing the work of beauty apply more usefully than in college or graduate writing programs.

The first part of this chapter is divided into topics all of which are meant to help us avoid floundering in the attitudinal lagoon of academia. When we teachers and our writing students identify which attitudes are only reactive or *natural*, we can see they don't help us with literary inventiveness.

Getting Past Thinking about Unfairness, Widespread Though Unfairness Is

Occasions come up in writing that are so unfair that we would do best simply to agree to ourselves aloud or in our journals, "That is wildly unfair," and not think about them anymore. Unless you mean to give up your writing to become the leader of a major psychosocial rebellion, thousands of horrible situations can't be cured. It is a great help to student writers to point out to them that the distribution of talent, of good earlier schooling, of useful family background, of good M.F.A. writing teachers, and, as everywhere, of money is unfair and always has been throughout human history.

"Talent" or "gift" is given out so unfairly that we can hardly grasp it. We may know that it's no coincidence that Papa Mozart's children were such good musicians, but what about when a writer can like lightning turn out beautiful phrases and strange metaphors whereas no one else in that person's family does much better than "How about those Vikings?" And what about those classmates whose hastiest first drafts read like Yeats and who have gone to the same either poor or mediocre schools the rest of us have gone to? Best label it "unfair, that's all," and do not meditate on it. And if somebody keeps going on about the unfair distribution of talent in your presence, you can say firmly, "Right. Totally gross, like much else," and walk away from the conversation.

After the unfair distribution of talent, the second unfair reality is that only a few Americans get to go to even passable elementary schools. Still fewer get to go to good high schools. Businesses and nonprofit organizations find it harder every year to recruit starting-level support staff who can spell, never mind organize and write a civil business letter. Some M.F.A. students never had a high school English teacher who read their papers at all.

Virginia Woolf got brought up in a literate family where thousands of words were used every day. Words are how we symbolize reality, and they bring extraordinary perspective to any family using them with variety and quantity. Perspective is humor. Humor lets us keep any oddball perspective we like without feeling we had better throw stones at such and such a person who keeps either a conventional or a different oddball perspective. Once you have agreed that it is unfair that some families are cultivated and some are not, think no more about it. People of every era have become authors, although their families, who theoretically loved them, pulled off every psychological trick in the book of bullying expressly to stunt their efforts and diminish their originality.

Another present-day injustice is that when you take a course in writing at college, or when you enter an M.F.A. program, you will occasionally be taught by fearful people. These are English teachers or writing teachers who have made themselves read right through the work of Foucault, Derrida, Lacan, de Man, and others whose ideas they secretly don't like. These teachers resent critical thinking so irrelevant to the creative process. What's more, these teachers may experience Foucault, Derrida, Lacan, and de Man as reductive or hard-nosed. Yet these same professors or instructors are afraid to confess to their own feelings. They even lead students into reading the same critical canon. Not all creative-writing teachers kowtow to "textural studies" or other loveless approaches to literature, but chances are that every M.F.A. student will be taught by at least one such teacher. Ironically enough, the distribution of teachers brave enough to teach love of literature instead of dissolution of literature is unfair, as unfair as the distribution of literary gift.

The word *philosophy* means "love of knowledge." If you are an M.F.A. student or a college student or a teacher of college English or M.F.A. coursework you will have to guard your original love of reading as well as you can. Try not to indulge in self-pity about horrible teachers wasting your holy time. It helps to recall that there have always been appalling schoolmasters. It helps to remember that most M.F.A. students will grow up into college instructors with one glaring fault or another.

No movements are so sluggardly as those that gradually gather momentum to counteract vicious pedagogy. For example, long after

Thomas Arnold, the great reformer at Rugby School, British masters went on caning boys. They knew that caning young boys did not encourage intellectual interest. Caning didn't even help the Empire, although the model would suggest a promising introduction to bullying. Prep and public school masters knew all that, but they went on caning boys because they knew the drill. Creative-writing teachers and scientists—likely most of us—are prone to going on teaching false concepts once considered to be true because we are afraid to stop and we know the drill.

The final endemic injustice is that some graduate students and some college students and some writers have money all their lives. They have time to write in. They don't need to be exhausted. They don't have to write at night. They don't hold a "day job," so no one tells them not to quit it. They don't need to ask their spouses to take care of the children for an extra couple of hours over the weekend so that they can write. What's more, such inequity of income survives in any kind of culture. Twenty years ago a few reports from the Soviet Writers' Union made it clear that a lot of Russians worked appalling hours on collective farms while a handful of writers were pensioned to be writers. There must have been tens of thousands of Russians, old Bely and Chekhov lovers, who weren't ever given a chance to become writers. And as for America, with our modified capitalism, some people lay hands on grants, but no one, not even experienced teachers, has figured out a way to give the serious poor, let alone the middle class, any time to write. No one has worked out how we might teach writing to homeless people. And only very few have put their minds to the problem.

We can suggest to undergraduate English majors and M.F.A. candidates that they think of the world's unfair splatter of luck as being of two kinds: first, the undeniably unjust circumstances that one can't do anything about, at least for now, and, second, other undeniably unfair circumstances against which one might organize a sensibly focused protest in the future.

Breaking the Natural Habit of Being Neutral about Much of Life or Much of What One Reads

For the last twenty years it has been stylish to assume that anyone who is neutral instead of fervent on a given subject, or who responds slowly to new stimuli of any kind, is probably repressed or experiencing some other psychological difficulty. That may occasionally be so, but in most cases being neutral, having no particular opinion on a subject, being vapid, are only bad habits—bad habits that writers, more than others, should overcome.

Families bring up their children to have that bad habit. Neutrality or indifference especially suits fearful people because if you ask them, "Well, what *is* your opinion of Derrida's work then?" they can say, "Well, you know, there are two sides to just about everything." Social workers teach that a person's past fearfulness may have vanished, but the *habit of acting fearful* or indifferent lingers, providing some banal comfort to the person. Clinging to that banal comfort is death for literature. Let me give an example.

In the fall of 1985 I was still respectful of the English classroom process called peer reviewing. I allowed a class of freshmen to look at each other's work. The comment always came in a deadbeat tone of voice. The peer critics would speak far down at the gravelly bottom of their voices. They said things like, "Well, I thought that the sentences were effective," and "I thought generally the tone was good," and "The voice seems strong," and "I thought it flowed well." Without missing a beat those experienced eighteen-year-olds hefted every cliché of low enthusiasm, and they were uniformly low-key, no matter how fascinating the papers in hand. Casual civility was their style.

A woman described her last summer's job in Alaska, which she worked in order to pay her tuition bill. She and her mother worked in the fisheries, their job being to stand along the line and gut the icy salmon as they came by on the belt. Up-line from the ten or twelve women in their section, men beheaded the fish. Everyone worked with their hands in and out of nearly freezing water.

One payday the women heard the men shouting and laughing especially loudly. The news joggled down to the women. The guys were taking $10 contributions for a jackpot to be paid to a fellow who swore he would grab a live salmon and eat its head off right there for everyone to see.

The scene reminded me of the first scene in *Jude the Obscure,* when a pig's pistle comes flying over at Jude, thrown by women making cheerful coarse jokes.

That writer's peer reviewers found "the sentences effective." They thought the story "flowed well."

At last I realized these young people had being trained to be low-key literary techies. Since that time I have taught many sets of graduate students and college students. No matter how affectionately these groups of writers (especially graduate students) drink together and share manuscripts with each other, when one of their number does an *extraordinary* manuscript, they usually miss it. It gets the usual noncommittal, civil, turgid indifference. The students are not cynical or even unpleasant. They are even free of envy until one of them gets published. They may have to work to quell envy all their lives. They may have to remind themselves, "I'm glad that this good writer, my colleague, picked up some honor. I'm glad. I am also sick with envy but I am 87 percent glad and only 13 percent envious." For now, before any friend is published, as they begin their upper-level writing course work, they have to break the habit of not noticing when something wonderfully intelligent has happened right in their midst. They need to stop missing the historical moment.

Let me suggest a *literary* rather than a psychological cure for the habit of offering noncommittal responses to our own or other people's literature—or to our own ideas or other people's ideas, or even to life as it presents itself to us.

In several ways the poem by Edith Wharton below is a horrible poem, but its curious subject is how to stop making slothful, low-level responses to life. The subject alone makes it valuable. In this work Wharton reminds us that a lot of people have died without being able to live out their lives. Wharton refers to World War I soldiers killed when they were eighteen years old. She suggests that being grateful for merely being alive might keep us alert in a wholesome way. For example, if one of our colleagues has written something sad, we can regard that sadness as very likely the sadness of millions and millions of people or creatures who didn't and now never will get around to writing it down. Here Edith Wharton says that our job is to live and write intensely since living and writing are a privilege:

THE YOUNG DEAD

Ah, how I pity the young dead who gave
All that they were, and might become, that we
With tired eyes should watch this perfect sea
Re-weave its patterning of silver wave
Round scented cliffs of arbutus and bay.

No more shall any rose along the way,
The myrtled way that wanders to the shore,
Nor jonquil-twinkling meadows any more,
Nor the warm lavender that takes the spray,
Smell only of sea-salt and the sun.

But, through recurring seasons, every one
Shall speak to us with lips the darkness closes,
Shall look at us with eyes that missed the roses,
Clutch us with hands whose work was just begun,
Laid idle now beneath the earth we tread—

And always we shall walk with the young dead—
Ah, how I pity the young dead, whose eyes
Strain through the sod to see the perfect skies,
Who feel the new wheat springing in their stead,
And the lark singing for them overhead![1]

Edith Wharton (1862–1937) is best known for her novels and short stories. This poem may be half-putrid, but it is only half-putrid: it is half smart as a whip. It suggests that we keep the cruel truths of life just under the skin of our love of life. Wharton doesn't write so wisely and well as Viktor Frankl, but she, too, had hold of a major idea that he wrote so powerfully about in *Modern Man in Search of a Soul*: one must consciously decide that life has meaning and then live in the constant presence of meaning.

Breaking the Habit of Relentless Informality

Why would we bother with formality? (Have a look at the footnote on the List of Abbreviations in the Appendix, about sharing English department scholars' traditions versus less formal social scientists' conventions.) Oddly enough, formality makes writers value their own invisible insides better than slob language does. But a good writing teacher feels edgy about establishing any formalities in a writing class because writing classes are typically full of nervous people. The conventional wisdom is that informality relaxes people. True enough, but it also fails to invite people to indulge in deep feeling. I suspect informality seems relaxing only because it is familiar. If a mix of formality and informality were familiar we might feel just as relaxed.

I suggest we practice just a few superficial formalities as a way of modeling respect for students' work.

For example, most college freshmen have just survived three or four years of neglect by their overworked high school English teachers. To recoup the neglect: a typical student load for a public high school English teacher is 150 students. If the teacher assigns weekly papers and writes even the tiniest comment on them, that teacher would be reading 150 papers a weekend. Fast reading might come to four papers an hour. A weekend, if we omit the three nights' eight hours for sleep, consists of seven hours on Friday, sixteen hours each for Saturday and Sunday—a total of thirty-nine hours. Thirty-seven and a half hours would be needed to read all the students' work. That leaves one and a half hours for love, raising children, active sports, and eating meals.

As a result, high school teachers either don't assign weekly or even biweekly writing, or they assign it but they don't read it. Here lies the real cause of American young people's shocking inability to write prose. If the Congress allocated and designated enough money for public schools so that every high school English class were made up of fifteen students, the problem would be solved.

I can offer an example of what it is like to be taught English at a private school (with twelve to fifteen to a class). One very brief comment from only one high school teacher in itself made me hang in with my childhood wish to become a writer. The teacher had written only "The stuff of which stories are made is here." Adolescents are so willing to feel mentored or encouraged by the tiniest remarks! That one was enough for me. That teacher had twelve of us in one senior section, twelve in another. We all wrote weekly. She could have written, "The stuff of which stories are made is here" to twenty-four of us in six hours of reading of papers. Presumably she could knock off that work on Friday afternoon and Saturday morning. If the Congress were to provide enough funding for American public schools to make twelve-person classes possible, public high-school students could get the same individualized encouragement I had.

But, for the present, college freshmen generally have not sat in any classes of twelve people. They may have done little writing or none. What writing they may have done may have received a short salute or it may not have. For my freshman composition class I bought bright-colored folders, not the university bookstore kind with the college football team colors and a receiver carrying the ball. I wrote the name of a first-year composition student on each folder.

At her first conference with me, one of my students watched me flip open her folder, take out her paper and a carbon copy of my earlier note to her, and a few notes I had made on her class participation. She looked amazed and delighted. She exclaimed in a tone of the greatest surprise, "Have you really got a folder for each one of us? You mean each one of us," and she emphasized *us*, "gets a folder?" She perhaps felt less like a face in the crowd because an adult human being had gone to the trouble of making a folder just for her. It reminded me that Czeslaw Milocz wrote sardonically that American life was, of course, wonderful after living under the threat of Communist police, but it was lonely. At least the NKVD or KGB had a file on you. They cared.

My student saw that her creative work did not get shrunk and freeze-dried into a grade book with nothing but alphabet letters in long horizontal lines.

When a writer's teachers attach a typed, separate note to a paper being returned, he or she feels more respected than if there were only marginal notes on the paper itself and a sentence or two at the end. That is because a typed note has a formality about it. Typing a note tends to make you, the teacher, contain and summarize your feelings about the work. You can write, "Dear So-and-So, please see all the marginal comments. Some of it is quite specific, some not; some is only my personal response to remarks of yours. I loved some of the things you said. See praise [here] and [there]. Please note that I wrote *Grrr* in the margin." *Grrr* is an abbreviation for the sound *gurrrrr.* (See the abbreviations list in the appendix.) *Grrr* stands for an animal growling. It means that in a certain line or place the student's work fell far below the level of work we are trying for in our group. It can stand for the fact that I have repeatedly given certain students in class or written on their papers suggestions that they have ignored for the twentieth time. This growl apprises them of my personal indignation. I keep my own humor together by using such abbreviations, but I do want to show human indignation. An attached note sometimes goes on to say, "Please pay special attention to [such and such] where I've marked it in the margins. You'll see that on this note I have put a green spot at the top of page one. That means I want a revision." Or, "You'll see where I have put a red spot. That means I'd like you to read the passage bracketed in red aloud to the class if you'd be willing. I will ask your permission when the class begins." Or, "You may notice that I have put a red spot *and* a green spot on your paper, and that means I'd like you to read some of it to the class to illustrate a literary point beautifully done, but I'm also asking you to do a revision. Yours faithfully," and I sign my name. I use the word "faithfully" because it is such very hard work to teach people writing that one must constantly remind oneself to be the servant in this huge cause—learning to do literature together. Besides, writers need some promise of good faith from their instructors.

By way of formality for the sake of simple courtesy, it helps to ask students' permissions at the beginning of each class to read their work aloud. It helps to say, "Ms. So-and-So and Mr. So-and-So, or Kordell and Hines, will you please read aloud the red bracketed part on your papers, when we get that far, because it illustrates things we'll be working on in class today." It needs to be clear that any student can say, "Actually, I'd rather not." And you then will say, "Right, OK," and move with dispatch to the next one and say, "Josh, may I please read aloud the part I've marked on your paper because I want to use it to illustrate such and such a point?"

There are several advantages to having a typed agenda for each class session, only one of which is formality. (The two actual agendas reprinted in the appendix were used in an advanced creative nonfiction class in 1999, taught at the University of Minnesota.) An agenda shows, for starters, that the teacher bothered to plan the class session. Many creative-writing classes are not planned. When students know a session is planned they feel genuinely served. An agenda also helps the teacher to stay on task and get specific subjects covered. If we are really teaching and not just offering a feel-good hour of literary scatter, we do have subjects to cover, even if they are invisible subjects. We teach certain skills, too, some of which are nuts-and-bolts literary craft and some of which are elegant literary craft. Some of our lessons, unfortunately, have to consist of K–12 grammar principles that our half-schooled students have missed. When those topics are listed verbatim, everybody knows how much there is to do during that session. A wise, kind-hearted teacher can ask the group if anyone would like to add anything to the agenda. My personal style is seldom to ask because I like a pacey agenda. Miscellaneous questions can be brought up in conference or via e-mail. If the agenda lists handouts to be passed out, people take the handouts more seriously. They should. Putting together handouts is a lot of work.

Occasionally it helps to present a given class member's work by memory to the group. This shows enthusiasm for that writer's effort, and it reminds the whole group that the core of our work here is literature, not social relations. The work, the work, the work—as Henry James would say. He suggested that people not talk about writing but just "Do it. Do it. Do it." The work is not about tracking one's own personality. Writers fret away too much time thinking of themselves as "a writer." "What should I do with my life—as a writer?" The better question is, "What literature shall I write just now?" (See the discussion under "Teaching the Psychological Work of Valuing Literature Itself More than the Literary Life," on page 208.)

I have found it helpful *not* to suggest that students about to read their own work first ask the others for quasi-technical help of some kind. According to an unfortunate American student-writing tradition of the last ten years or so, a student about to read aloud says to the group, "What I'd like help with here, please, is whether you think the voice is consistent," or, "I'd like help with the pace." I think such stuff is not only ridiculous but in its mealy way it is controlling. It says, "I want your opinion *only* on such and such." Besides, it is scattershot use of audience. A writer often needs a critique of a totally different sort from the one he or she may choose to ask for. A writer typically asks for help with "voice," when what he or she needs is help with sincerity and clean-cut language. Too often student writers ask for *technical* help when what they need is to work on scope or depth of *vision.*

You can teach grammar to an "advanced" class of writers quickly by adding a box with grammar tidbits in the lower left or lower right corner on each agenda sheet. Teacher and class can run through the material briefly, and students have the agenda to take home. In the 1960s it was assumed that if writers learned logic (grammar, in our field) they wouldn't be free spirited. That was not true, but "being turned off" by grammar became fashionable. The following decades have produced more and more students who know little sentence logic. Any writer had better cultivate a positive liking for the logic of the English sentence.

A strong, if much less becoming reason to teach good usage is that there are still some secondary schools and colleges in the United States in which usage skills are still taught—and these students thus gain an advantage in career choices over students who don't learn to organize their thoughts well enough to speak clearly. When college freshmen don't know any grammar or usage, English department instructors typically send them to a "writers' lab." That sounds like a fine compromise until one sees that these writers' labs are often run by fellow students whose own usage is appalling. Writers' labs are a mixed bag, although it is bad form to do anything but praise them. An alternative: an instructor who is teaching writing, even upper-level writing, can tuck in brief lessons on the mechanics of English.

Rendering unto Caesar What Is Caesar's—Useful Machiavellian Psychology for Teachers and Writers in Graduate-School Programs

A caveat: when everyone renders unto Caesar what is Caesar's, what happens is that Caesar gets richer and richer and everyone else gets poorer and poorer. This is true in things psychological as well as with empires. Psychologically speaking, we live our lives in an occupied country where much of the control is out of our hands. The people who control the work site have the power. In an M.F.A. program, people in control can either grant you the degree you want or withhold it.

There are certain tactful practices both instructors and students had better take note of. Hour for hour, most writing classes taught in M.F.A. programs are themselves staffed with teachers who are not authors but fellow M.F.A. students or adjunct faculty. These teachers may have published one or two short works. They are roped into teaching whether they want to teach or not because they need the income. Their presence alone means that the direction of the whole M.F.A. program and of the English department may well be out of any artistic control. The whole enterprise may bravely fly the flag of literature, but it is mainly driven by the principles of available labor.

I think we writing teachers can dodge around a number of the abuses without sacrificing either our students or ourselves. If we want to bell the cat (reform the creative-writing program) that is one thing, but we shouldn't make any of our students do it.

Specifically: American M.F.A. students must get As. Even undergraduate writing students expect an A on every paper.

The only serious issue here is: how can we use grades to indicate the gamut of performance from excellence to mediocrity without sacrificing a student's requisite 4.0 grade level?

I finally solved this dilemma by making up my own grading system for graduate-level creative writers, consisting of eight grades: A+++, A++, A+, A, A–, A––, A–––, and F. I also sometimes give one or another kind of an A followed by a slash and then an A, B, C, or F on the other side of the slash. (See the grading suggestions in Exercise 15, "A Nearly Impossible Writing Exercise," in the appendix.) The meaning of an A/B is that I thought the writer deserved an A for a fresh idea or exhilarating metaphor, or for the essay's scope or for its delicacy. The writing itself was jejune or slothful, so I added a slash and a B.

Back to the use of A+++ through A––– and F: since everyone knows that each M.F.A. candidate must receive an A as a final grade, it's best to announce you will give As to everybody, unless you find stanzas by Adrienne Rich or paragraphs by Rebecca Harding Davis pillowed into a manuscript the student claims as his or her own. That stunt deserves an F for crookedness. I like to announce the grading policy well ahead to allay fear. I usually ask for six to eight very short papers and several serious if short revisions in a course. I want to let student writers know that there will be no end-of-term trouble with grades. The A+++'s through the A−−−'s tell people to write and recite fearlessly. Freedom from fear is important because fear-laden people simply don't think up metaphors. The mark given to the right of the slash gives my opinion of the students' craftsmanship.

My grading may be so ridiculous that people jeer when they hear of it, but it's more honest and expressive than a lot of the graduate-level grading that has been normalized all across the United States. Grading is so depraved that we teachers may as well do it as expressively as we can without putting our students' academic careers at risk.

A final word on rendering unto Caesar what is Caesar's—in our case cooperating with the dictates or customs of whatever writing program we have joined as teacher or student teacher: when we undertake to write creative nonfiction we are already in a rebel or gadfly or change-agent mode. We are in that mode even if our writing goals are purely aesthetic or purely self-expressive and have nothing to do with public idealism. We are in the rebel mode because we are standing up for our inward selves. Standing up *for* anything involves standing *against* something else. We are standing *against* our most conventional, easy-living selves. Just standing against our usual easy-living selves is rebellion enough for a lifetime.

We feel the strong pull of our conventional self when we're writing. For example, you pause in your writing because you are trying to get something right. Your conventional self says, "Look, here's what most people agree on about this. Can't you just put that down for now?" Your conventional self hates agitation, especially agitation that may not yield some wonderful new insight or metaphor. Your conventional self is tricky, too, so it adds, "Can't you just put down just *something* for now . . . so you can get on with your life?"

If you listen carefully to how the expression "Getting on with your life" is used, you hear its message: (a) I mean to repress some intransigent memory, or (b) I'm going to leave some particular injustice uncorrected, or (c) I am going to blow off some demanding truth or other. "Getting on with your life" is one of the cagiest phrases your conventional, self-centered mind-set will use to bring you down.

So we teachers and students of writing are involved in a kind of guerrilla action against our own conventional selves—enough scary enterprise for the moment.

Breaking the Psychological Habit of Wanting to "Feel Good about Yourself" All the Time

The superego, Freud's term for that part of us that absorbs instruction from dominating parents, is out of style now. Good thing, in the sense that, of course, we want any slavish licking up of advisories and papal bulls to be out of style. Yet it saves time if one can take *some* advice quite directly. It shows psychological strength to be able to stay in the room, despite the pain, just in order to learn.

Let me give an example. At the Associated Writing Programs' Conference in Albany, New York, in the spring of 1999, I argued in a panel that some women writers were trivializing huge subjects by making announcements like "Every woman has a Holocaust inside her." By saying or writing that she had experienced her own Holocaust, a woman writer was trying to make it clear that women bear pain that men can't or don't imagine. On the other hand, the woman who said this was trivializing an experience that by definition has to do with whole peoples. Holocaust, or genocide, means "whole peoples being killed by another people or members of another race or another people." A holocaust cannot refer to something going on inside one person.

Further, it's tasteless for Americans to make anything like such a melodramatic claim unless we are Native Americans who have survived a genocidal experience ourselves. People so distant from the massacres of Rwanda or Bosnia, Germany or Russia or Turkey, should not let themselves use such language about anything lesser. It's such self-aggrandizement—taking the language of others' intense experiences and wrapping it around yourself—to make yourself feel more glittering, to dramatize yourself. I complained about such trivialization in our panel. A woman stood up and said, "Wait a minute—what's going on here? I feel as though we're being chastised." So they were—they were being chastised for being so greedy with language and so self-aggrandizing and self-oriented. She was able to distract a roomful of people from the question of language and onto the question of whether or not she and the others in the room were feeling good or feeling abrased. She could not make herself return to the issue of appropriately or inappropriately attaching strong language to ourselves. She was so magnetized by her own woundedness of ego that she could not focus on the issue of leveling down words like *holocaust*. She could not grasp and consider the practice of insidiously normalizing what happened to the millions murdered.

Self-dramatization isn't so bad, but if we attach strong language or weighty references to the description of our experiences, we absolutely will level the language, just as cheery TV advertisers using themes from Beethoven's Ninth Symphony and the William Tell Overture leach out the intensity of our musical hearing.

If teachers support a few psychological standards such as making oneself learn instead of wanting to feel good all the time, then students will be freed to take artistic risks. They will stop clinging to feeling comfortable.

I taught off and on for a few years with a brilliant philosophy professor, John Dolan. We ran an ethics and literature course together: I taught the class for six weeks and he visited; then he taught and I visited. John joined many class discussions during my six weeks. I asked dozens of questions in his six weeks.

During my six weeks, John offended several students by leaping into the discussion and cleanly labeling things evil or good. He praised certain thinkers a good deal. He praised Thales and Gauss and dozens of philosophers and mathematicians who interested him. By the time my six weeks of the class were over, some students were in a more or less constant rage over John's values. (Two students despised him in particular because he was not a cultural relativist.) They were unaccustomed to someone running a class with verve and love of certain particular virtues instead of 1990s communication skills. They could scarcely stop trembling long enough to take in the content of his remarks.

John wasn't present on the last day of my class. I took the opportunity to say, "Listen, you're going to have John Dolan for the next six weeks. I want to suggest something to you up front. John doesn't do any twentieth-century feminist process. He just doesn't. He doesn't do what is thought of as 'sharing.' He doesn't share. He speaks. He may not even get around to asking everyone for their input on every given issue. He *will*, however, courteously answer every question any of you asks. He's going to offer you what he is sure of. You will be so annoyed.

"I want to urge this idea: first, John's a genius, and therefore if you spend your time being deaf to his ideas because you feel cross about his process style or non-open-minded teaching style, then you'll waste his genius. So just for these six weeks, why don't you learn to quiet down. Sit down as if a very beautiful snowfall were starting. Don't insist on 'relating to the snow' and all that. Just sit there and let the snow fall on you. Later you can think about all the ideas that you received. Still later, you can respond.

"The idea I'm suggesting is that most of your instructors have very high-end communication skills. See if you can put up with just one class without—for the sake of not wasting serious genius."

The roomful of people looked at me balefully. I finished up by saying, "Good supportive schmooze is not everything. Sometimes we need sharp concept and resolute language. Dolan does little schmooze, but he does some first-rate *good* thinking—good thinking often being different from schmooze."

I so wanted to convince my students that writers, more than others, need to stay in the room to learn whatever they can from the Dolans as well as from the merely comfortable instructors.

I offer one last disciplinary suggestion: creative-writing students frequently allow themselves to be and stay ignorant. In their essays they frequently say, "Well, who knows how many people feel that way!" or "Why such and such a university professor ever did such and such I'll never know," or "What so and so had in mind when he said such and such we can only guess." Essayists should call up someone or get on a Web site or call a reference librarian at a good public or college library and unearth the particular fact.

I urge that we practice using unequivocal language with one another, both those of us who teach and those of us who are learning creative writing in colleges and universities. We should be as definite as we can, even if we are forced to change our minds later. But we should exemplify to one another clear, unequivocal language.

The Psychological Work of Getting Clear of Local University Hatreds, Faculty Folk Wisdom, and the Lackluster Jargon of Our Trade

Certain styles get going in any academic department. Graduate students in that department naturally take such styles for professional models.

When I was a graduate student, people constantly talked about Robert Lowell's poetry as though it were simply wonderful. Actually, much of it was New England trivia, and in his later writing Lowell did a lot of moaning over his own problems. Lowell had a good ear for the use of harsh sounds, barking vowels and short-sound endings and dissonance. We talked about his good sound, not his self-centered content. We talked about John Donne and about *irony* because T. S. Eliot talked about John Donne and about irony. But irony isn't such a wonderful artifact of feeling. We tried to arrange juxtapositions in our prose that would strike readers as irony. Our style was to talk about juxtaposition. Whatever Cleanth Brooks and Robert Penn Warren[2] talked about, we talked about.

Today's graduate school herds give what James Wright used to call "little sneers" at famous men primarily because they're both dead and white. People even sneer at Matthew Arnold's strange, psychologically intricate essay on culture—an essay that is as much about class workings as it is about culture.

I think that as a teacher you will be doing yourself and your students a great service if you keep clear of all pet hatreds of your department. Local hatreds lead us to jeer at greatness, perhaps so that the jeerers' own less considerable philosophies will take on more consequence.

For the sake of looking at an example, let's say we feel like jeering at the old dead white male Matthew Arnold. What shall we jeer at? Matthew Arnold said that there were really four forces of culture. I look over his list with some repugnance, defensively, because I prefer my own lists enumerating things 1, 2, 3, 4. But this time, I make myself stick with Arnold's list. His list lays out four ideas that we're always trying to teach creative writers and trying to practice ourselves:

1. the power of intellect and knowledge,
2. the power of beauty (by which he means the love of beauty),
3. the power of social life, and
4. the power of manners.

Carlyle and Ruskin both jeered at the middle classes for being so merciless to the poor—for being so greedy. Matthew Arnold was more subtle. He suggested that the real problem was that the middle classes were so narrow-minded that their minds or hearts were constantly insulted by excruciating boredom.

Arnold could have been speaking of our time. He complained that the critics who should have been helping writers be inventive were too fond of technique. With this trumpet blast—critics being interested in technique and not in content—alive in my ears, I tell myself, "Perhaps one should hate Matthew Arnold for some reason, but let's not steer graduate writing students away from his lists—not because they must accept his philosophical listings but because he had scope enough to write down this list, and writers need models of artists who have committed themselves to ideas."

An English department's group opinion can sour the love of our subject. You may think, Oh, well, I can shake off local jeering on one or another subject. But it is hard work to clear your ears of the residual effects of the ongoing politically correct dislikes voiced by other professors or students. Schiller says the artist should "direct his gaze upward" (see Chapter 4). That is *very* hard to do. In an e-correspondence about loving one's subject, John Dolan, the colleague mentioned earlier, wrote:

> In the meantime I am conscious that all writing, and especially all philosophical writing, is *rewriting* and, accordingly, I attempt to give my students plenty of opportunities to rewrite the papers they are assigned. When teaching logic at the

> undergraduate level, I arrange many hours of weekly "workshops" (most led by undergraduates who have demonstrated a particular love of the subject) which give the students an opportunity to work together on problems and explore the subject in the presence of someone already at home in it.

I was so struck by his saying that what made undergraduates able to be good TAs was not expertise but their *love of the subject.*

Perhaps the habit of trivial, local hatreds—scorning this or that author or enclave of authors—gets going because we think we must run English departments largely on small talk. Even in famous English departments the professors make small talk. The faculty rarely ask one another to pause in the hallway to recite poems or tell essays or enact scenes. What if most small talk in any college is actually a mistake, the dumb road taken, as Frost would say, and it is making all the difference? Perhaps small talk, far from greasing the ways of friendship, actually isolates us from one another.

Graduate and undergraduate students hear our small talk at meetings. They are neutral on the topic. They may not have considered small talk a workplace issue on which one needs to make up one's mind. One way to see if one has any particular philosophy about a topic is to make a list. Here is my list of the pros and cons of workplace small talk:

Some Points in Favor of Faculty Small Talk

1. It is normal.
2. It allows flexibility. Sometimes it distances people. Sometimes it brings them closer.
3. It can be very funny. English faculty members are often delightful and especially funny. Small talk is perfect opportunity for funny anecdotes.
4. It avoids fights.

Looking at the Ph.D. subjects of a particular English department we see experts on the work of Rebecca Harding Davis, Rudyard

Kipling, and Sharon Olds. If I found myself crowded into a corner during an end-of-term party with the Davis person and the Kipling person, my own ignorance would drive me to small talk. I might ask whether my colleagues knew that members of the Portland State University English Department use elephant dung in their gardens not because cubic inch by cubic inch it is more organic than cow manure but because there is such a lot more of it.

Points against Faculty Small Talk

1. Small talk makes people feel cynical because it shows you that the other person doesn't trust you with anything that really interests him or her. (One might be better off just going for it—e.g., trying to convert the Kipling lover to Alice Walker.)
2. Small talk wastes chances for off-the-cuff theater. What if the Kipling person could, instead of responding to my inane communiqué about elephant dung, do a dramatic telling of how the stupid tailor bird prematurely mourned Rikki Tikki Tavvy's death just because it saw him follow Nagaina down her tunnel? What if the Rebecca Harding Davis expert could reproduce the rich-people-slumming scene in "Life in the Iron Mills"?

Although it may not be known for this use, e-mail is a great blessing to college faculty and students as a way to talk briefly about subjects that are *not* small talk. Serious conversation can take place between teachers and students via e-mail. It's a perfect medium for responding instantly to substantive questions. (A caution: I don't allow students to send me any class assignments via e-mail—that is, no papers or revisions of papers may come to me electronically. I don't want to read literature in the ugly e-mail format, and I don't want to invite a virus from students' file attachments.)

E-mail enables people to reach each other at all hours. Students who stay up at night writing and who want to talk about literature can send an e-mail without disturbing anyone. And electronic talk almost always is more fervent than telephone talk.

Some American folk wisdom is specific to students and faculties of graduate schools. One current axiom at the University of Minnesota is the expression "I know I ought to let it go." By this is meant: I should drop the bag of memory, and forget such and such an injustice in the bag. Another is, "I know I ought to keep an open mind." Quite often it's infinitely better to keep a closed mind. Open minds are wonderful for receiving fresh data, fresh evidence in a case, or conflicting evidence that we weren't aware of before. But keeping an open mind can also mean drawing no boundary between bottom feeding and exacting principles.

I recommend that teachers of graduate writing courses point out to their students "A List of Useful Sentences for Writers in a Tight Spot," in the appendix. We probably ought to add a sentence along the lines of "Sorry, I have a closed mind on this subject. Closed for now, at least."

People determined not to succumb to academic convention run the risk of taking overly strong stances. All of us are bound to be horribly mistaken from time to time. We need to have enough spirit to say, "Right, it turns out I was horribly mistaken. I am now backing off from that particular stance."

Ways to Help College- and Graduate-Level Writers Experience a Literary Change of Heart

Teaching Writers Who Have Done Little Reading

As recently as thirty years ago anyone taking a graduate writing workshop very likely had read much the same canon as others in the class. Teachers and students could cite examples to one another as parallels to the work being done in the class. Everybody could make the connections. That's not the case these days.

Because student writers are coming from different kinds of backgrounds, the best way to run a class is to start reading students' own work aloud early in the semester or quarter. This way the students have each other's work as a little body of literature to refer to.

I ask students deliberately to remember each other's work in class discussion. It helps when we can say, "You remember two weeks ago when Susan's manuscript gave us a perfect example of using adjectives stacked up in the predicate instead of in the nominative part of the sentence?" or "If you remember, Wayne took up this whole vexed problem of the dominating military father not quite the same way, but nearly the same way Bill is telling us about today." Keeping each other's texts in mind won't make up for the fact that few of the students have read *The Decline and Fall of the Roman Empire,* but at least it will give students the experience of working from common text *with love* instead of working from text coldly and alone in the library.

Teaching the Psychological Work of Staying Focused on Major Subjects and Major Feeling

Sometimes it's helpful, as is explained elsewhere in this book, to jot down your major considerations in life, just to keep them upward in your mind. It is the habit even of faculty members to have friendly conversations with one another on a nonphilosophical level. Even highly educated people expect of themselves only fragmented comments on life as it goes by. They don't really expect to relate one thing to another. Even though the wise environmental enthusiasts of the 1980s forced upon us the fact that all things, like it or not, relate to all other things, people don't really expect to put together a philosophy of life. They don't expect their own minds to be gathered enough to say, "This is where I am on this issue." They expect, instead, to remain in a kind of wordless suspension or abeyance, a wobbly neutrality like horses not "gathered" for a jump because they suppose the jump is vaguely far ahead.

Neutrality is one of the worst attitudes writing students can adopt. So I suggest that we occasionally remind ourselves of the old existential concerns of loneliness, death, freedom, and meaninglessness, as Irvin Yalom,[3] the highly cultivated group therapist, neatly named them, and let these ideas color our other interests—our loves, hatreds, our general enjoyment of life.

If the major subjects and the major feelings are not engaged now and again, student writers will, from habit, expect to form opinions about only *the periphery* of things. I want to say very fast that I feel some sympathy for people getting stuck in peripheral ideas.

Here is an example from my life: I am now trying to read up on some subjects I paid no attention to in college. I am reading philosophy. I am learning Icelandic. A few other subjects that interest me now weren't accessible to the general public when I was in college—among them are theories of ecological patterning. I am reading two of those theories. But it is very hard to get hold of and hang onto the absolute center argument, so to speak, of a philosopher or a bioecologist. If I were at an academic meeting at which both Søren Kierkegaard and Simon Levin showed up and we three got squeezed into a corner, I would want to make a grateful remark to each of them. Chances are, however, that my thanks would come out as praise of some minor point each had made, not the major deep point that truly excited me. When you're on the spot, it's easier to think of the little stuff. And just in case you have gotten the author's center, core, most deeply felt principle *wrong* somehow, you won't be offending him or her or making a fool of yourself if you make some peripheral remark. So I feel some sympathy for hesitant, evasive talk.

Of course, peripheral remarks float around creative-writing program gatherings. No wonder we tell each other we enjoyed each other's work because of the "writerly tone" or the "voice." Student writers, TAs, and the rest of us acquire a dangerous habit, however, if we always fishtail around in such shallows. The habit is dangerous for this reason: what if a young faculty member has just published a book that we have all read. We wander over to him, glass in hand, and say, "I have just finished your *Mein Kampf.* It was amazing! I could hear your voice all through—it was so wonderfully clear!" What we need to do is to speak to him about his content.

Teaching the Psychological Work of Valuing Literature Itself More Than the Literary Life

I offer here four mechanical suggestions to help keep your focus on the work itself. The first is the method of red-bracketing student papers

I've already explained. Reading aloud in class passages that I have bracketed differs from a student's reading a whole paper in order to receive comment from their peers. Red-bracketed material is used only to illustrate something present or not present in writing—either good or bad—usually good. I try to show parallels between students' work and similar effects achieved by famous writers. Students then see themselves as colleagues of successful writers. When these successful writers are young and newly successful, such comparisons are encouraging—in a nonegotistical way. The student *doesn't* think, "I must be good if she's talking about me in the same breath as she talks about Jane McCafferty or Steve Adams." The student may instead get the message: "She is talking about me as being a colleague of these serious, awfully good, published writers because we all face the same problem—how to do sensuous, philosophical tasks when all we've got to work with is English sentences."

Apropos of red-bracketing, I sometimes ask people deliberately to be the guinea pig, or the Mutt of the Class. *Mutt of the Class* is obviously an absurd term, and people ask, in an appropriately disrespectful tone, "What's that, for the love of heaven?" The Mutt of the Class is what Edwardians would have called a Horrible Example—someone who has done some literary task badly.

In our schmoozy world, most creative-writing teachers would never publicly announce that someone has done something badly. If you do it, you need to be prepared in the very next minute to show how the Mutt does something else well, even if not in that same manuscript. Further, I never choose anybody to be Mutt of the Class who hasn't got a general, abiding confidence. If a student has a good deal of confidence, being the Mutt of the Class sharpens his or her self-discipline: everyone has to learn that we are all capable of bad as well as good work. Some writers whom I have asked to be Mutt of the Class have later during the course said, "I'm so glad that you called my bluff on such and such." They felt truly *seen.* But playing that role does take humor on their part. Any kind of serious research or any kind of serious scholarly work, and absolutely any kind of serious creative writing, requires humor.

Here's how the dialogue goes. "Listen, I need a Mutt of the Class today to show something that *doesn't* work. There are practices writers really need to avoid. I could be wrong. In fact, I want all of you to weigh in on this, if you will, but I am asking now if Bill and Ward will read aloud the red-bracketed parts of their papers so we can discuss them."

No one turns down being Mutt of the Class. We discuss each Mutt's passage. Sometimes people stand up for it. They say, "I didn't see that at all. Carol, you are so wrong on this. I thought that was a very strong passage that so and so [the Mutt] wrote." The Mutt-defender gets practice in intellectual bravery, standing up for truth.

It's helpful to appoint a truth-keeper to protect weak or fleeting voices in your class. I got this idea from Dr. Sara Hunter, a psychologist who has visited several of my writing classes. Dr. Hunter assured our group that some of our bravest and best ideas are fired off so rapidly that if we don't encourage them right there, right on the spot, they simply vanish and we never see them again. Put another way: sometimes a valuable neuron firing didn't catch our attention.

For instance, a mild-mannered person, or someone whom members of the class have already read off as too vapid, too passive to count, might say something quite wonderful. Sometimes that person aggravates the situation by presenting his or her notion with such irritating torpor that the others scarcely take in the content. The truth-keeper must intervene at that point: "Wait a minute, everyone. So-and-so just spoke, and I think we need to hear it again."

That gives me a chance to say, "Let's hear it. What was that? What did I miss here?" Instructors can miss a good thing. Students need to know that the instructor missed a good thing.

The sluggish speaker then repeats what he or she said, speaking more confidently this time because now two people are giving their attention—the leader of the class, and the truth-keeper or ombudsman.

The truth-keeper has to be brave, I explain at the start of the course. The truth-keeper must protect the class from the instructor. I believe in fairly directive instruction in teaching writing because writing is such long, hard work. One shouldn't shilly-shally about. Writers have so much to learn in such a short time. As Chaucer wonderfully said, "The lyf so short, the craft so long to lerne." I don't always take time to promote a democratic process. Without the truth-keeper, therefore, there's the danger that only one person's—the instructor's—totalitarian voice will go on and on. An alert truth-keeper will notice that a lot of people have been waving their hands because they want to speak, but Bly seems to be overriding them. The truth-keeper says, "Carol, we need to hear from those voices."

Providing that check and balance makes a pleasant experience for a class. It's happened four or five times for me—when I've had a truth-keeper brave enough to do it. Each time the truth-keeper's intervention has raised everyone's spirits, including mine. I suppose it's some sort of proof that democracy actually still works somewhere. We feel wistful for democracy, grateful when might gets checked by right.

Our psychological task in focusing on the writing, rather than on this writer or that writer, is subtle: we must screen back our need for personal flattery, yet we must keep our personalities—of which the ego is a vibrant part—engaged in whatever's coming down.

Teaching a Brief History of the English Language

Young writing students benefit in two serious and several minor ways from learning a little language history.

The first benefit has to do with learning technique. Nonfiction writers wake up to the difference in *texture* between Latin-based and Saxon-based words. I notice that writing students scarcely grasp the point when they are lectured to about prose that has too many soft-sounding, abstract, Latin-based words or too few punchy, concrete Saxon-based words. I tell them it is no accident that angry people do not shout "Copulate thee!" to one another—but after dutifully leering or giving a bark of a laugh, students still don't see the point. If you narrate a very few historical events, however, they wake to some sense of how language changes. Explaining the following few events can be helpful:

1. Roman legions invaded the Celtic island they called Britannia in 43 A.D. and stayed, for the most part south of Hadrian's Wall, to the end of the fifth century. Britain's place names are rich in Latin words—for example, the common ending *-chester* or *-cester* or *-caster* derives from *castrum* (fort). Even in the United States we still use a few terms from those Roman provincial administrators. A small *d*, meaning "penny" in England as late as 1973, derives from *denarius*, a silver coin worth a quarter in Roman-

British times. We still buy our nails in sizes of 6*d*, 10*d*, 16*d*, in American lumber stores.

2. In the fifth and sixth centuries, Britain was invaded severally by Germanic peoples. Again and again Germanic forces shoved the British—who were Celts—to the west. The Germanic invaders were principally Jutes, Angles, and Saxons. The island then became an Anglo-Saxon land, not a Celtic land. Our words *England* and *English* come from *Angle*. (The French call England *Angleterre*, or Angle Country.) The general language of the people for several centuries afterward was a mixed bag of dialects that we now call Old English, or Anglo-Saxon. This was a language thick with its thud of double consonants and short words whose vowels were deep and long. It takes time to speak Old English. You can't rattle it off.

3. Then more northerly people, the Danes, came to the island as invaders. They entered by harbors and generally left their language mark at sea level, not in the uplands. Scots in the lowlands are Andersons, but in the highlands they were MacAndrews. The Firths came from the Old Norse *Fjörð* which shows up still in Icelandic *Fjörður*. There was such endless fighting throughout these various Germanic people's holdings, that the English tended to welcome any king who promised to be strong enough to stop the internal strife. The English had sophisticated laws. They had sophisticated structures for administering justice.

4. William the Conqueror came across the English Channel in 1066. The Conquest, as it is called in England, was a huge success for the French and a cruel devastation for the English. Practically overnight the Normans licked up the wealth of the English villages, castles, and countryside.

All government and business were soon conducted in French. If you wanted to make a living you had to learn the language, so the English did. French words replaced most abstract words. English words for concrete objects stayed put. Hence by the time Chaucer (1340–1400) was writing, English had two very different kinds of vocabulary in use—Germanic words and Latinate words. We call Chaucer's language Middle English. To this day, then, if you want to write short, clean, concrete language, you use Germanic-based words. If you want rhetorical flow and sailing pronouncements on major eternal subjects, you use Latinate words. If you are a bureaucrat you use as much Latinate language as you can so that what you say will sound like sailing pronouncements on eternal major subjects even when it is drivel.

We writing teachers are constantly scolding students for turning out imageless (abstract) Latinate language. But our spirits also drop when we read only concrete words. What suits English is a mix of both the smooth Latinate abstractions and the robust Germanic concrete words. Following is a perfect example.

> In the waste fields strung with barbed wire where the thistles grow over hidden mine fields there exists a curious freedom. Between the guns of the deployed powers, between the march of patrols and policing dogs there is an uncultivated strip of land from which law and man himself have retreated. Along this uneasy border the old life of the wild has come back into its own. Weeds grow and animals slip about in the night where no man dares to hunt them. A thin uncertain line fringes the edge of oppression. The freedom it contains is fit only for birds and floating thisteldown or a wandering fox. Nevertheless there must be men who look upon it with envy.[4]

Note how fresh and civil the well-chosen Latin-based words strike us—*curious, uncultivated, oppression*. They are beautiful because they are set among harsh concrete objects with long sounds—*barbed wire, thistles,* and *mine fields.*

To write like Loren Eiseley one needs a good ear, and that good ear is aided by knowing some English language history.

The second and stronger reason for teaching language history is that we teachers need to take every chance we can to attune American minds to feeling that what has *gone before* has reality. History is a kind of treasure. Of the various aspects of the "dumbing down of America" the most harmful is fainthearted egocentrism—an inadvertent ignorance of anything that is "other"—partially caused by ignorance of the past.

The *long* past is *very other.* What is now past, even if it is past by hundreds of years, still needs to feel like human gossip. The writer's imagination should *want* to encompass it. Curiosity about history seems to lie blessedly close in the brain to curiosity about *why* and *how* anything comes about. The sooner you feel curious enough to make some hypotheses about why such and such happens in life, or how such and such happens, the sooner you can put together respectful, humble guesswork on any interesting matter without being scared. Respectful, humble guesswork is a classical task of essayists.

Lesser reasons for teaching the history of the English language include building cultural confidence so student writers can raise some inner shields against defeat. Cultural confidence comes of knowing miscellany in one's field. That sounds stupid, but miscellany that at first glimpse looks like peripheral trivia often turns out to have meaning. You feel shielded from despair or defeat if you know even a short history of your own tools. You realize *we have been here before*. For example, most young Americans do not know what it is like to be conquered by foreigners. Writers should know and be able to reimagine a few particulars about how a country's civility breaks down when it is overrun by another country. Even ten-year-olds would have some idea that food and fuel supplies disappear, but no ten-year-old would think of how quickly beaten people must *learn the invader's language*. You have to sell *him* the eggs tomorrow and next week and forever that your leghorns go on laying. Practical life straps you down in a new way because the gentry and your fathers and brothers got licked at Hastings yesterday. Next week you will shine a Frenchman's shoes because he and his fellow officers will have taken over the best houses in your village, one of which was yours. He will want to learn a little English, in order to give you orders, but he will expect *you* to learn a *lot* of French because otherwise you won't make it as a hanger-on in his establishment. But he also has a spotty, complacent curiosity about your language. "So what's your word for *maison*?" he asks, waving all around to indicate what used to be your home and furnishings. "Hus," you answer—the Old English word for it, pronounced *hooce*. "*Hooce*," he repeats benignantly enough. He writes it down, spelling it *house*, French phonetics for the sound *hooce*. You are nearly done shining his boots. Rag and one boot still in hand, you lean over the note he made and you see *house*. "House," you say. And we've pronounced it *house* ever since.[5]

I would recommend that English teachers look up three or four narratives showing how it happened that English is full of Latin and French words.

Teaching the Psychological Work of Praising What Deserves Praise

Enthusiasm is a *psychological skill.* It's usually called a mind-set, but the fact is, it is a combination of willpower and luck, like any other psychological skill.

Enthusiasm can be taught in several ways. Often babies are taught it by mothers and fathers and others who care for them. Those caretakers model enthusiasm for their children. One often sees young parents bending down over a section of sidewalk with their young child. All three are studying some ants crawling along in the crack. All three show interest and enthusiasm about the strangeness of an ant's life. They show respect for it, too: the parents don't kill the ant in front of the child just because they could. Those parents could model the normalcy of killing, but they don't. This respect for ants makes a tremendous difference in that child's life.

When grown-ups read aloud to a child and they themselves get a kick out of the antics of the story animals just as the child naturally does—when grown-ups, for example, read *Charlotte's Web* aloud and they enjoy the plainly revolting materialism of Templeton—children rejoice. They pick up the adult's enthusiasm for the no-holds-barred truth about Templeton.

With creative-writing students, maintaining enthusiasm is complicated. Often there are genuinely clinically depressed students registered in a class. After depressed people have written a few creative nonfiction papers or stories, you can suggest that they make some lists of good things, without denying any bad things. One need not deny evil. One need not deny depression. But if something is wonderful, a depressed writer needs to *practice* saying so. So far as I can tell from my experience, if a depressed person identifies and praises something good, this work has nothing to do with healing. I suggest praise to him or her for only one reason: acknowledging goodness helps the student write with greater scope.

Writing exercises can *increase* the mood swings of a writer. If there's anything we need in order to keep actively scanning across all of our truths, it's to be host to huge, opposite responses at every level of our emotional range. Some things are wonderful. Some things are dreadful. Some things are in between. Some things we're in doubt about.

Setting ourselves to distinguish our own values and then developing appropriately different responses for certain aspects of life vastly improves our agility. It enables us to praise something wonderful when it happens. We know how to wall off other emotions for the moment. Access to even a glint of enthusiasm raises tone.

11.

Teaching at Writers' Conferences, Community Retreats, and Summer Short Courses

What These Courses Are, and the Burgeoning Population Who Use Them

When you sign on for a community writing weekend or a writers' conference or a summer writing course you count on a convivial experience. Conferees and faculty alike are voluble, and the teachers are usually, if not always, honorable about reading the writers' work carefully and offering individual conferences. Typically, the individual conferences are honest and courteous and are focused on the writers' work in hand.

Famous writers give guest performances at summer courses and conferences. These are welcomed. The conference staff prepare enthusiastic introductions of the authors. People on staff and visiting celebrities hug one another up front. Writers in the audience feel hopeful and cheerful. Maybe literary success will rub off on them, too. In any case, those stars up there are some part of what the conferees paid for.

Most literary conferences are not a gyp. They follow exactly the agenda printed up in the promotional material.

The largest population of student writers in the United States consists of people taking one- and two-week writing courses or retreats and attending writers' conferences. Most of the attendees have as their *first* priority paying more attention to their *own* ideas than to the American noise in their lives.

It is amazing how Americans, despite our generally brutal culture and our hit-or-miss educational backgrounds, long for the reflective life that Socrates commended. Unmistakably, under such expressions as "I want to make sense of my life," what most of us really want to do is connect our sense impressions to our principled thinking, the process discussed in Chapter 5. We long for the very practice the mind has potential to do: connecting everything. People who have these longings show up in summer writers' conferences.

They seem to want to do what Friedrich Schiller described in *On the Aesthetic Education of Man:* Schiller was convinced that people intend, if they are conscious enough to recognize this intention, to uncover or recover something wonderful that lies waiting inside themselves.

Yet writers of all ages are also fearful of confessing to having any philosophies inside themselves. They need reassurance that feeling and thinking are OK. Once reassured, they are grateful to quit talking about "wanting to polish their skills." They may even attend to their own story without feeling constrained to reconstruct by guesswork their great-grandparents' immigration to America.

Because thousands of people now attend creative-writing classes in order to save their personalities, we who teach them must be extraordinarily respectful of individual ideas. I assume, and I shall go on believing it, that personal philosophy is best learned through creative writing, and that a good deal of that learning can happen in creative-writing coursework.

When short-course students arrive with their luggage and their writing equipment and their laptop, if they've brought one, they look like an ordinary gaggle of human beings. They are a scattering of young people, a good many middle-aged people, and even more older people. One could mistakenly assume: "Well, these are people using their holidays to have a good time in a writing course. They want to do light fluff, perhaps. They want to read their journals aloud to others. They do not want to focus on any intense feelings."

Intense feelings don't show on their faces as they ask about their rooms and the soap and where the public classrooms are. As teachers we need to remind ourselves: we don't know who these people are. They may have spent thirty or forty or fifty years doing other things. Each might be full of strong memories or irate philosophies or spirited enthusiasm about life—at the least, each is a vessel of miscellaneous information, whether or not the individuals themselves value that information. We teachers need to decide, as we greet these fourteen or fifteen or sixteen or twenty people, that we do not know which one is the Abraham Lincoln or the Mary Oliver or the Rebecca Harding Davis of that particular group. Therefore, we must teach *the whole group* as if they *all* had fantastic potential inside them. Only cultural abuse or negligence has kept them from writing until now, perhaps.

Others actually do show up at writing courses for fun and only for fun. Large numbers of people take Elderhostel courses, for example, just for intelligent fun. They typically have golf plans for the afternoon of your class. Some are suffering through your writing class in the morning because of spousal agreement. Retired people naturally want to fill their life with some interesting learning, but that doesn't mean they will agree to slave over a manuscript during your week working with them. Fun-loving seniors sitting before you sometimes listen and sometimes do not listen to others' manuscripts. Frequently they make witty remarks instead of giving thoughtful responses. Their attitude is, "Look, I've worked all my life. I'm not doing it here." In that case the best a teacher can do is keep his or her eyes and ears open to anyone in the room who *would* like to learn about writing, and make sure those who are interested gain something. One can figure, with Elderhostel groups, heavily populated as they are by retired, married couples, that half the couple had the idea of going to this Elderhostel program and the other half did it out of affectionate tolerance or otherwise a razor-edged marital agreement that if I do this Elderhostel writing course for you then you have to come to my championship mud-wrestling demo. A lot of attendees sleep during class sessions; as much as 50 percent of the class may sleep during morning classes and 80 percent in after-lunch classes.

People in weeklong courses need to be encouraged to take an interest in one another's work. Doing writing exercises gives the group a common interest. If you offer writing exercises at the start of the week, people then can read to each other. The writing exercise about work (Exercise 9 in the appendix) is great in a summer writing course. Some participants are much happier asking and answering questions about work than about their private lives. Others get some practice in empathy. They can ask for further detail. They can use this practice in empathic inquiry not just on each other, as they're doing here in the class, but on themselves, later, as was discussed in Chapter 3—self-empathy being one means of learning how to write more thoughtfully.

People need actual training in taking an interest in other people's work. It's astounding how indifferent or neutral people can be unless chaffed by their instructor to attend to what others are saying. We've all seen panels of three or four writers or speakers, especially at writers' conferences, where one panelist speaks while the others don't even try to *look* as if they're listening. They even tap pencils. A whole classful of students like that can be deadly.

I've spoken directly to summer-writing class members for being disrespectful while others are reading their writing aloud. I once pulled a rude person aside after class saying, "You know, you clearly didn't take any interest at all when so and so was reading aloud." This middle-aged scholar, who spoke three languages fluently, was astounded that I would ever expect her to show any interest. Being courteous was not part of her moral code. Nor did it occur to her that she could learn from other group members. Teachers probably ought to remember, since people read so little nowadays, that most people are attuned to a fairly low-key life. When one listens to other people, expecting to hear something either numinous or intellectual, one is living out an odd, *high-key* expectation. Yet if people haven't got such an expectation, we may as well teach it.

How can we improve these short writing courses? From the beginning let's help people leave the world of the *cute anecdote*. Short writing courses are vulnerable to cute writing. Some people who want to learn to write, but are unused to sitting in classes of writers, have typically done some heavy reading of *Writers Journal* and other manuals written to help people turn out popular articles, stories, and novels. These people feel that they must produce something humorous and light—attractive, charming fluff. The faster we can get them through the cute anecdote and onto something else the better. All the rest of their lives they can write fluff, but our job, if we're their teachers for this one week, is to help them explore their own deeper interests. We might suggest that they tell themselves, "I am far from home. No one will know what I do here. I don't have to do enchanting fluff. While I am here my writing doesn't have to make the cut of funny dinner-table conversation at home."

We might suggest that they use the week in either of two ways: to plan and start their next writing project, or to try to write in a totally new vein. The exercises we offer might lead them to try experimenting with new subject matter or approaches.

Sometimes we can say, "Yes, go ahead, try something you've never done before. You might even read some of it aloud to this group. And also, why don't you make a list of fifty-four of your personal ideas about life. Do it tonight and I'll look at it tomorrow if you like." Making lists of the invisible aspects of life might be new to them.

Very occasionally asking students to write up philosophical outlooks and have a conference with a teacher about it afterward can undo a little of the negligence they have experienced. Sometimes not. In any event, a weeklong workshop is the perfect place to try. When I suggest such an exercise, sometimes experienced writing-retreat attendees tell me, "I'd feel a perfect fool if I did something like that." My response is, "Just go ahead and feel like a perfect fool. Here you are, far from home, in this retreat with a bunch of other people from outside your own life. They don't know you. You don't know them. You don't need their good opinion. You can do something very earnest without fear. Don't let yourself fear. That's a conscious choice—whether or not to feel fear. Do not fear whether you're doing something stupid or not. Literally no one who matters in your life will know. I will be behind you all the way on this. I will read whatever you write—with interest—as long as it's sincere. Don't bother to do any gags, no tongue-in-cheek. No devil's advocate drivel. Do it, do the list tonight, and let's have a look."

Three Populations We Don't Serve Well Enough So Far

In the main, writing teachers don't serve the very poor, the medium poor, and the highly educated, privileged middle-aged and older people very well.

The first of these, the very poor, are scarcely recognized as potential writing students, yet they need what writing can do as much or more than the rest of us.

We do not have good writing programs for people who get into shelters or who sleep on the street or in condemned building spaces. In some cases there is mental illness or substance abuse going on, making it even harder to reach these people. Nor have we programs designed for people living underneath bridges. No one I've heard of has figured out how to provide them with portable-sized notebooks, pencils, and directions to teaching sites. No one has taught them how to make themselves get to a writing site. We also have a poor record for designing programs for very, very disturbed and beaten-up kids from psychologically or financially unprivileged families. Social workers design great programs for adolescents, but they aren't any good at teaching kids how to *separate themselves from the group*—a psychological exercise that any writer has to learn. I will not say more about teaching the very poor because I have failed, so far, to think through a workable program for serving them.

Teaching medium-poor people at weeklong writing retreats is currently handled differently by each teacher because we have no guidelines. Money is such a weight on our minds that it feels socially incorrect to acknowledge that someone is in different straits because he or she is *poor.* It feels more democratic to pretend poverty and wealth have no reality. The logic we're using is the same logic of some 1950s educators who taught deaf children to learn certain cues so they could pretend they were not deaf—when what they needed to learn was signing.

From time to time any good organization running summer writing courses provides scholarships, occasionally or steadily, for a few people who otherwise couldn't afford to attend. A situation in weeklong writing courses that wants special attention is the occasional, very welcome presence of nontraditional, nonliterary, or very poor students. By very poor I mean people who didn't have the money or opportunity to go to college and take English courses. These people obviously do not come from the same place as the majority of the people in a summer-retreat class. Sometimes a summer class registers two or three people who are not fashionably broke: they are just plain poor. Usually the writing group can be made a comfortable place for either uneducated or very poor people if they are assured that they won't be called on to do anything they aren't prepared for.

But being made to feel comfortable in a group is not the same thing as being taught anything. As soon as scholarship students arrive at the retreat camp or conference center, they overhear jaunty conversations among the old boys and girls. They may feel dismayed. This weeklong course could be a week of crashing self-esteem. They feel like new kids. There are dynamics and philosophy for preventing that from happening.

Borrowing from stage-development theory, for starters, the teacher might explain that there are no *types* of people. There are badly read people and well-read people. No one can know about literature until they read some. For now, the people who have given time to studying literature look very advanced. It would be best to divert the attention of the nonliterate person away from the group and the brilliant-sounding remarks of those accustomed to peer reviewing language and other swill. Otherwise the less well prepared person might spend the whole week in disconsolate envy.

It's a good idea to double the amount of individual conference time you give to inexperienced students. Show them what slave labor rewriting is and how we all must do it. They can quickly adapt to the week's writing if they have several half-hour conferences—a lot of supportive but demanding attention from the teacher. They must be invited into the core idea of creative nonfiction: turning your own real life into literature. An obvious means to that end is to encourage writing about daily work.

We consider ourselves to be thinking citizens who have terribly demanding sex lives and terribly demanding reading lives, who take in entertainments, who go on holidays, and so on, but in fact, hour for hour, Americans are a people who spend most of their lives in the workplace.

Our workplaces vary tremendously. Anybody in a summer writing course who's had any job at all can write beautifully about that job. Usually, therefore, inexperienced writers of any background leap at the chance to write about work. And if that's their strength, that's what they should write about, at least for starters.

But people are forever more original than we suspect. I ran a New England workshop group, one of whose members had no experience in writing at all. She had enrolled in the program through a scholarship. She was noticeably unlike the other people in the class. The others were a mix of Yale undergrads, middle-aged arts administrators, and other comparatively lucky people. Even the women who described themselves with that ominous 1990s phrase "in transition" were better off than the scholarship writer was. Even if those women in transition had been laid off or fired, the jobs they were laid off or fired from were better jobs than the scholarship writer had held so far, and the next job those women would interview for would be better than the next job the scholarship student would interview for.

I made a pedagogical mistake. I went with my gut instincts, teacher's gut instincts built up over eight or nine years of teaching writing classes. I asked the scholarship student if she would like to write about her work life. Would she like to write about her family life? Clearly she was an agreeable and intelligent person, so wouldn't she like to do some nonfiction about work or family? For two of our five days together the truth didn't get through to me. She simply hadn't much feeling for those subjects. I asked myself, well, what did she have feeling for? For me she had done obedient, lifeless writing. She was cooperative but also brave. She said, "I don't see what you're trying to get at here." I said, "I'm trying to find out what it is you're really like and what you would actually *like* to write about." "Oh," she said. "That's easy. I like nature. Mostly, that's what I like. I like it a lot. Well, not all of it. But I was brought up near a mill by an old river, and I'd like to write about that." "All right!" I said. "Let's hear it. And get it in this afternoon so I can look at it tonight and be back to you about it tomorrow. See if you can sign up for a conference for early tomorrow afternoon." I asked her to write hastily because we had so little time in that weeklong course. I had already wasted two of her days. All the rest of the week she described one or another aspect of the unused mill, the river's bend, the grace of it, although the mobile home where she lived was noisy and she had no space to herself.

Ever since that experience I ask students for a list of what's good in their life. I don't let people settle for writing about things they are only mildly interested in. I have learned that teachers have to be ready for 180-degree surprises, such as that young woman's loving nothing so much as she loved the mill race and the few particular trees that hung over it.

I have never seen a writing program that is really suitable for those who are mature, well educated in literature, and who have read all their lives. Based on what I have seen, the attractive, weekend writing retreats designed to appeal to the rich play into the clients' lifelong habit of "having a good sense of humor about themselves." Much humor is great. Other humor is a slick winding-sheet to hide meaningful stuff in their heads. Rich people are taught to be humorous, not earnest—they do not want to bore others in the living room—but tangentially that discipline works against their being serious about themselves.

Privileged, educated people now in their fifties, sixties, seventies, eighties, and nineties probably make up the last two generations' few hundreds of thousands of people in the habit of reading books for pleasure and who have listened to books from age one on. They are a literate, book-loving lot.

Now that they have time, they would like to write up their own lives or write stories or a novel or detective stories. They are not particularly well served by most short courses or by summer courses such as those offered in famous writing centers. At this point in their lives they have not only their lifelong taste for literature but also a kind of accumulated, every day more wistful taste for the *meaning of life.* (Smart people of all backgrounds want to get close to *meaning,* all the more eagerly when near or in retirement.) So these people go to a writing class. There they usually find a much younger teacher who by their lights is ungrammatical, unread in traditional canon, and acculturated to stereotyping old people as amoral hobbyists. Not good.

I can see that making "The Privileged" a category of student writers would sound crazy, even to an arts organization used to phrases like *diversity* and *multiculturalism.* Still I think it is a sensible idea.

When I was a board member for The Loft, the Minneapolis writers' organization, several times I suggested that we design a writing course especially for privileged old English majors who didn't get around to doing much writing of their own until late middle age. I suggested we frankly advertise for such students in the local papers. We could even put a small classified in *The New Yorker* along these lines: "Listen, if you are a mature, financially secure person with a love of reading, who's never had the time to do any writing, we can help you, etc., etc."

A few of The Loft's directors and all the members of the major-gifts committee listened civilly, but the executive committee of The Loft board straightaway labeled the idea crazy. It flew in the face of two central philosophies of The Loft—first, that we were a democratic organization giving inexpensive writing courses at night to people not served by the various colleges of the Twin Cities; and, second, an underlying, if unspoken, conviction that the rich have caused the problems that The Loft spends its time and funding and passionate imagination trying to rectify.

I've been rolling the issue around in my head ever since. We all agree to certain truths: the writing process itself wakes you up to insights about yourself you never would have dreamed of if you hadn't taken to writing. Writing helps habitually sardonic people become humorous and earnest instead. Writing helps people who tend to see themselves as victims take hold of themselves and point at the veiled predators. Writing helps scatter-minded people stay on task. Writing helps extroverts and people stuck in "concrete thinking" to take an interest in their own invisible selves.

It follows, then, that writing might help mature, privileged people to take an interest in parts of *themselves* that class markings or habit have allowed to atrophy. It might also follow, then, since the whole world would change if its lucky upper classes were to change, that it might be a good move to *help* the privileged get such fresh self-knowledge.

Even if such a highly politicized insight were useful—not just a rustle or outright howl from the liberal wilderness—why ever would a writing teacher suggest that privileged, cultivated writing students have a category to themselves? Lucky people are presently mainstreamed into the nation's writing conferences and weeklong and full-semester university courses in writing. Why not just keep them there, along with the others? An aside: not only do top professionals and executives take some of the usual writing courses around the country, but large corporations are keen on offering writing courses as part of their own human-development programs. They bring in speakers and writers at amazing expense. Some of these consultants are fascinating. A good many are debilitatingly dumb. Corporate human resources officers are not stupid: they know when bad consultants are charging thousands of dollars a day for fake thought and the most heavy-footed sort of group facilitating. But they have no guidelines or benchmarks for sorting through the available writing professionals. Consultants are canny, too. They know how to talk to human resources officers. Churches get amazingly gypped by smooth "creativity" consultants, although plump corporations are the usual target.

In 1996 I complained about the sludge of fakey psychological dynamics. I was cross because along with one hundred intelligent people I had wasted a day being "facilitated" into a stupor.* I lost some friends and won some new ones by writing a newspaper article about the profound stupidity of the facilitators. Clergy thanked me for identifying the problem. They had apparently been feeling wrathful for years, but they didn't know where to go with their indignation. Church leaders naturally feel unsure of their own judgment: after all, a smart writing consultant talks "spiritual journey" to the clergyperson, and the clergyperson thinks, "Well, I am supposed to be *for* spiritual journeys." And people of the cloth learn early that they can't scorn tiresome phrases like "spiritual journey" because congregations express themselves in an incorrigible procession of such fad-driven phrases.

So dubious clergy, desperately looking out their vestry windows, listen to the consultant explain how he or she will take the conferees "to a safe place," where they can find out "who they are" and "begin their spiritual journey." In the end, the consultant gets the job—$5,000 or $10,000 for a Saturday.

*The Loft had planned a whole day's retreat for staff and key national and local literary people to do mission airing together.

That kind of offering is enraging to a formally educated person.

It goes without saying that regardless of background, human beings who want to write have many psychological dynamics in common. We find it hard to concentrate. We find it hard to keep up our confidence. We may begrudge the hours and hours of creative work we expend that come to nothing.

Nonetheless, some psychological pressures are specific to, or disproportionately weighty, in mature, educated, privileged people. Social workers teach professionals how to draw "eco-maps" for the poor. Circles and hatched lines show which community connections and sites comfort or terrify very poor people, particularly those still learning English. If writing teachers made eco-maps for the rich, or at least if we deliberately identified psychological pressures specific to the rich, we might be more successful in helping the rich explore *their* own psychological habitats.

I began to think of this in the early 1990s. In 1997 I was asked to join a panel for the fifty-year class reunion activities at Andover. We were four panelists—three Andover old boys and one Abbot old girl (myself). (Abbot is now part of Phillips Academy, so our panel was coeducational.)

Our subject was to advocate a meaningful, as opposed to a merely luxuriant, retirement. My contribution was an idea for how people could write something a lot franker and even more satisfying than the usual personal memoir. Everyone knows what the usual memoir is: a three-generational retrospective in which family skeletons are kept sealed tight in schmaltz. I told the Andover men that any sixty-seven- or sixty-eight-year-old professional, military, or businessperson is a practiced whiz at trimming memos so they don't offend anyone in the organization. If some still living uncle was such a sadist that the American Dental Association threw him out, any nephew knows to keep that out of the memoir.

My suggestion, therefore, was that they write not one, but two memoirs. They have time. Both projects are good. One memoir can be the usual one that the family has been begging them to write, full of old-fashioned Christmases. The other memoir is to be secret, to give them a chance to write, *without fear*, of happenings that may have secretly delighted or galled them over the decades. This memoir was to be *absolutely* secret. The rich don't have the trouble the poor have in keeping something private: they can afford a safe. They can put the secret memoir into the safe each night. They can leave instructions in the will for the future destruction or publication of the memoir.

The title I gave to this exercise was "A Guide for Lucky, Privileged, Mature People on How to Write a Private Record of Your Own Lives." Those men cordially seized and carried off my two hundred handouts. Since then I have slightly amended the proposal of a secret memoir. (In the appendix of this book it appears simply as The Andover Format.)

If some psychological pressures are really specific to mature, educated, privileged people, we should list them. A list of this kind is no better than a hypothesis, but useful societal insights usually do start out as only hypotheses. Lots of useful truth gets stuck for decades and decades as just someone's hypothesis because (a) there were no sociological tools to prove it, or (b) someone with cachet didn't want it proved, or (c) the person with the theory had previously offered so much off-the-wall stuff that people thought it wise to let this one slide by, too.

Here is a hypothesis I find valuable for writing teachers.

A Tentative List of Psychodynamics Especially Strong in Privileged Educated People of Mature Age

1. Liberal-arts-educated people between the ages of fifty and ninety have been encouraged to be aesthetic in their lifestyle, not ethical. Their way of seeing literature (or attending plays or listening to music) is an approach learned when they were just kids and were taken to the museum or to concerts.

What happens at a museum? You see the interesting stuff behind glass one by one, and nonegotistically learn facts about it on its own terms. If it's a modern, interactive museum you still experience its displays on their terms, not yours. You get to play with the buttons, and so forth—but such play involves no interaction with your mind. You do not connect the museum topics with your own life. The museum subjects are just *interest-*

ing things. When you were a child you were not expected to go look at Millet's *The Gleaners* and then race home to Fed-Ex your piggy bank to the National Farmers Union. You learned to be *interested*, not *moved.*

Adolescence does something special for rich kids. They enter the stage of rebelling against their parents. In their minds, as with any adolescents, "parents" and "parents' values" flop together. Teenagers can run a gratifying rebellion, therefore, by (a) galling their parents by going out for junk values, or (b) galling their parents by going out for morally *higher* ground than their parents' modi vivendi. CIA parents' kids take Peace Studies and talk up the course at dinner. CEOs' kids talk about multinational organizations orchestrating poverty for Third World poor and the American poor.

Smart parents will *fragment* those adolescents' ideas by good-heartedly approving of the peace studies course and any other projects that push boundaries. Way to go, Trevor. Way to go, Persis.

This pleasantness tends to idle back the young idealists' motor. They vaguely think, "How complacent, how confident Dad and Mom sound! Obviously nothing in the world that I can do can scratch the surface of the evil stuff *they* are doing. So of course they can afford to be pleasant. Besides, they have always had really nice manners. They've always had them. I've got them, too. The problem of ongoing evil in the world is insoluble then? Well, for now, I will write poems and journal entries about it." That is a part-conscious monologue in such young people's minds.

Now the young people look at *The Gleaners* again. This time they may feel wistful about those poor women bent over picking up corn while a male, on horseback, what's more, watches in the background. But wistful does not mean change agent. Wistful means attractively sensitive to universal sadness; change agent means protesting against specific powers that be. A reason that the rich regularly give more money to theater, dance, and orchestras than to literature is that watching plays, watching dance, and hearing music do not affect the change-agent parts of the mind. They affect the aesthetic parts. A terrific scherzo, no matter how spirited, does not lead its listener to say, "Oh, dear, now I've heard that, I am afraid I shall have to go out and free our serfs, or knock down a nuclear tower."

2. Financially safe women between the ages of sixty and ninety are in a subset by themselves. Their power usually comes from marriage or trust funds, not from lucrative positions they themselves have held. They have

paid dearly for the power of marriage, however. Typically they have spent years being helpmeets.

It is pleasant enough work being a helpmeet. When you are doing it, you are making up half of a loving team who together withstand whatever sadness life brings because you have each other. Women in that position needn't develop their own philosophy of life. The bad news of their not having been encouraged to have their own philosophy, however, is that they have been actively conditioned *not* to develop it. Their philosophy is halted at marital and familial loyalty. Loyalty is a tribal value with genuine honor tied into it, but it does entail no commitment to any universal principles. Interestingly, such loyalty shows up as only stage two on virtually all moral stage-development schemes.

If a woman has a commitment only to her specific family, she has no conscious commitment to universal principles. She has built no philosophical shape, so to speak, for her various impressions of life. She is philosophically fragmented. Fragmentation does help her stay on the gravy train, at least. It pays off. It means that she need only accommodate others in the same nest. Aunt March took Amy, not Jo, to Europe. Jo was "too decided." Amy knew how to work the family system. Jo was democratic.

A present-day genius on rich women's psychological fragmentation is not a psychotherapist, but the short-story author and novelist Jim Harrison. His "The Woman Lit by Fireflies" is about the class abuse, so to speak, of rich women. Most novelists writing about the rich don't know what the rich are like, so they make wild guesses. Not Harrison: "The Woman Lit by Fireflies" is an astounding view of how society wastes the personal potential of rich women. Woolf and Cather and Sandoz are authorities on how society wastes the potential of *poor* women. I feel grateful we have Harrison, so accurate, so incisive, on the rich.

3. Middle-aged rich people have little muscle for working in an ambiance of likely failure, ambiance in which writers of literature have to work. (Scientists, like us authors, can't know ahead of time just what truth they are looking for, so they are always at risk to fail, too.) Anyone who plans a story ahead does not grasp that a serious, good story cannot *be* planned ahead. The process itself gives us the real plot. The true gift hides in the mind for a horribly long time.

In the nature of things educated, well-to-do people are able, organized, and practical. They assess needs and show up for meetings if they said they would. They volunteer to chair tiresome committees. They finish jobs they take on. They are *not*, however, used to pegging away at some project that *may fail in its entirety*. They take on sure things. Who would knock themselves out for two years starting up a Friends of the What's-it Symphony with the idea that the Friends were as likely to fail as to succeed? None of their acquaintances ever proposed that they work privately at some project likely to fail, so it is not one of their expectations. In fact, they feel that in return for conscientious effort, they are *entitled* to success.

One needs particular muscle to face likely failure. The poor know all about spending hundreds of scarce dollars applying for jobs—getting together good-looking documentation, scaring up clothes that suggest that your aims are a support-staff-level position, *indoor* work, not field work. The nonrich typically have to go through this process several times in a life. Most job applications come to nothing. Because of this, poor people are likely to have an easier time than the rich in devoting themselves to really chancy projects like writing literature.

4. Privileged people hardly have the expectation of what we could call Ruining Your Life for Art. Jung pointed out long ago that writers are a great trial to themselves and their families. Writers' everyday lives are drenched with their work. Writers are *always* at some sort of top pitch. Recently I was having radiation for breast cancer at the same time as a friend. One day she said, "When all this is over, let's go skydiving." She was getting up a group. They wanted to live on the edge. They duly skydived the following spring. She loved it and felt no fear. I realized the reason I turned down the idea was 75 percent fear (of course), but the other 25 percent was this: I am a writer. I'm already jolting along on the edge all the time without dropping the one body I have out of an aircraft.

The majority of people in their fifties or sixties or more are not like writers. If they have money they do pleasant things with it. They don't work sixteen hours a day, and why ever should they? Those who have shown up in summer-arts programs of mine have been marvelous, spontaneous, courteous, curious members of the class sessions, but they usually found it a hard go to concentrate on overnight writing specifically assigned. They mentioned "better things to do" and they explained they weren't going to "throw away this wonderful opportunity to see rural Vermont" or wherever we were. It would have been very hard for them to switch that philosophy to: "I don't want to throw away this wonderful opportunity to write. Anyone can tour the lower forty-eight."

Another reason educated, privileged people do so handsomely in the class sessions of a writers' workshop while ducking the *actual writing* may be that sitting in a class is "being stimulated"—an experience they are brought up to. It is like going to a museum or touring the Houses of Parliament with a guide. When you are "being stimulated" you needn't be doing any work *inside* yourself. In fact, you are encouraged to look *out* of yourself all the time, not back in. Oh, look, there's the wool sack! Oh, look! There's a story by Jim Harrison!

Privileged, educated people of middle age and better are a thousand times superior students with respect to reading literary assignments. Part of their privilege is that they so often know a *lot* of canon, not just *the* canon of English and American literature* but canon of other literatures, canon of science, canon of history. It's wonderful to get to teach people who know about Marco Polo Bridge. It's wonderful to teach people who have read Howard Zinn but also Arnold Toynbee. They expect pleasure and interest from looking up things—reading Wendell Berry, let us say, not for the pleasant old-style-rural-values stuff Berry's best loved for but for his sharp, universally applicable essay, "Solving for Pattern."

Privileged, educated, mature people are in general more psychologically naive—plainly *unconscious*—than most of today's student writers. They comprise what I hope will be the last two generations who can't see any harm in lightly kidding young people for taking life seriously. They are the last generation, I even more fervently hope, who, without having read *any* psychological theory of the last forty years, feel that lightly jeering at all psychology is a classy behavior.

My personal view is tremendously biased. I feel deeply that American culture is psychologically absurd with its many biographies written by Ivy League–educated people claiming that now, when they are so very old, only *now,* they are sorry they made nuclear subs—they shouldn't have done it (Rickover)—or they are sorry they kept pursuing the Vietnam War (McNamara)—they shouldn't have done it—or

*As if we could agree on one.

our nuclear policy was a mistake (Gen. George Lee Butler). In another twenty years must we dread a new lot of autobiographers, at age seventy or eighty, confessing they feel bad that they kept the 1990s and 2000s sanctions against Iraq going? That is, the lucky, no matter how reflective their educations, stay immune to any public conscience all the years they make money—and then, safe in old age, with their portfolios as bulky and cozy as bullet-proof vests, they write apologiae. I ardently agree with Colman McCarthy, who wrote in *The Washington Post* (Dec. 17, 1996) that he wished General Butler had been wiser back when he could have made a difference.

Perhaps our writing classes are not the place where privileged adults can learn to drop their class-induced immunity to other people's suffering. But what if writing classes *are* the place? Just in case writing classes *might* be venues where the lucky could become ethically conscious, we probably ought to design classes to accommodate and support such wakening of heart.

All I have thought of so far for a weeklong course is my usual pack of exercises plus The Andover Format and a starting list of readings: Lopate's *The Art of the Essay*, Maugham's "The Three Fat Women of Antibes," Wendell Berry's "Solving for Pattern," Scott Russell Sanders's *Writing from the Center*, Richard Leakey's *The Sixth Extinction*, Ronald Blythe's *Akenfield*, George Orwell's "Why I Write," Virginia Woolf's *Three Guineas*, and Dava Sobel's *Longitude*.

Each of those works either illustrates or outright discusses different aspects of what it is to put together and enjoy one's own theory of everything, and urges that we do it now, in good time.

12.

Some Issues of Aesthetics and Ethics of Writing Literature

> Do not venture into its [the world's] equivocal company without first being sure that you bear within your own heart an escort from the world of the ideal. Live with your century; but do not be its creature. Work for your contemporaries; but create what they need, not what they praise.
>
> —Friedrich Schiller, from *On the Aesthetic Education of Man*

I love Schiller for being two hundred years before his time in seeing ethical development as a dynamic of psychological growth.

This chapter provides a few psychological explanations of the difference between literature that is aesthetic and literature that is both aesthetic and ethical.

Some Psychological Dynamics of Aesthetics and Ethics

Let's say that when we sit down to write we do it to find one or more of the following kinds of psychological excitement: we want to discover ourselves, we want to change the world by showing readers what life is like in some particulars, we want to make something extraordinarily graceful, or we want to escape into our literary hobby. Likely when we start off, one of these yearnings is probably a good deal stronger than the others, and therefore we are conscious of it, but the others may be small parts of our motivation, too.

I think it is useful to see our literary work in terms of psychological wants or needs because then we can talk about it and make fine distinctions. Chapter 3 on how to ask yourself (or others) open-ended empathic questions gives us some tools for keeping our *feeling* foremost and refining it. Traditionally, literature teachers tell a writing student, "All right, you have all this feeling. Now let's attend to the *craft* of it. For now you must put aside the feeling." That proposal comes of a retro philosophy—the "craft fascism" Aldo Alvarez identified. Let's drop it in favor of a holistic plan: for starters, let's decide to see the whole job—writing this piece of literature—as a half-blessed, half-cursed hodgepodge of strains, pulling this way and that way, some of the pulling being for the sake of our careers.

The greatest pull on all writers is the aesthetic pull. The American culture wants everyone to learn a *skill*—not some body of thought that might rear up and ask for reform. The younger our students, the more societal pressure there is for us to teach them to be aesthetic achievers, not people of moral ideas.

Some famous writers' works get taught as if the authors were only private-life stylists when in fact they were moral geniuses. High-school English students aren't being taught that Whitman wanted us to love the earth and devote our income and labor to others, to hate tyrants, and to dismiss whatever insults our soul (some of the advice given in the "Preface" to *Leaves of Grass*, 1855).

Mark Twain's "The War Prayer," a jarring satire against war and clergypeople's pious enthusiasm for war, is almost never taught. Few American college students know that Mark Twain wrote with wrath against American imperialism in the Philippines.

Virginia Woolf, constantly praised for being not only a stylist but a *precious* stylist—given credit for giving the novel a new psychological intricacy—is rarely recognized as the author of *Three Guineas*, in which she adjures everybody, especially women, to quit evading the linkage between the fact that wars got financed but women were so uncapitalized that they couldn't go to university. Even keen feminists, who should know better, habitually represent Woolf as a stylist rather than a moralist.

A fourth example is Leo Tolstoy, whose essays tell us that people ought to follow their conscience—not their nation's orders—when it comes to deciding to hurt groups of other people.

Apparently it is unpleasant to take a stand on ethical situations. Here are two questions about trying to mature from being merely a lover of beauty to someone who loves both beauty and justice:

First, why are proponents of aestheticism so resolute in not paying attention to literature as a treasury of humanitarian idealism? I think of T. S. Eliot's complacent statement: "When Whitman speaks of the lilacs or the mockingbird his theories and beliefs drop away like a needless pretext."[1] And why not let people linger in the more comfortable of the two stages—aestheticism being much easier than justice-seeking? Why fuss?

There are likely several dynamics that lead English teachers of high school, college, and even graduate-school students to pay so little attention to what stories or poems or essays are really *about.*

- Teachers are afraid to invite scorn from colleagues. Earnest idealists generally take a beating from cynics. Even Copernicus wanted to dodge scorn. He wrote that "the scorn which I had to fear on account of the newness and absurdity of my opinion"—he is referring here to his idea that our universe is solar-centric, not terra-centric—"almost drove me to abandon a work already undertaken."[2]

- Some teachers may not have developed much interest in justice.

- Teachers tend to follow the academic herd—they exhibit a natural passivity. Since T. S. Eliot was one of the two or three greatest poets of our time, an unconfident teacher of writing might well don his scorn for humanitarian content.

- Teachers are constantly forced by state, federal, or university authority to make their students acquire certain "skills," and thus there is little time left for teachers to consider context seriously.

Tricky author skills, not ideas, get too much emphasis in high school texts for English and American literature. The literary selections in the anthologies adopted for public high school use are nearly always splendid. Nonetheless, one can tell from the "unit questions" at the end of the chapters that what the authors of these texts really admire is tricky methodology, as if the principal job of a writer were to control the readers' feelings. How opposite such trickery is to showing young people what literature has to say about life!

The second question, "Well, why *not* let people linger in the more comfortable aesthetic (preethical) stage? What is wrong with writing about our lives, writing them up beautifully, and sparing our readers the moral shrillness?"

Lawrence Kohlberg assumed that the people in the lower stages—let's say, for the purposes of applying stage theory to literary affairs, people in the aesthetics-for-their-own-sake stage (Schiller's and Orwell's stage two)—feel perfectly confident in their ideals for a time. They are happy to be out of the previous stage, in which they used to think that nothing really counted if it didn't yield immediate, concrete benefit to themselves. Now they are in love with beauty, so they feel, as the social workers say, "good about themselves" in their beauty loving. It was a good step to have taken! they logically feel.

Perhaps an author's parents honored only the simplest, physical tastes in life. These parents may have made remarks like this: "If you major in English, where's that going to get you? You had better take up something that'll do you some good!" Despite that dreary chiding, the youth grew up to be an English major, the English major grew into an author, and now that author may well feel justified in spending years congratulating himself or herself for having bravely escaped the world of deadbeat practicality. For a long time this author's pegging away at the literary craft, writing beautifully, feels as good as an ideal needs to be.

But sooner or later some advocate of fair play like Epictetus or Marcus Aurelius or Matthew Arnold or George Orwell or Virginia Woolf comes along and says that *art for art's sake* is shallow stuff considering that while writers are writing precious phrases rich industrialists are starving poor people, and old men are sending young men to war, and when old and young men go to war the effort uses up the money that others need in order to live. A person can feel extraordinarily cross when told that his or her highest goals are self-centered—or worse, *precious.*

"Art for art's sake" comes into style and goes out of style. The ingenious scholar Gene Bell-Villada has given us a stunning, absolutely fresh insight: Art for its own sake, he says, appears to exist as major movements *only in Western industrialized cultures.*[3]

Bell-Villada, an English professor at Williams College, has written a literary history of the two centuries of art-for-its-own-sake authors. Clearly Bell-Villada regards these aestheticists as refugees from social conscience. They are writers who guide their skills carefully around any moral unhappiness.

I want to append an idea to Bell-Villada's. What if the core principle of Western industrialized culture is that if you inherit a full deck and then play those cards right, you have a *right* to be happy? You needn't fret because many people are poor. The classical question about one's *right* to happiness is fascinating. Perhaps the reason that only Western industrialized cultures have hosted art-for-art's-sake fads is that authors, like others in a greedy climate, get debauched: they pick up on how happily, how gracefully, the extremely rich stay immune to the calls of the poor. Authors build up their own sort of immunity: they work to build beautiful literature, and then they go into that literature to hide from pain. People who write beautifully can feel awed and glamorous and proud just about every working hour. They can, like T. S. Eliot talking about Whitman, write off social conscience as niggling. Bell-Villada's *Art for Art's Sake and Literary Life* do sure battle against craft for craft's sake. Of Aldo Alvarez's remarks about "craft fascism," discussed in Chapter 9, a major one is psychological: if the conversation in writing classes is only about craft, we get no assurance that it is sensible and right to care about the rightness and wrongness of things. Moral anxiety has no psychological critical mass if we never hear it named.

Bell-Villada leaves readers with the following as a question:

> Among the basic questions that have led me to research and write this study are: Why does Art for Art's Sake exist at all? What is it about Western culture in these past two or three

> centuries that has prompted this way of thinking? None of the answers thus far presented are, to my mind, fully satisfactory. The routine textbook or handbook accounts can sometimes verge on the tautological: *l'art pour l'art* sprang to life in the steady march of man's ideas simply because it did, and no one really knows why.[4]

Hiding in aesthetics, stalling before taking the next step, works for a while. We stall. Besides, compassion looks like a slippery slope. Once we've started in on it, where's it going to end?

To illustrate the difference between aesthetics and ethicality, here are two short pieces of writing, both about large cats in twentieth-century zoos. Jorge Luis Borges's paragraph is from his essay called "Blindness." He describes what it is like to be losing his eyesight.

> In the course of the many lectures—too many lectures—I have given, I have observed that people tend to prefer the personal to the general, the concrete to the abstract. I will begin, then, by referring to my own modest blindness. Modest, because it is total blindness in one eye, but only partial in the other. I can still make out certain colors; I can still see blue and green. And yellow, in particular, has remained faithful to me. I remember when I was young I used to linger in front of certain cages in the Palermo Zoo: the cages of the tigers and leopards. I lingered before the tigers' gold and black. Yellow is still with me, even now. I have written a poem entitled "The Gold of the Tigers" in which I refer to this friendship.[5]

And here is Rilke contemplating a Paris zoo animal.

THE PANTHER

His vision, from the constantly passing bars,
has grown so weary that it cannot hold
anything else. It seems to him there are
a thousand bars; and behind the bars, no world.

As he paces in cramped circles, over and over,
the movement of his powerful soft strides
is like a ritual dance around a center
in which a mighty will stands paralyzed.

Only at times, the curtain of the pupils
lifts, quietly—. An image enters in,
plunges into the heart and is gone.[6]

In 1998 the essayist and teacher Scott Russell Sanders came to The Loft, a writers' organization in Minneapolis, to give a master course and teach a few private students for a month. I went to one of his Saturday-morning classes. Sanders handed out copies of the Borges quote, then asked everyone to read it. We each took ten minutes to write a little personal comment, which we read aloud to the group. I was sitting on Scott's left. He started on his right.

People made appreciative and sensible comments about Borges. Nearly everyone noted that you could tell that he's a very sophisticated person, that he writes elegantly. He writes with the kind of easy informality that comes from a poised mind. Borges made wonderful connections between his childhood memory of the tigers' yellow fur coats and the fact that now, as he is losing his eyesight, yellow is "faithful to him." He can still see it. Everyone said it was a lovely piece of writing. People picked up on his classy, nonwhining tone.

By the time it was my turn, I had cooled off. I had been cross for over ten minutes. To my mind, that roomful of people had followed the worst psychological style of groups. The first two or three people had made their appreciative remarks about Borges's exquisite writing. Then everyone said more of the same. No one was horrified that Borges considered imprisoned animals only in light of the aesthetic pleasure their yellow coats gave him. Borges was indifferent to the tigers' own realities. These creatures were serving out life imprisonment without right of habeas corpus or a jury trial. In fact, they had committed no crime at all.

When I had my turn, I said that this paragraph was self-centered; it typified the aesthetic stage of young writers or of old writers who get stuck in art for art's sake. Borges was oblivious of cruelty because he was engaged, even fascinated, with his own thinking about what the color yellow meant to him.

Later I read the rest of his essay. Not surprisingly, it is very much the essay of an entitled, but also a very intelligent person. Borges felt entitled to address without distraction only the subject he wanted to address. Suffering tigers is just landscape. The yellow of the tigers is just landscape. The yellowness itself was all that was useful to him, so he used the yellowness.

In his poem "The Panther," on the other hand, Rilke does not talk about himself at all. Rilke is a consummate poet, yet he was not self-centered. Rilke tries to imagine, through empathic hypotheses, what cage life is like for the panther. Rilke hypothesizes that a great will, confused, goes round in ever tighter circles. We can't ask a panther empathic questions in German or French or English, but we *can* do empathic guesswork. Rilke says that there appears to be no end to the panther's suffering. The panther must feel as if there are a thousand bars between him and the world. Only now and then does the panther's eyelid stir; he makes out what's going on between the bars. Then, Rilke says, a picture goes in. A powerful feeling—a stillness—springs up all through the cat's limbs and stops at his heart.

If we look back at Schiller's three stages or Orwell's four stages, or if we carefully glance over Dr. Loevinger's upper two stages, we can see that one cognitive accomplishment of Homo sapiens is a love of the world's beauty. A more profound accomplishment, however, for which we do not abandon our once-acquired love of beauty, is seeing others not as amusing or charming landscape but as creatures with their own fates to bear and their own lives to live.

So I said, in Sanders's group, that I felt angry at Borges for not caring about the Palermo tigers. Everyone grew still, but only out of good manners. Next they looked annoyed. Up till then the group had been talking all *in one ambiance.* That ambiance was affable. It allowed for discourse—some literary critiquing and some mild enthusiasm for an awfully good author. Then one person makes an unpleasant remark.

Scott Sanders said, "Well, it's true. Borges is an aesthete, first of all."

To anyone living at the purely aesthetic level, not only is it OK to experience others' suffering simply as background for a poem or for a passage of prose, but it is in good taste. Apropos of leaving aestheticism behind, we can interrogate our rough drafts in a new way. We can ask ourselves, "Is my rough draft like Borges's paragraph? Is it like Rilke's poem? Is my rough draft anything that Schiller might have called 'in a compassionate relationship with all our fellow beings'?" Schiller's Ninth Letter discusses the complexity of staying apart from the culture at the same time as one feels affectionate for one's fellow human beings in the culture. He wanted us not to be "of" our culture, but still to maintain a general sympathy for it.

A magnificent aspect of Rilke's many-sided genius was how he took the time to urge other poets to keep themselves to themselves. In this passage, taken from his famous little advisory called *Letters to a Young Poet,* Rilke warns his friend to stay conscious—consciously to keep watch lest he merge into the general cultural sludge.

> It is true that many young people who love falsely, i.e., simply surrendering themselves and giving up their solitude (the average person will of course always go on doing that—), feel oppressed by their failure and want to make the situation they have landed in livable and fruitful in their own, personal way—. For their nature tells them that the questions of love, even more than everything else that is important cannot be resolved publicly and according to this or that agreement; that they are questions, intimate questions from one human being to another, which in any case require a new, special, *wholly* personal answer—. But how can they, who have already flung themselves together and can no longer tell whose outlines are whose, who thus no longer possess anything of their own, how can they find a way out of themselves, out of the depths of their already buried solitude?[7]

I want to draw attention to a kindly, oddly loving aspect of most stage-development theory. When you begin to read the theory, you feel comforted, in the most unlikely sort of way. You feel that kind overtures are being made—made by egalitarians, what's more. You feel the authors' profound wish that we would all, fast as we can, stop being just creatures averaged and generalized by society and become our own persons. You feel the authors' faith in the process, as well—

that is, that such "individuation" or "self-fulfillment" is possible for everyone provided that each of us decides to undertake the work. Stage theorists, most remarkably Kohlberg and Loevinger, are rather like the distant bugle sound from a cavalry come to save us. Their philosophies are curiously like the philosophies of twentieth-century psychotherapists: that is, in both professions the idea is that we start as mere creatures of nature, but each of us can turn into our own person. Here is the best part for writers: turning into one's own person is what saves you, not being "a team player."

Both stage-development theory and psychotherapeutic philosophy rouse us to pay attention to something in the distance, or so it feels. Next, you may notice that what you want to pay attention to is, indeed, at some distance, but the distance is not so spatial as it is temporal. This becoming your own person is a goal already inside each of us, but not yet showing to our duller selves, like something still over a horizon. We want to "raise" it, as the old sea captains said, looking through their glasses.

The only drawback to reading anything so encouraging as stage-development philosophy is that we become aware of how thousands, perhaps millions, of our species do not make it into individual, original personality. They stay stuck in the phase of Schiller's "natural man" or in Kohlberg's premoral stage, stage two. So we can't just count on automatically growing into anything like the psychological level we are capable of.

Our efforts to think and feel beyond simple love of family or love of nature are a fragile enterprise! We will have to keep reminding ourselves of how this civilization, the stuff nonfiction writers write about, works out cruelly for some, cruelly for all at some times, cruelly all their lives for still others.

Literary colleagues may assure us that such thinking will make us shrill. "I used to love your work so much," they will say, "back when you just described how people are and you didn't press for change." Such friends and colleagues far prefer rereading Woolf's *Mrs. Dalloway* to reading *Three Guineas* all through once. In *Mrs. Dalloway* the character Hugh Whitbread was still only an emerging shadow of a villain. He was still just one of Woolf's aesthetic achievements—an interesting character vaguely benefiting, but only vaguely, from being a privileged player in "the system." By the time she wrote *Three Guineas*, Woolf recognized the Hugh Whitbreads as the beneficiaries and manipulators of unethical entitlement because by then she had asked the question: "Who is the victim for whom this civilization doesn't work out fairly? And now that I have shown you the victim, we had better ask who, exactly, is the predator?"

Of course, the Woolf of *Three Guineas* is less charming than the scrupulous but still merely sensuous novelist of *Mrs. Dalloway*. It is odd how easy and gratifying it is to think of men in ascot and waistcoat and striped morning pants, yet how awful it is to think of a major perpetrator of war and poverty (not just to women—to everyone) in that same morning dress! We may wish that someone had not pointed it out to us that the villain often wears the correct school tie, but the psychological fact is that once it *has* been pointed out to us we are pinned. We will look at Hugh Whitbread but see poor women's buckets and dead soldiers' heads and limbs on the beach.

Once we creative nonfiction writers have asked either question, "Who is the victim for whom this civilization doesn't work out fairly?" or "Who exactly is the predator?" we can never go back. We will never again equate a sojourn in the wilds with a spiritual journey. From then on, we will see the wilds wistfully, as someplace not yet intruded on and misused by our lot. Enjoying nature is from then on only escape, a pleasant one, of course.

We will be less obvious writers. We won't exasperate one another with long essays that "celebrate" this or that pleasant experience while we ourselves take no clear sides and feel no pain.

We can never undo any insight once we've had it. Stage development cannot go in reverse, so once started, "think we must"—as Virginia Woolf says.

> Think we must. Let us think in offices; in omnibuses, while we are standing in the crowd watching Coronations and Lord Mayor's Shows; let us think as we pass the Cenotaph; and in Whitehall; in the gallery of the House of Commons; in the Law Courts; let us think at baptisms and marriages and funer-

> als. Let us never cease from thinking. What is this "civilization" in which we find ourselves? What are these ceremonies and why should we take part in them? What are these professions and why should we make money out of them? Where in short is it leading us, the procession of the sons of educated men?[8]

Distinguishing Hack Work from Literary Artifice

A good deal has been said in this book about aiming or not aiming at an audience. There is a vital distinction to make between hack work and proper literary artifice.

When we revise *content* in hopes that such and such a large audience will like it the better, then we are hacking. For example, we are hacking if we change the perfectly good sex in our work into really scary stuff because, word is, a huge audience out there prefers S and M.

A thoroughgoing instance of hack writing is cited by Ted Kooser in his essay entitled "Lying for the Sake of Making Poems."[9] Kooser describes how a poet has chosen, in a biographical poem, to alter what was in real life an amicable relationship to a horrible cruelty perpetrated against a child. When questioned, the poet explained that she felt the horror version would have more impact on an audience.

If she thought about what she was doing, she might look at herself and say, "I have apparently decided to drop from the rolls of people who write literature. I have decided to join the people who will do anything, such as major lying, in order to sell. I have looked at the market, and the market likes sensationalism, so I gave it to them."

On the other hand, when we revise a nearly finished manuscript to give it *richer image or language or sharper juxtapositions of bright scene or argument,* we are not lying, because we are not changing the content. We are exercising our craft of literary artifice.

Normalized Indifference Is Our Comfortable Stance on Any Subject until Something Jars Us

Normalized indifference works well for people who don't need to think for the rest of their lives, but it doesn't do for heroes or for authors. It is no accident that Joseph Conrad tells us, on the first page of *Lord Jim*, that Jim had been raised in a country vicarage. His father gave sermons about virtue-related subjects, as must Church of England vicars, rabbis, and priests as a matter of course. Conrad says Jim's father preached about virtue, but without disturbing the sensibilities of his conservative parishioners.

We know Conrad worked fast as an author: here he works so fast that one scarcely notices what he's doing. He lightly, lightly suggests: if virtuous talk that dodges any actual application of virtue is the normal intellectual nature of our childhood, might we grow up to be bystanders—unable to connect the phrase "courageous action" with actually jumping down into the pitching longboat to help the other midshipmen save drowning sailors? Further, do we feel *entitled* to be bystanders while others do the heroics—again I refer to Jim early in the novel—so entitled that as we watch our fellow officer candidates doing their dangerous work we feel scornful? Jim felt scornful, because this harbor rescue job was such a minuscule occasion. He told himself he was waiting for some decent, serious occasion: *then*, oh, *then*, he'd come through all right. We know from the novel that when the greater occasion came, he funked it, too.

As aspiring heroes and heroines and aspiring authors, then, we may need to be vigilant in our current literary scene, where craft counts for too much and content for too little. But it is hard to be vigilant about, say, cruelty, when no one else is paying attention. Here is a perfect instance. M. F. K. Fisher, the amusing essayist who has greater scope of subject than most writers even fantasize about having, is writing about a funny scene. She was tooling around provincial France. It got to be lunchtime, and, passionate eater that M. F. K. Fisher was, she was delighted to find an old country inn. It was the off-season. The maidservant who welcomed Fisher was in ecstasy because she admired Monsieur Paul so much. Monsieur Paul was the chef. The servant girl was "almost frighteningly fanatical about food." The servant both guided and coerced Fisher through course after course of the most fulsome but also the most exquisite noon lunch of her life. Somewhere in the middle of the courses, the waitress brought out a pail of water with living trout in it.

> "Here is the trout, Madame. You are to eat it *au bleu*, and you should never do so if you had not seen it alive. For if the trout were dead when it was plunged into the court bouillon it would not turn blue. So, naturally, it must be living." I knew all this, more or less, but I was fascinated by her absorption in the momentary problem. I felt quite ignorant, and asked her with sincerity, "What about the trout? Do you take out its guts before or after?" "O, the trout?" She sounded scornful. "Any trout is glad, truly glad, to be prepared by Monsieur Paul. His little gills are pinched, with one flash of the knife he is empty, and then he curls in agony in the bouillon and all is over. And it is the curl you must judge, Madame. A false truite au bleu cannot curl."[10]

Fisher has so light a touch that we can ask ourselves, is she simply reporting an amusing narrative about a nation or at least a waitress and a chef and a lunch eater, all three of whom are nuts about good food, normalizing the torture of the truite au bleu that gets its good-looking curl from agony? She does better: one passion can override and squash other principles right out of mind. If you have a crush on your superiors in a workplace, as had that waitress, you had better figure you will be scornful if someone says, when Monsieur Paul opens up that fish alive and then burns it to death, will it hurt?

Rebecca Harding Davis hasn't the light touch of M. F. K. Fisher. In fact, she was often a clumsy writer. Her cunning was not in craft but in the exactitude of her psychological discernment. She knew that privileged people are conditioned to be immune to the sufferings of the poor. True, everyone knows that, but Davis recognized several discrete *kinds* of that immunity, and she managed to work several manifestations of that immunity into one short scene of her long short story entitled "Life in the Iron Mills."

This story takes place in an ironworks where the labor is hot and grueling. One ordinary worker named Wolfe is making statues—artistic statues, with some taste to them—and he leaves them around at the edges of the looming furnace room where the iron is smelted.

One day some big shots from the iron mills and the social leaders of the town have a look at these works of art. Partly they are slumming. They are half ready to have some attractive, wistful things to say about the sadness of this poor man trying to do art. Two of the characters are only at the stage of Schiller's coldhearted practical man. Two, Mitchell and Dr. May, have incipient compassion. Their class background and their habits have normalized cruelty, however. They feel a little something, but it escapes them. It gets lost "in the imagination of their hearts," as the Magnificat puts it.[11]

> "Raining, still," said Doctor May, "and hard. Where did we leave the coach, Mitchell?"
>
> "At the other side of the works. —Kirby, what's that?"
>
> Mitchell started back, half-frightened, as, suddenly turning a corner, the white figure of a woman faced him in the darkness,—a woman, white, of giant proportions, crouching on the ground, her arms flung out in some wild gesture of warning.
>
> "Stop! Make that fire burn there!" cried Kirby, stopping short.
>
> The flame burst out, flashing the gaunt figure into bold relief.
>
> Mitchell drew a long breath.
>
> "I thought it was alive," he said, going up curiously.
>
> The others followed.
>
> "Not marble, eh?" asked Kirby, touching it.
>
> One of the lower overseers stopped.
>
> "Korl, Sir."
>
> "Who did it?"
>
> "Can't say. Some of the hands; chipped it out in off-hours."
>
> "Chipped to some purpose, I should say. What a flesh-tint the stuff has! Do you see, Mitchell?"
>
> "I see."

He had stepped aside where the light fell boldest on the figure, looking at it in silence. There was not one line of beauty or grace in it: a nude woman's form, muscular, grown coarse with labor, the powerful limbs instinct with some one poignant longing. One idea: there it was in the tense, rigid muscles, the clutching hands, the wild, eager face, like that of a starving wolf's. Kirby and Doctor May walked around it, critical, curious. Mitchell stood aloof, silent. The figure touched him strangely.

"Not badly done," said Doctor May. "Where did the fellow learn that sweep of the muscles in the arm and hand? Look at them! They are groping—do you see?—clutching: the peculiar action of a man dying of thirst."

"They have ample facilities for studying anatomy," sneered Kirby, glancing at the half-naked figures.

"Look," continued the Doctor, "at this bony wrist, and the strained sinews of the instep! A working-woman,—the very type of her class."

"God forbid!" muttered Mitchell.

"Why?" demanded May. "What does the fellow intend by the figure? I cannot catch the meaning."

"Ask him," said the other, dryly. "There he stands,"—pointing to Wolfe, who stood with a group of men, leaning on his ash-rake.

The Doctor beckoned him with the affable smile which kind-hearted men put on, when talking with these people.

"Mr. Mitchell has picked you out as the man who did this,—I'm sure I don't know why. But what did you mean by it?"

"She be hungry."

Wolfe's eyes answered Mitchell, not the Doctor.

"Oh-h! But what a mistake you have made, my fine fellow! You have given no sign of starvation to the body. It is strong,—terribly strong. It has the mad, half-despairing gesture of drowning."

Wolfe stammered, glanced appealingly at Mitchell, who saw the soul of the thing, he knew. But the cool, probing eyes were turned on himself now,—mocking, cruel, relentless.

"Not hungry for meat," the furnace-tender said at last.

"What then? Whiskey?" jeered Kirby, with a coarse laugh.

Wolfe was silent a moment thinking.

"I dunno," he said, with a bewildered look. "It mebbe. Summat to make her live, I think,—like you. Whiskey ull do it, in a way."

The young man laughed again. Mitchell flashed a look of disgust somewhere,—not at Wolfe.

"May," he broke out impatiently, "are you blind? Look at that woman's face! It asks questions of God, and says, 'I have a right to know.' Good God, how hungry it is!"

They looked a moment; then May turned to the mill-owner:—

"Have you many such hands as this? What are you going to do with them? Keep them at puddling iron?"

Kirby shrugged his shoulders. Mitchell's look had irritated him.

"*Ce n'est pas mon affaire.* I have no fancy for nursing infant geniuses. I suppose there are some stray gleams of mind and soul among these wretches. The Lord will take care of his own; or else they can work out their own salvation. I have heard you call our American system a ladder which any man can scale. Do you doubt it? Or perhaps you want to banish all social ladders, and put us all on a flat table-land,—eh, May?"

The Doctor looked vexed, puzzled. Some terrible problem lay hid on this woman's face, and troubled these men. Kirby waited for an answer, and receiving none, went on, warming with his subject.

"I tell you, there's something wrong that no talk of *Liberté* or *Égalité* will do away. If I had the making of men, these men who do the lowest part of the world's work should be machines,—nothing more,—hands. It would be kindness. God help them! What are taste, reason, to creatures who must live such lives as that?" He pointed to Deborah, sleeping on the ash-heap. "So many nerves to sting them to pain. What if God had put your brain, with all its agony of touch, into your fingers, and bid you work and strike with that?"

"You think you could govern the world better?" laughed the Doctor.

"I do not think at all."

"That is true philosophy. Drift with the stream, because you cannot dive deep enough to find bottom, eh?"

"Exactly," rejoined Kirby. "I do not think. I wash my hands of all social problems,—slavery, caste, white or black. My duty to my operatives has a narrow limit,—the pay-hour on Saturday night. Outside of that, if they cut korl, or cut each other's throats, (the more popular amusement of the two,) I am not responsible."

The Doctor sighed,—a good honest sigh, from the depths of his stomach.

"God help us! Who is responsible?"

"Not I, I tell you," said Kirby, testily. "What has the man who pays them money to do with their souls' concerns, more than the grocer or butcher who takes it?"

"And yet," said Mitchell's cynical voice, "look at her! How hungry she is!"[12]

I quote this whole passage from Rebecca Harding Davis's work here because the author presents several different psychological pain-avoiding mechanisms: the more civilized the man, the more ingenious the mechanism by which his own mind contrives to keep itself immune. Each man illustrates a mind-set that either coarsely or subtly desensitizes itself to human beings—authors or readers.

We should try to recognize when we are writing for what could be called "museumgoers." We should especially recognize when we ourselves are acting like museumgoers. The museumgoer mind-set gives us these conscious goals:

- being interested in a civil, dispassionate way;

- feeling delighted (by beauty, charm, or humor); and

- feeling nondirectionally stimulated.

(Chapter 11 discussed museumgoing as a cause of psychological fragmenting.)

Interest, delight, and stimulated feelings are kept intact in a habituated museumgoer: the inner mind does not let its own memories intrude on the present interesting, delightful, or stimulating moment.

I was once taken to "The Screens" at the Guthrie Theatre in Minneapolis by two season-ticket holders. Jean Genet's characters screeched at us about one thing or another, frequently telling the audience to fuck themselves, as Genet liked to do. It was repetitive stuff, I thought, and I asked the two who had paid for my ticket if they would like to leave at the intermission. They looked shocked. They never left a play. To them playgoing was a discrete activity. They couldn't possibly find this play interesting since they hadn't any interest in the Algerian War, and the play certainly wasn't delightful. It failed to elicit interest or delight, but—hold on—it made the cut for being *stimulating.* Genet rifled insults at the playgoers. They intended to feel gratified at the stimulation.

Such playgoing is an adult version of little children's "parallel play." Toddlers play amicably together but with different toys. They do not interact, but they are pleasantly stimulated by one another's presence. Genet did his thing; the season-ticket holders did theirs.

An oddity in literary news: it is not so hard to write for privileged audiences as it was ten years ago. One reason is that privileged audiences are now nearly starved for beautiful language and fulsome plot in fiction; they are starved for beautiful language and some decent philosophy in nonfiction. The end of the 1990s and the first years after the year 2000 is a wonderful time for writing nonfiction, because crummy America has exasperated a growing crowd of readers. These people, who seemed to take cover in museumgoing in the 1970s and 1980s—that is, they paid no attention to strident authors' social news—are now tolerant of the vagaries of creative nonfiction, and they want to feel that a decent idea broods over it.

How the Old, Familiar Dynamic Called Pain Avoidance Affects Creative Nonfiction

Pain avoidance is often referred to by helping professionals as the greatest motivation of our species. Let me suggest three ways in which pain avoidance vitiates the literature we want to write.

Pointing to but not Elucidating Some Subject or Scene

Most of the poems that irritate nonpoet readers like me are poems clearly pointing to some event in the poet's life without ever telling us what is going on. Here is a poem by William Stafford that is just talk: he doesn't tell us readers enough so that we can join whatever his feeling is. Instead he does the trickery of rhetoric at the end, repeating the image of turning on the light twice, to ratchet up feeling. I will add that although this poem is a perfect illustration of a *point-and-dodge* poem, this poet at his best was a wonderful writer, one of the very best.

When beginners point but do not elucidate, we teachers bawl them out, as Roger Angell once did me in a story for *The New Yorker* in which he said, "Fix it. You have nondirectives in here." But the old hands like William Stafford we let go without complaint: it was enough, we think, that they produced as much beauty of line and idealism of thought as they did.

THE DAY AFTER THEN

He adjusted the blinds for the morning sun;
office-floor-wide the light streaks ran.
His things there—where had their value gone?
Cold it was, cold at his work.

He could hold still and slowly turn
all that was under his hand at noon,
there where the sunbeams were shaken—
like threads, like long promises.

Listen, you nearest who should know all:
night brought a strain that came down the hall
and muffled the room in the rest of the world.
And he turned the light on, turned it on,
turned it on.[13]

Stafford promises a dramatic incident then dodges away from telling us what it was. We should take seriously how little poetry intelligent readers read. It wouldn't hurt to analyze our creative nonfiction the same way we might analyze poems: that is, ask if the author is trying our patience by keeping secrets while pretending to tell. This is such a common form of literary pain that we may not have noticed it—the author wanting to sound off on some issue, but being too niggardly or frightened to reveal what happened.

Not only constant class abuse and constant cultural abuse can build the *pointing-and-dodging* habit in a writer. Writing in a journal can habituate pointing and dodging. Since at least any first draft (and often the only draft) of a journal is solely for your own eyes, you have no discipline. You just point to "that horrible night in October of 1998," and you needn't say what happened. You scarcely need even to point. If you keep a journal for five years, you may have given yourself the habit of not elucidating anything.

Literary tradition isn't so good as psychology about encouraging people to reveal painful truth. Literary tradition says one should not let "author-intruded anger" tear the skein of the work. What happens, however, if one upholds that standard, as two courageous poets, Linda McCarriston and Kristin DeSmith, and one courageous prose writer, Richard Hoffman, have recently pointed out, is that the author feels constrained to be beauteous and lyrical, even "forgiving" and "healing," in writing about subjects that ought to be handled down at the precinct station, with names mentioned.

Resisting Writing about Adult Life

I discourage adults from repetitively pulling up memories from their childhood and making a lot out of them—such as memories of bygone Christmases. Childhood descriptions and nostalgia are a bad magnet for an adult who means to write serious literature. Even as you're writing up some childhood happening, saying, "I will never forget the Christmases, and so forth, and so on," your own writing models for you the idea that childhood had more feeling to it than adult life does. It didn't, and it doesn't. The whole business of adults' trying to find meaning in life is to realize that our innermost meaning lives in our *adult* lives. Adults have much more imagination than children have. We need to get into that imagination and build it some more and believe in it. I'm afraid that writing childhood descriptions promotes an ongoing discrediting of adult loves and passions and hatreds.

Nonetheless, for people under twenty-five, childhood is their area of expertise and a resource. They need every encouragement to write about childhood. They are the authorities of their own life stories. When young people are stuck in generic patriotism or spurious nostalgia—the dullest of human emotions—respectfully let them be stuck there for a while. For young people, love of country and wistfulness about place are artifacts of noble feeling. Those subjects are brave structures in their heads. In grown-ups, the middle-aged, and the old, pining for the past can be an addictive emotion that eats up all others, but that isn't the problem during adolescence.

Resisting the Idea of the Existence of Enemies

Talking about actual opponents on a given issue or opponents in our workplaces is fearsome only in that one can be fired, and literary skills—which happen to be the only skills most of us are trained in—don't teach us how to oppose something that was just said in a meeting. If no one in a department has the social-work or counseling skills to be able to agree to disagree, as it is sometimes described, then that department is likely to have an unpleasant word with anyone who opposes the general drift. The person will be regarded as someone who won't get with the program, a personnel problem, not an intellectual challenge. I haven't any solutions for that. I can assure writers loath to recognize the presence of enemies in a given setting that they had better recognize the presence of enemies if indeed they are there.

Writing about enemies will not curdle the more agreeable parts of your essay.

What does spoil an essay is the author's attempt to blend black and white into "gray areas." In current culture, recognizing this thing called "gray areas" is still a little in style, despite the fact that black behavior (counting black as bad) and white behavior (counting white as innocent) do not blend. They remain, like oil paint and water-based paint, swirling discretely in the same can.

For example, Andrew Carnegie spoiled and shortened the lives of tens of thousands of his ironworks employees, adults and children, because of the unmitigated cruel hours, conditions, and dismal pay he inflicted on them. Then he fixed up every U.S.A. town with a really nice library with a copper dome. The libraries do not make up for the manslaughter. They do not lighten Carnegie's black behavior to gray.

An ethics professor whose class I visited suggested we imagine a very skilled surgeon who has operated on hundreds of people and cured them. Then the surgeon murders five patients on the operating table because he didn't like them. He is not a gray surgeon. He is an evil surgeon. The evil he did was not "balanced" or lightened by the good.

What will freshen up our nonfiction is straightaway to confront people who cry, "Oh, but you are seeing everything in black and white!—when there are so many gray areas!" I always ask for one example of a gray area. So far the examples given have been partly evil behavior laved over with partly philanthropic behavior.

Well—but we have such a taste for amiability! We are disposed to be grateful that our little towns have libraries. Why must we hearken back to Carnegie's horrible labor practices?

We must keep all the bad news in memory along with the good, so that as history makes itself, yesterday and today and tomorrow, we will have the habit of discerning between enemies and friends.

An author's reason for using the language of hostility is to *mark the difference between victim literature and predator literature.* I finally learned that no evil (from one person's point of view) happens in a vacuum. One particular evil is wonderful for someone else, which is why that someone else made it happen.

I learned that lesson while working for the National Farmers

Union. The little farms didn't disappear of their own accord. The great grain companies could have eschewed forcing American farmers into a half-century-long price war with Third World farmers, but they didn't. Wrecking the little farms was profitable for the big grain companies. They made a lot of money while they drove American farm families off their land.

For some reason I couldn't get that through my head for years. I was brought up on women's schmooze like other American women who are now in their sixties and early seventies. Intelligent women were supposed to be *balanced.* People talking about the evil done by grain companies look angry and shrill: schmooze philosophy writes off any shrill, out-of-control people as losers. Deciding that outraged people are losers is a prime, number one exhibit of pain avoidance. It's also a gigantic copout! It is knowing there is evil out there and choosing to pretend it isn't real.

My own hands have taught me in a small way. I am presently returning a northern meadow to forest, so that in sixty years it will look something like, perhaps even better than, the way it looked before early-twentieth-century dairy farmers cut it over for pasture. I plant hundreds of acorns then protect the baby oaks from grass. The tall meadow grasses, brome and quack, have powerful roots: they win their way more by root than by seed. I have to yank up their root extensions by the tens of thousands; that grass knows that once those baby oaks get going they will grow into huge shade trees and will drink up all the good of the soil and deprive the grass of the good of the sun.

Finally I came to see how, unless we are fooling ourselves, we have already taken sides. Good guys, bad guys. It is amazing how old a person can get before facing the fact that in life, one thing is nearly constantly at the throat of something else nearby. Rabbits are the enemies of tree planters, the Easter bunny notwithstanding. Yet rabbits wish to live. It is curious how you learn tolerance for enemies once you admit they *are* enemies and name them. Still, in tree planting, as Richard Hoffman pointed out about incest, the predators have to go. Taking any active part in life, like planting, is secular. Actually it is a shock how secular and practical life can be. One cannot pose as a forgiving person once one realizes that the rabbit may have promised never again to chomp down the baby trees flat to the ground, but he will do it, again and again.

How does this realization affect the literature we write?

First, if we do not identify any particular perpetrators, our writing about a given evil, such as incest, will be centered on the *victim,* and our work will get to be labeled as *victim writing.* Such narratives need to be known as *narratives about predation.* Linda McCarriston points out that such literature is testimonial, not confessional. If someone raped you, you *testify* that they did. You don't *confess.*

An odd psychological dynamic causes muddled thinking: it is less depressing, oddly enough, to think of oneself as a *victim* of incest than to focus openly on the *predator* and name him or her. It is hard, unpleasant work to study a predator's drives or urges, then design for him or her a hostile environment. Medical people do this more cleanly than authors do: they know you don't go on treating ulcers with a bland diet when the cause of ulcers is the *h. pylori* bacterium. Doctors deliberately design a hostile environment for those bacteria. What we want in a doctor is someone who will kill bacteria. What do we want from an essayist? Not a bland diet.

When essayists offer a bland diet, predators remain safe and free in the streets. One of the best authors writing about facing evil is Richard Hoffman, whose powerful essay called "What's Love Got to To with It?" was mentioned earlier. The essay discusses the psychological dynamics of people who have been raped by their parents or other adults, but then later *feel that they ought to forgive the rapist* and "get on with their lives," so to speak. These victims often insist that they *have* forgiven the rapist. When you say, "I ought to let it go," or "I know I ought to have forgiven," and "One ought to forgive," using, as Hoffman points out, a kind of vague, intransitive form of the transitive verb *forgive,* what you are really doing is making a false claim for peace. You want to be at peace to avoid pain. Besides, the point is to look nice. This "letting it go" or forgiving predators and letting them glide away without any imprisonment or other punishment is an advanced form of a psychological artifact of our "New Age, no-fault, moral universe"—Hoffman's wonderful description of a culture, of the 1990s especially, in which there are no serious values.

Hoffman describes his dismay at seeing a play written by someone who carefully tracks the horrible psychological damage done to a young girl who's been raped. The playwright records her final claim that she absolutely forgives. "Forgives whom?" he asks. This wanting to feel healed or to be on the side of healing as opposed to being on the side of blaming lets predators live to rape another day.

The latter part of Hoffman's essay tells about some response he has received to his own writing,[14] in which he writes about being raped by his athletic coach. He received letters from people who were grateful because there are coaches out there whom no one dares speak about. Literature occasionally joins the escapist middle-class crowd in pretending that it's enough to *feel healing feelings* or to *feel forgiving feelings.* Those healing feelings are just that—they are *not* the psychological work of talking from appropriate rage. This false comfort of the once-raped person who scrabbles to keep in a healing mode for the rest of his or her life makes possible such rationalization and hiding and cover-ups as, Hoffman points out, the very word *pedophile*—or somebody who loves children—ought to be *pedoscela*—Latin conjunction *pedo* for children, and *scelus* meaning evil. Somebody who rapes children is not a lover but one who does evil to children. One of Hoffman's most salient points is: one cannot "forgive" a rapist who still says that he did it out of love. Hoffman says, "What is forgiveness if no one has acknowledged wrongdoing, nor asked for it, nor changed their conduct? What is forgiveness in the case of a serial offender preying upon the helpless? What if turning the other cheek is, in fact, offering up the next child?"[15] The pressure of what Hoffman calls our "no-fault, moral universe" is *not* to point, *not* to blame, *not* to judge, to let the predator go and then, finally, to write lyrical literature about it.

Writers should be willing to be sad if only in order not to dodge bad news. An overload of talk goes around our need to build self-esteem and to feel "comfortable with" such and such a circumstance, but the greatest nonfiction writers are the ones who are willing to put up with extremely uncomfortable, miserable thoughts, for days and weeks and years on end. Perhaps it will buck up our spirits to know that Goethe, Lincoln, Bismarck, Schumann, Tolstoy, Robert E. Lee, Martin Luther, Winston Churchill, and Virginia Woolf all suffered *major depression* in their lives.

Perhaps we should say the opposite of what women writers, perhaps men as well, are so constantly telling one another: "You are too hard on yourself." We are too *easy* on ourselves if we try to be happy and confident when the news is bad.

The following poem by Sid Gershgoren is the kind of writing that, like journal entries, helps the beginner—but it ought to be dropped later in favor of more complex subject matter. It reads beautifully, like angel scat, but it is too slight.

The full moon rising—
how slowly it punctuates
the gathering dark.

A man and his horse,
alone in the autumn field—
clouds and alfalfa.

Between the rainstorms,
in a sudden shaft of light—
confused butterflies.[16]

Such a poem helps beginners experience a moment's small flutter. That is a useful start for males who might think they shouldn't be writing anything delicate. Once an essayist or poet has been working for as long as a year, however, it is time to put his or her brains together. If there's doom to register somewhere, by then a grown writer should register it.

Falsifying What Could Otherwise Be Interesting Psychological Evidence about Homo Sapiens in One or Another Setting

History has much to show us about lying in memoirs.

There was no general use of psychology before the twentieth century. Even today, huge pockets of educated people are absolutely unconscious of how certain psychological dynamics work in themselves, in crowds, in anyone—and they are still less aware of how hopefully one can work with those dynamics. But once you consider some of the dynamics that make people go, it is like studying geology—the study of what makes the planet go—once you get hold of that excitement, you want truth and truth and truth. You can direct and redirect your own mind, changing values as you learn this or that truth, a little like the way we all change depths of idea in the writing process. You can actually change your inward habits, something like the way you can fire and refire your imagination by teaching it to make and test hypotheses.

It was one thing for Thoreau to lie about details in *Walden*: he didn't know that a century later people would passionately mull over how human beings can come to the principles he reached. We also would love to know what, if any, dynamics might have taken him even further. Like a literary traditionalist, Thoreau (and Herodotus long before him) knew the traditional means of getting one's idea across and moving the reader. These means included some tampering with the facts. He didn't leave us clean psychological history.

Let me give two specific examples of how our expectations are higher now because psychology, that baby art-cum-science, is here and growing to help us. Say that we want to research these two horrific, repetitive behavior problems in our species:

1. How is it that a remarkably small number of leaders or plotters can create a critical mass of people willing to implement genocide?
2. How many times must a normally intelligent human be exposed to evidence of Very Bad News before that person is impressed enough *to think about it*?

The first question has been and is being studied by the world's cadre of genocide scholars, such as Israel Charny, Robert J. Lifton, and Erik Markussen. Their findings are amazing and invaluable, even if most people have not yet heard of them. Let's look at the second question instead, since that one has to do with all of us.

Let's say a literary person keeps a journal and affects an interest in the question of how long a person can remain immune to suffering. She decides to visit Wannsee, a mansion where a conference was held at which Hitler and ranking Nazis worked out the Final Solution, now something of a specialty tourist site, like Dachau. This well-meaning memoirist flies to Berlin.

This topic was discussed on the America Online Writers' Club message board folder called "Integrity and Art in Fiction." This message board was the only one of all the AOL Writers' Club folders that was never craft-centered or commercially motivated. It was founded by Jerome Brooks deliberately to serve as a place for civil, literary discourse. Now and again, when a junk culture gets so strong that the intellectuals lose confidence, someone builds a tiny island, traditionally a little literary journal. Jerry Brooks, under his AOL name of Live2Write, did that with this folder. It lasted three years before rage addicts—fourteen-year-olds and alcoholics and other surfers—took to flaming through the AOL sites, leaving obscenities on the message boards, the way they were later to do on the Internet itself. Its three years were a gem of American literary discourse.

Before I present my contribution to the discussion, here is a synopsis of the Message Board so far: A Jungian therapist and author had made the suggestion that it is OK to adjust the truth here and there in memoir to conserve space, avoid repetition, and keep a simple cast of characters. These adjustments are usually called "conflation" and "composite characterization." Bearing in mind how wonderful it would be if we could figure out exactly how people get immunized from feeling much of anything about genocide, I posted the following response.

> If the memoirist has lied, then we haven't useful information we need. For example: let us say the memoirist said she went to Wannsee once and her life was changed by the horrors she felt and subsequently got proactive about. Wannsee is the mansion and estate outside Berlin where Hitler's people did a retreat in January, 1942, in which they decided formally on The Final Solution for Jews. Now, let's say that the memoirist actually, in truth, did what many people do: they go to a museum for a psychological horror history in that way, and they are mildly interested, even mildly disbelieving, the first time, but they go again. This time they have a kind of immunity to feeling horror. "So?" they say. "Things have always

> been tough all over, I mean, we can't f——cry all the time, life's too short. . . ." They pull out any number of other immune-response tools that I suppose are practical.
>
> Then someone drags them again to Wannsee—and there it is. They feel it. They feel us all as a species in a planet who must, please, somehow learn to get smart about our minds and have mercy on each other.
>
> But it took *three* trips. For the sake of psychological history we need to *know* it took exactly three visits there if that's what it took. Not *one*. So we know that particular denial-cum-nondenial pattern. So we forgive ourselves for being hard-nosed if we ourselves have been hard-nosed about something. So we look askance at ourselves right now—if we are traveling to see some artifact—and belay our cool; so we say to ourselves, "This particular thing doesn't seem to move me much—but I should bide some time—because I may be defending against it."
>
> So I am for truth, inch by inch. Change the hair color, yes, tell the reader you are changing names—but otherwise stay with the truth. But there is a very strong movement not to stay with the truth and it has a lot of promoters.[17]

In summary, on bending truth to make a fact denser, more accessible, or prettier: that wasn't so wrong to do before exact truth had the psychological value it has now. But in the twenty-first century, when we know the tremendous value of exactitude, fudging memoir details is like dipping a computer into a river to make it shine.

There have been outbreaks of opinion about the lying in American nonfiction.

A case of lying serving to weaken the document is written up by Celia Dugger in her *New York Times Book Review* article entitled "Fatal Abuse," in which she's reviewing *The Book of David: How Preserving Families Can Cost Children's Lives*, by Richard J. Gelles. Celia Dugger says:

> Mr. Gelles has also sapped his argument of much of its power and its credibility because David's case, the heart of the book,

> is actually a "composite." Mr. Gelles begins with the boy to whom he gives the pseudonym David Edwards, but adulterates his story with facts from other cases of children killed by their parents or caretakers. He also alters facts about the boy's parents and grandparents, as well as clinicians' descriptions of the case.
>
> He says these changes are necessary to protect the privacy of the people involved, though he does not explain why this should be true in the case of a mother sentenced in a public trial to 30 years in prison, all but four of them suspended, for killing her son. The decision to tamper with the facts effectively denies his readers the ability to evaluate the case on which he has built the "children first" policies he promotes. It also deprives his story of much of its human drama. The death of a composite child is not as moving as the death of a real one.[18]

Readers rightly feel bruised and condescended to when an author lies to them. Here is the comment of a psychotherapist on a book by Marsha Aldrich, *Girl Rearing*. The psychotherapist posted her remarks in the AOL Online Writers' Club message board folder called "Integrity and Art in Fiction":

> Today I went to a bookstore in search of a "memoir" written by a professor at Michigan State University where I may be moving soon. I thought I'd see what's there in terms of published writers. Marsha Aldrich, *Girl Rearing*—newish book, lovely writings as far as I could tell from skimming. But what put me off enough not to buy the book was a brief note at the beginning that while much of the book [her life story growing up in the 50s] is true, she added both fictitious characters and events. I had heard that this was done so why am I put off? Occupational/moral hazard, because as a therapist my main purpose is to discover the "truth" in people's stories? Moral purity because I like and value truth?
>
> But here's the thing; what is "memoir" then and what is fiction?[19]

Let me quickly dispatch the question of *inadvertent lying* in literature.

Of course there is inadvertent lying. Often, in our present-day climate of memoir—in which "anything goes"—when I insist we authors mustn't lie, some people reply in a sage tone: "Yeah, but you can't tell the truth anyway. Nobody remembers anything right."

Of course, we do remember a good deal wrong. There will likely always be blunders made in recording the past. I recently published a short memoir in which I got two major facts wrong. I was therefore delighted to read in William Manchester's three-volume biography of Winston Churchill that Churchill remembered totally wrongly how familiar he was with what Hitler was doing in 1929, 1930, 1931, and 1932. At the time, Churchill was researching Hitler's activity on his own. Unlike most English statesmen, he had read *Mein Kampf*. He was extremely interested in and frightened by Hitler's goals. But Manchester reports:

> In his [Winston Churchill's] World War II memoirs he wrote of his stay in Munich, shortly before the Nazis came to power, "I had no national prejudice against Hitler at that time. I knew little of his doctrine or record and nothing of his character" but that is an astonishing lapse of memory. By then he had been well informed about Hitler for two years, had published several appraisals of him, and had repeatedly warned the House of the imminent threat in central Europe.[20]

Here is another, more gratifying instance of bad memory in an otherwise reliable, experienced journalist:

> Vernon Bartlett, a British journalist with a large following, spent forty minutes in Hitler's study. Afterward he wrote of his host's "large, brown eyes—so large and so brown that one might grow lyrical about them if one were a woman." Actually, Hitler's eyes were blue.[21]

Deliberate falsehood is as different from false statement made through bad memory, however, as is deliberately shoving someone versus accidentally bumping into someone. To argue that you may as well lie in memoirs because you will make some mistakes anyhow is like saying you might as well give someone a good satisfying shove since you might have collided with him or her anyhow.

Hatred of Literature by Those Left Out of It and Sometimes by Those of Us Who Participate in It

Hating any kind of feeling or thinking slightly more elegant than your own has been observed most famously by Nietzsche and given a name—*ressentiment*—for how it plays out in matters of social class.

Here's an example from my own life: at fourteen I went away to school in Massachusetts to be surrounded by fourteen-year-olds who had been to country day schools. Not only could they play musical instruments; they knew how to *work* at music. They could concentrate. As I dragged back and forth between the enforced study halls and Draper Hall, a dissonance of sounds from pianos flung down from the third-floor practice rooms. Some of my classmates could even itemize, from the French plays we had to read, evidence of the differing temperaments of Corneille and Racine.

I became a living individual case of what Toynbee would have called a culture that experienced too great a challenge to manage. My feelings ran at two levels—the bottom being a vapid, filthy sludge of resentment and fear overlaid by an equally powerful, opposite current, which was excitement and gratitude for getting my first shot at the thinking life. I was in danger, like Schiller's man (described in the discussion that follows), of shrinking back from using willpower to live a meaningful life. I see this same phenomenon in some writing students who are held back, inside themselves, as if by a weir under the surface.

I find it amazing that Schiller could at the beginning of the nineteenth century see behavior so clearly from the *psychological* side, instead of from the outwardly ordered systems outlook. Because most writers nowadays won't come across his insights, here is a passage specifically about the psychological artifact we can call *hatred of whoever fulfills more of our human potential than we ourselves even reach for.* I suggest that by far the best way to read Schiller is to remember all the time that he is talking in terms of psychological dynamics, not about the big draw in his day, called reason. He wrote about how people's feelings delimit their insights for a while—how they stay stuck at some nihilistic idea for ages and ages—and how being nihilistic comes naturally to us. Schiller was a man of his time, so he used the word *reason* the way Greeks did, for what *we* now think of as realistic, open-minded, open-systems approaches to how systems interact and change one another as they grow. I suggest you read his core passages, like the one I quote here, not thinking "reason" but thinking "psychological confidence enough to have a philosophy." That should help keep you clear of postmodernists' knee-jerk discounting of eighteenth-century idealism.

A handy way to think of the man Schiller describes is to see him in front of a television set. Imagine him as a fellow who has received almost no instruction except the influence of the U.S.A. junk culture. If he once went to Sabbath or Sunday school, he may have heard some abstract concepts named, but they were not much discussed. Now he is twenty-five and he has forgotten them. He doesn't regret losing them. No one ever said that church and school talk had anything to do with real life. From the TV he hears only flattery. The Buds are for him for what he does. If he does nothing, that's good enough. Figure this way for this American: no one has ever said to him, "Bestir yourself."

Here Schiller tries to think through what's going on inside this person that blocks him and blocks him.

> Unacquainted as yet with his own human dignity, he is far from respecting it in others; and, conscious of his own savage greed he fears it in every creature which resembles him. He never sees others in himself, but only himself in others; and communal life, far from enlarging him into a representative of the species, only confines him ever more narrowly within his own individuality.[22]
>
> . . . But even if Reason does not mistake its objective and confuse the question, Sense will for a long time falsify the answer. As soon as man has begun to use his intellect, and to connect the phenomena around him in the relation of cause and effect, Reason, in accordance with its very definition,

presses for an absolute connexion and an unconditioned cause. In order to be able to postulate such a demand at all, man must already have taken a step beyond mere sense; but it is this very demand that Sense now makes use of to recall her truant child. This, strictly speaking, would be the point at which he ought to leave the world of sense altogether, and soar upwards to the realm of pure ideas; for the intellect remains eternally confined within the realm of the conditioned, and goes on eternally asking questions without ever lighting upon any ultimate answer. But since the man with whom we are here concerned is not yet capable of such abstraction, that which he cannot find in his sphere of empirical knowledge, and does not yet seek beyond it in the sphere of pure Reason, he will seek beneath it in his sphere of feeling and, to all appearances, find it. True, this world of sense shows him nothing which might be its own cause and subject to none but its own law; but it does show him something which knows of no cause and obeys no law. Since, then, he cannot appease his inquiring intellect by evoking any ultimate and inward cause, he manages at least to silence it with the notion of no-cause, and remains within the blind compulsion of Matter since he is not yet capable of grasping the sublime necessity of Reason. Because the life of sense knows no purpose other than its own advantage, and feels driven by no cause other than blind chance, he makes the former into the arbiter of his actions and the latter into the sovereign ruler of the world.

. . . Even what is most sacred in man, the moral law, when it first makes its appearance in the life of sense, cannot escape such perversion. Since its voice is merely inhibitory, and against the interest of his animal self-love, it is bound to seem like something external to himself as long as he has not yet reached the point of regarding his self-love as the thing that is really external to him, and the voice of reason as his true self. Hence he merely feels the fetters which reason lays upon him, not the infinite liberation which she is capable of affording him.[23]

If we are writers we should recognize those periods when we are tipping between hatred of literature and longing for it. We might have to dive into ourselves and break from something that has us stuck.

Still, all hatred of literature or philosophy is by no means the pathetic effect of cultural deprivation. Some hatred of literature is *deserved.* I mentioned earlier so many beginning writers' tendency to *point at* some vexed subject *but fail to elucidate it*—the process I called "pointing and ducking."

I have always actively disliked about three-fourths of the poems that have come my way. It has never been politically correct to say one disliked most poetry, so I kept that dislike more or less to myself. The 1960s California culture with its swampy tolerance gave us a correct way to talk about art one didn't much like. It was all right to say, "I don't get into poetry," or "I don't do poetry," which was even better until the phrase got worn out. The criticism, if there was any, was of oneself for not doing poetry.

Eventually I realized what particular quality I so disliked: it was poets' pointing and ducking. The poet mentions some scene or people or place and indicates that it is of great moment, but never tells us what it is all about. I would not blame anyone for being antiliterature or hopelessly middle-class for disliking the following poem by Patricia Hooper.

THE STATUES

Imagine for a moment we are in
a garden:
        wasn't there
a place like this in which
we used to walk, the trees
so undisturbed, the flowers
almost motionless, and where
it seemed that time was stilled?

And the statues—weren't they
always about to move
their perfect fingers, touch
each other's arms?

There was a river, yes,
but it was out of sight
beyond the pond,

and fountains that were filled
once only, since their water
fell to the shallow pool
and was returned.

The gods, you said, referring
to the statues. Yes,
we stood among them once,
not of them but apart
from time which kept on passing
somewhere else,

the place where we'd return.
Was it because
we met so seldom there that we were given
a moment's presence large enough
to hold us?

        Or was it
because there would be no future
that we were held?[24]

This issue was discussed earlier in the chapter, with Sid Gershgoren offered up as sacrifice. I mention it here because there's ethical, as well as aesthetic fallout to such poetry.

When poets and nonfiction writers deliberately write coded verse for themselves, they are making literature utterly indifferent to ordinary men and women. A culture can bear any amount of private-hobby literature, I expect, but student writers should be conscious of these issues: will I be an artist of only my own private occasions? Will I write with the corner of my eye upon the res publica?

A Psychological Tool for Ethically Minded Writers

Every kind of writing has its particular ways of boring readers. I happen to hate pretty writing on nostalgic subjects worse than the relentless thud of moral writing, but moral writing can be so boring that tears squeeze out of any reader's eyes.

A cure: instead of falling for the conventional wisdom of taking every argument to its logical extreme, let's look at the logical extreme, so to speak, and then take the argument back, away from the logical extreme, and *toward the middle range* of life. For example, let's not look at a bully and then theorize (aloud or to ourselves) that that kind of bullying, "taken to its logical extreme," ends up as genocide by Hutus and Tutsis or genocide by Yugoslavians or genocide by anyone. Instead, let's read about the Hutus and Tutsis and Yugoslavians and look for small samplings nearby, within our own range. Just this one practice can keep us clear of a good deal of conversational generalizing.

For one thing, as Edward Hoagland says of ordinary, low-key life, most of us live in the middle range. We are not torn up by the gigantic passions of *Anna Karenina* and *War and Peace.* We live in what Hoagland calls "stasis." Most people's lives go on, not moving much, generally staying the same.

Hoagland's comments help us to avoid grandiosity, but they still leave open the chance for us to take such huge human circumstances as do move us when we hear of them (like genocide) and see if their sad or brilliant scatter falls *in any small way on our range of life.*

Taking events to the middle range, instead of to the logical extremes, gives us a way to base our nonfiction or poetry upon our own lives yet to keep our work lit by huge events that have transpired elsewhere. This particular practice alone can save us from turning out diurnal, provincial drivel. All we have to do, for starters, is ask, Do any of the great happenings of history and science come to rest in my fields or my apartment building?

In his poem "The Groundhog" Richard Eberhart seems to say, "All that I have to work with here is the corpse of a groundhog and the fact that I am not a particularly inspiring professor at Harvard. Does anything great rightly apply?"

Eberhart's poem is so perfect an example of honestly putting large meaning into the perspective of *middle-range life* that I offer it to non-fiction writers as an ideal model. It's odd how Eberhart uses such an elegant, modern, passionate psychological logic in this poem. Other poems of his don't show it, but this one does.

Notice that he never claims great human passions for himself. He doesn't claim to "relate to" the big stuff. Yet knowing it's out there has filled his heart.

THE GROUNDHOG

In June, amid the golden fields,
I saw a groundhog lying dead.
Dead lay he; my senses shook,
And mind outshot our naked frailty.
There lowly in the vigorous summer
His form began its senseless change,
And made my senses waver dim
Seeing nature ferocious in him.
Inspecting close his maggots' might
And seething cauldron of his being,
Half with loathing, half with a strange love,
I poked him with an angry stick.
The fever arose, became a flame
And Vigour circumscribed the skies,
Immense energy in the sun,
And through my frame a sunless trembling.
My stick had done nor good nor harm.
Then stood I silent in the day
Watching the object, as before;
And kept my reverence for knowledge
Trying for control, to be still,
To quell the passion of the blood;
Until I had bent down on my knees
Praying for joy in the sight of decay.
And so I left, and I returned
In Autumn strict of eye, to see

The sap gone out of the groundhog,
But the bony sodden hulk remained.
But the year had lost its meaning,
And in intellectual chains
I lost both love and loathing,
Mured up in the wall of wisdom.
Another summer took the fields again
Massive and burning, full of life,
But when I chanced upon the spot
There was only a little hair left,
And bones bleaching in the sunlight
Beautiful as architecture;
I watched them like a geometer,
And cut a walking stick from a birch.
It has been three years now.
There is no sign of the groundhog.
I stood there in the whirling summer,
My hand capped a withered heart,
And thought of China and of Greece,
Of Alexander in his tent;
Of Montaigne in his tower,
Of Saint Theresa in her wild lament.[25]

Writing Creative Nonfiction for the 400,000

Here is a way to keep from feeling whacked one way, then the other way, now by the market-wise advisors, now by the holy-ground advisors—the first saying anyone is a fool who doesn't identify his or her market and then write for it, and the second saying that the very process of identifying a market and writing for it shuts down the best sites of your brain: figure that you are a person with a meaningful outlook and a certain taste in literary work. Your proper audience is others like yourself. If you write for yourself, you are writing for them.

People who live in major cities aren't depressed by that idea because they feel the presence in all those square lighted windows of so many millions that surely among those millions, for example 7 million in Manhattan alone, it's a sane guess that at least 400,000 of them have your very tastes. They can't all become writers, so we must write for them. Edith Wharton, in the poem quoted in Chapter 5, said we should write on behalf of the dead. In the same sense, since they can't do it, we have to write for the living, too, without lying or letting ourselves get frivolous.

We are probably not so original as we suppose ourselves to be. There likely really are 400,000 others like any one of us. Let us say that everything that we know so far about the brain suggests that each human being wants to work up to a kind of General Theory of Everything. If this is true, those 400,000 people who are like us will want to read our particular theory of everything because it may be theirs too, and they won't get around to writing it down for themselves.

If out of sloth or lack of confidence, we write only bits and pieces of sensory impressions, we won't have done as much as an essayist can do. If out of cunning or greed we choose some larger market than our 400,000 and lie to attract that larger market, we won't have done as much as an essayist can do. But if we stick with a plan to stay awake to our own ideas and our own strongest feelings, then everything we write will be lighted by every other thing in our minds.

The Appendices

Appendix I

Fifteen Writing Exercises

There are already dozens of splendid writing exercises in print. Most are designed to waken the memory or to give beginning writers confidence in their own life stories.

I have a different purpose for the sixteen exercises presented here. Each exercise emphasizes either moving from idea to sense impression, or the reverse—moving from sensory experience to one's inner judgments. The idea is that when consciousness and imagination are brought together, the most subtle and long-lasting literature results.

Under that concept lies another one: it is that Homo sapiens has an innate propensity for pulling consciousness and imagination together. The moment we say to ourselves, whether grimly or gladly, "I want to *write*," we begin to warm ourselves at the firings of our own minds. Those flaring neighborhoods want nothing so much as to connect this particular given moment with hundreds of our previous impressions.

These exercises are designed to help us do it.

Four Exercises about Background or Place

1. Writing without Clichés about a Beautiful Place
2. Ugly Place, Good Event: Ugly Event, Good Place
3. Pathetically Shallow Use of Places Once Full of Serious Enterprise
4. Paying Respectful Attention to Background Settings

Easy Exercises

5. Good and Terrible Qualities in Human Nature—An Exercise for People over the Age of Fourteen
6. Ignatow Poem Exercise
7. A Catty Vignette
8. An Essay Pot—A Group *Talking* Exercise
9. Writing about Work

Elegant Exercises

10. Attending to Other—Specifically, Attending to Relatives, Nonhuman Creatures, or Plants
11. Increasing One's Affection for Utterly Ordinary People
12. A Writing Exercise for Extroverts
13. An Irritating Person Exercise
14. A Nearly Impossible Writing Exercise
15. The Andover Format

Exercise 1: Writing without Clichés about a Beautiful Place

No one need respond to all eight suggestions below. Mosey through them to see which one or more might bring up your feeling about one or another place. Then decide on a place to write about. The suggestions might help you think beneath the usual scenic remarks. Keep clear of anything the local chamber of commerce would say about your place.

1. It's best to leave out how you came to this place unless the reason is unusual. Perhaps you did not mean to come to it, but a relation begged you to—or you became aware of your mortality, wanted some time off from your usual thoughts, and chose this beautiful place. One of Chekhov's most vivid vignettes is about a man's wife having insisted they go to the country for a break. That story is the definitive tale in the genre of Horrible Vacations Planned by Others.
2. Who are the other present inhabitants of your beautiful place? Sometimes thinking about who else is around in a beautiful place may remind you about social class issues and animal populations.
3. Who are the past inhabitants of your beautiful place?
4. The geology or astronomy of the beautiful place: for example, 45 degrees north latitude, 72+ degrees west longitude . . . what is overhead at this time of year . . . planets, comets, dust, what rags of ozone remain to us?
5. Thoughts about your *own* life that this place wakes up in you.
6. What would be the *aesthetic* ideal future for this place?
7. What would be the *moral* ideal future for this place? In his essay "The Courage of Turtles," Edward Hoagland observes turtles with great focus. Hoagland has his sympathies for this creature so like a machine "with the governor set low." Yet he always bears human behavior in mind. It is we who drain turtles' swamps. It is we who imprison them in shallow, dry drawers, and sell them on the streets in New York. Like Goldfinger, people paint turtles, causing their deaths. A spacious essayist like Hoagland stays on task—here, turtles—but speaks from several worlds. And without the statesman's

posturing. He doesn't keep the high ground himself in the end; Hoagland dropped a turtle overside in water too deep. There likely are thousands of Marcus Aureliuses for every Hoagland willing to confess to ineptitude.

When we want to write an essay about a beautiful place, we can get dense models from poetry. Unless the poet is a liar, he or she has the same mission as the creative-nonfiction writer: to make vivid some personal sense impression and then let it sink to its hidden or slant truths. Poets are handy to learn from because their means of getting to hidden truths is metaphor. Metaphor is much faster showing than meditative prose.

A. E. Housman is best known for despising middle-aged army officers who smile at the doomed eighteen-year-olds before sending them over the top in the usual hopeless World War I infantry assault. But Housman wrote beautifully about the "woodland rides" full of cherry blossoms. His heart was *complex*. His description of cherry trees in bloom is better than most nature writing because Housman pulls in his own dread of death. He has lightly feathered it into his admiration of the white blooms. He had a literary and gutsy versatility. Versatility, in this case, means keeping major delight and major dread in the same poem without either diluting the other.

8. For ourselves then: say that we are out-of-doors in Vermont. A half-century has gone by since Mengele did his work in Germany. Years have passed even since the executives of Texaco made their famous racist sneers in a meeting. All three knowledges are in our brains: our present knowledge that the sky is still and chilled with snow; our past knowledge that we have not yet solved the problem of human beings enjoying hurting others; and our recent awareness that we have not yet found a way to teach those who love jeering and superiority to derive pleasure from something else instead.

Well, there is no law that says an essayist writing about a beautiful place need mention anything but the night full of snow in Vermont.

At our most generous, however, we essayists have something in common with radio operators in the shipping lanes at sea: we listen in our heads for every coded message. We know that if there were ever icebergs close by, icebergs will come again.

Exercise 2: Ugly Place, Good Event: Ugly Event, Good Place

The photography director of the film *Dr. Zhivago* had to insist, over much resistance, that painful scenes occur in beautiful places. He wanted to show the beautiful, huge white steppe with the white sky behind it. Suddenly black figures show up. They shoot one another, leaving young Russians, either Whites or Reds, lying dead in the snow.

One of the qualities of literature that I most admire is authors' carrying off two things at once—having so much passion about themselves or a given subject, yet making grateful observations of beauty around them at the same time. Authors can set an ugly action in an ecstatic place—or they can show members of our particular species feeling ecstatic or being courageous or virtuous in utterly indifferent or even outright ugly places.

This writing exercise asks you to set either a good event in an ugly or sad place, or chintzy or bad behavior in a beautiful place.

Exercise 3: Pathetically Shallow Use of Places Once Full of Serious Enterprise

One of the most important lessons for writers to learn is not to boast. It is especially hard for creative nonfiction writers not to boast. We tend to insist (because we believe it) that we ourselves are more sensitive, more observant, more open to the holiness of things than others. Well, what is wrong with feeling that we are more sensitive, more observant, and more open to holiness, and so forth, if we actually are? Here is the reason: such confidence is too much confidence. It blinds a person to the surprising depths of other people and to the greater significance of places other than the places we know.

Droves of Germans and Americans and French people drag themselves through the Russian Orthodox churches of Moscow and St. Petersburg. Many—not all—of their faces droop from tedium. Our feet hurt. If God meant, or still means, this much to the people going through with this old-style mass, He doesn't mean that much to some of us visitors. We long to listen to rock music back in the tour bus. We felt wistful when we heard the driver turn up the volume the very moment we left the bus. The driver didn't have to go into this church. We guess we aren't sorry that we chose to go on this tour to Russia but hey, I mean, it can get to be too much. I mean, OK, so Ivan the Terrible was terrible, but that was then and this is now.

We do not feel free to reveal our real feelings about old churches and old castles and the great rivers, with their empty vodka bottles floating past our boat. We feel we are supposed to *want* to see the great places of the world. But what if, in fact, we would much, much rather get home and for once get on top and *stay* on top of the dandelion situation in the lawn?

We may not *always* have lightweight emotions, but sometimes we have. At those times, we do not make the eternal connections to great places. Chekhov made dozens of his stories on the basis that some people are simply too shallow for the settings in which they find themselves. One can't really blame them.

Describe some place where great or infamous history was made that means very, very little to you. If Ivan the Terrible murdered all those people, ordering it, what's more, to be done slowly, forcing clergymen to watch the rackings because he enjoyed making clergymen cry, but go on eating crow, well, what are we supposed to do about it?

Describe a place like that—or describe any true occasion on which you yourself were too slack to *get* it.

This could be called *seriously* taking the low ground. An odd dynamic of deliberately confessing to having a banal personality is that, while doing it, out of the corner of your mind's eye, you may catch a glint off some bright coal in your mind's firing. I never count on it, though.

Exercise 4: Paying Respectful Attention to Background Settings

Whether we are writing essays or story, our narrative will have more life if we give account of some minor, background aspects—the setting, certainly, but also the mere *stage business* of the people being talked about.

Very simple example:

1. *No background.* The mother lion lay on her elbows, jaw hanging open. She was saving up strength for the night's hunt.
2. *With background business.* The mother lion lay on her elbows, jaw hanging open, saving up strength for the night's hunt. She and the two others had made a concerted stalk during the hottest hour of the day. In the end, one of the other lionesses had sprung too soon. They all three made off as fast as they could, but the zebra easily outran them. What divides the women from the girls is to have your nose trembling with the fragrance of zebra, but you must hold back, control, control . . . simply stalk. If you know you can only do a one-hundred-meter spurt, you must resist the impulse to leap too soon.

   Gradually the air cooled. The mother lion began to feel hopeful and businesslike again.

Here is a first-rate example, a passage by the mystery writer Freeman Wills Crofts, in *The 12.30 from Croyden.*[1] In this novel, Charles, a hard-pressed owner of an engineering firm, has successfully murdered his uncle for the inheritance. Charles has survived several police questionings, and every day he feels a little more normal. The police seem at last to have faded away, likely looking elsewhere for their man. Crofts first tells us that something exciting and horrible will happen, but *then* he goes into a quite bland description of Charles's ordinary if unpleasant business day, followed by a privileged male's evening, and only after that does Crofts get back to the main horror.

> Then one evening a dreadful and totally unexpected blow fell.
>
> Charles had had a tiresome day at the works. Owing to the nondelivery of certain materials an important job had been

held up and it looked as if it could not be completed in contract time. Everyone was working at high pressure and worry and frayed nerves were the result. Charles had brought home with him the relevant papers, intending during the evening to draft out a statement of his claim against the defaulting contractor. The matter was not straightforward, and he foresaw trouble and possible litigation.

Charles dined and read the evening paper while he smoked a leisurely cigar. Then about nine he settled down with his papers in the study.

He had the faculty of concentration. Soon he drafted out the main heads of his argument and then turned to give the detailed proof of each. He got on better than he had hoped, and at ten o'clock he thought that another half-hour should see him through.

A few minutes later he heard the rolling sound of a car and a ring at the door. Charles listened to Rollins passing down the hall. Then came the murmur of voices. There were heavy steps and the study door opened. Rollins announced, "Superintendent Lucas and Inspector French."

One glance at their faces told Charles that his hour had come. Both looked grave and troubled.

Exercise: Write about a certain intense situation, no matter what, but take time somewhere in the writing to give us some calm, mildly interesting, *minor business.*

Exercise 5: Good and Terrible Qualities in Human Nature— An Exercise for People over the Age of Fourteen

This is an essayist's *psychological* exercise, nothing fancy. The idea is this: everyone likely has four thousand more strong feelings and ideas than we stay in touch with. We are so used to living lightly in the everyday world—we are so used to naming only a few of the most obvious of our emotions—that we forget how many things we hate and love. Most people doing this exercise for the first time go into a fog after about the eleventh or twelfth item. That's *it,* they feel sure. But if they can keep themselves from scoffing and going for jokes, they will find the other twenty-five values, amazingly. Be sure to include both evil and good things on your list.

1. Please write a simple list of the thirty-six (or ten, or five; see the discussion of adolescent use of this exercise in Chapter 9, "Helping People in Middle and High School Learn to Write") most important abstract things of life. Explain them each in a sentence or two. Important: stay serious. Do not try to have fun with this exercise. Don't list Cheez-Its as a good thing. Don't list frayed dental floss as a bad thing. Be heavy-duty with this writing.
2. Now choose one of the thirty-six things to write a paragraph about. Please set it in a place. Please remember that you are trying to tell your readers about something they are utterly ignorant of. Assume that your readers are intelligent enough but weren't *there.* Unless you tell us, we can't be sure whether your experience was in Lofoten, Paris, or Little Walden, Essex.
3. Once you've done getting your paragraph down, go back over it all and take out any phrases or stereotypes you've heard before. Take out any ideas you picked up on television. (For example, if you heard someone on TV sounding off against U.S. sanctions against Iraq, but you honestly haven't any feeling about it one way or the other, don't enter "U.S. sanctions against Iraq" as a value on your list.) Replace any stale language you can spot. Then read your paper aloud to yourself. Various smart loci in your brain may now like to weigh in with other amendments. This gives you a marvelous chance to adjust your paper, to re-envision it, so that it is more like you and less like the work of just anyone drifting around the neighborhood.

Exercise 6: Ignatow Poem Exercise

This exercise is first-rate for shy people who are not used to hearing poetry or reading it—never mind hearing their own voices recite it. The purpose is to give people a chance to hear their own voice on a major subject. I have used this exercise with large groups of social workers, large groups of psychotherapists, and summer groups of writers—all those people who are wonderfully eager to think but are inexperienced in writing.

They are not used to reading poems and simply relaxing while listening. They certainly are not in the habit of reciting poems. They're not used to that slight *formality* one must muster to recite a poem. Hearing their own voices recite anything so formal as a poem helps them. It gives them confidence.

I ask them first to listen to me when I recite David Ignatow's extraordinary, beautiful poem called "Above Everything."

ABOVE EVERYTHING

I wished for death often
but now that I am at its door
I have changed my mind about the world.
It should go on; it is beautiful,
even as a dream, filled with water and seed,
plants and animals, others like myself,
ships and buildings and messages
filling the air—a beauty,
if ever I have seen one.
In the next world, should I remember
this one, I will praise it
above everything.[2]

I read the poem all the way through. Then I pass out copies. The class members have, often for the first time, a good poem in their hands. I urge people to memorize it. They never do, but I go on urging.

Next, they receive a copy called "*From* Above Everything" in which lines 6–8 of Ignatow's poem are missing. I ask each person to write their own three or four lines to fill that middle section.

FROM ABOVE EVERYTHING

I wished for death often
but now that I am at its door
I have changed my mind about the world.
It should go on; it is beautiful,
even as a dream, filled with

—a beauty,
if ever I have seen one.
In the next world, should I remember
this one, I will praise it
above everything.

When the group is large, I ask volunteers to go to the midaisle mikes. They are to read, all of a piece, David Ignatow's poem except for lines 6–8, with their own inserted lines fed in.

When the group is sixteen or fewer, I ask everyone to read in turn, without pause or comment between readers.

They hear their own thought then, given a boost from David's sound. They see both how hard it is to write a poem and how easy it is to write a poem. They notice, often for the first time, how a poet chooses carefully what to say. David Ignatow prinked a little. He said that the dream he was talking about was filled with water and seed, plants and animals, and others like himself, and ships and buildings and messages filling the air. That aggregate is more interesting than what most of us think of.

When I've given this assignment to social work conferences for attendees to read aloud, long lines of nondesignated poets have come up to the mikes. We listen to them all, an endearing quality of social workers being that they will listen without showing boredom or irritability. They tend to agree, by the dozens, that the world should go on. It *is* beautiful, even as a dream, filled with the beauty of small children, new babies, the world in spring, flowers, trees, and new lovers. They are right. All those things are beautiful.

But in the end, I ask them to go back to David's poem and to see how strange his selection of stuff is—the air full of messages—isn't that strange? Very strange. Then I ask people, if they're willing to take four minutes to revise their own three or four lines in the middle, to have another go at it. See if they can make their writing less general. If it is a creative-writing retreat of more than one day, I ask volunteers to read their first version again, the one the class heard the day before, and then to read their second version. Everyone then sees how one can narrow and sharpen and focus—the job of people who want to write literature.

The social workers generally refuse to revise their stereotypes (newborn babies) and generalities (spring, birth) because well-worn language is the professional, nonthreatening medium of social work. It suits the practice. Social workers have to be so alert to a thousand human subtleties as clients talk to them. And clients are constantly talking to them. I never press social workers to fidget about fresh language.

It is apparently wonderful for all kinds of people to hear their voices reading aloud without hurry, with deliberation, with long, strong sound. By hearing their own words set in among David Ignatow's, they feel bolstered and collegial with this good poet who is serious about life.

Of course, a few people scorn this particular exercise. Perhaps there is always, in any field, a contingent who feel that only a professional cadre is entitled to practice the work of that profession—for example, creative writing. In those snobs' view, all nonprofessionals should just sit and watch. They are not allowed to pray, but they must sit nicely in church.

Exercise 7: A Catty Vignette

Sometimes a class or group of writers clearly droops. The students are sick of careful reflection and artful craft. Then I ask them to write a catty vignette. Life pours back into their faces. And once, actually, an intelligent woman who was a Minneapolis entrepreneur of consequence grabbed the exercise handout and said, "OK, *this* I can do!" and dashed out of the room.

This is a completely secular exercise. It has no high purpose. It doesn't necessarily connect up the brain's various neighborhoods full of elegant ideas with this very moment's sense impressions. Writing gossip, no matter how pungently, does not help one develop one's philosophy. If anything, it gives us a moment of jazzy regression: a minute ago we were mulling over something philosophical and useful but now that we are asked to write "A Catty Vignette" we go back to our old thirteen-year-old selves. We think up some mean remarks describing some other thirteen-year-old who makes up her eyelids so she looks like a scary national border crossing.

But there's an occasional use to doing a piece of writing that is *worthless but exact* (not just that we might mine it later).

I learned this indirectly from a psychotherapist. I thought of this psychotherapist, whose name was Chris, as a professional who was saving my life and other people's lives with her wise, unegotistical, constantly attentive skills. I battened on her well-timed confrontations, her interventions with injustices, and so forth. I associated all she said with the high ground.

One day Chris said, "Well, once a month I never really get out of bed." I asked, "What do you mean you don't get out of bed?" She said, "No, the fact is I leave my pajamas on all day, and I'm lucky if I say anything civil to anybody. I don't answer the phone. I drink a lot of coffee, and I take a few naps during the course of the day. I take a nap in the morning, and I may just take another one in the afternoon. I don't read anything any good either. It's a day off," she said. She added thoughtfully, "Yup, I take a day to fuck off."

Curious that she deliberately did this blasphemy—deliberate shallow use of a day—and used U.S.A. junk slang to describe it, too, my mind came up with three or four responses straight off. For starters, I took her down off the pedestal of Awesome Guru. Apparently she was not a guru since she didn't do the guru thing of languorous-but-sedulous-self-congratulation. She was willing to look utterly ordinary. My mind settled back, like Alice gotten too big to squeeze through the tiny door. Too bad. Like Alice, however, my mind landed on the solution. (Alice happened on the little bottle that said, "Drink me," that would shrink her.) My solution was threefold.

1. People may well be the wiser for being part-time slobs.
2. People need to give up forever that pleasure called loving one's leader. Especially writers need to get past followership.
3. The slight heartbreak one feels when a charismatic leader turns out to be either part-liar or part-slob is a good ambiance for writing literature. Slight heartbreak—the general terrain of it, like a field of talus we had once taken for a stunning mountain—is perfect landscape for the middle stage of working on any manuscript.

Every so often a creative nonfiction group needs to squat foursquare on some low ground. Vignettes are the perfect narrative form for essays in any case. Nowhere does our own temperament, whatever it is, show better than in a vignette. We can't hide it in rhetoric.

George Orwell and Jane Austen do catty vignettes so differently that I offer one of each here. First, here is George Orwell presenting an appalling working-class boardinghouse in Lancashire mining country:

> Partly blocking the door of the larder there was a shapeless sofa upon which Mrs. Brooker, our landlady, lay permanently ill, festooned in grimy blankets. She had a big, pale yellow, anxious face. No one knew for certain what was the matter with her; I suspect that her only real trouble was over-eating. In front of the fire there was almost always a line of damp washing, and in the middle of the room was the big kitchen table at which the family and all the lodgers ate. I never saw this table completely uncovered, but I saw its various wrappings at different times. At the bottom there was a layer of old newspaper stained by Worcestershire Sauce; above that a sheet of sticky white oil-cloth; above that a green serge cloth;

> above that a coarse linen cloth, never changed and seldom taken off. Generally the crumbs from breakfast were still on the table at supper. I used to get to know individual crumbs by sight and watch their progress up and down the table from day to day.[3]

In Jane Austin's *Sense and Sensibility*, an inconsiderate man holds up the line in a retail jewelry shop:

> [T]he Miss Dashwoods found so many people before them in the room that there was not a person of liberty to attend to their orders; and they were obliged to wait. All that could be done was to sit down at the end of the counter which seemed to promise the quickest succession; one gentleman only was standing there, and it is probable that Elinor was not without hope of exciting his politeness to a quicker dispatch. But the correctness of his eye and the delicacy of his taste proved to be beyond his politeness. He was giving orders for a toothpick-case for himself, and till its size, shape, and ornaments were determined, all of which, after examining and debating for a quarter of an hour over every toothpick-case in the shop, were finally arranged by his own inventive fancy, he had no leisure to bestow any other attention to the two ladies than what was comprised in three or four very broad stares; a kind of notice which served to imprint on Elinor the remembrance of a person and face of strong, natural, sterling insignificance, though adorned in the first style of fashion.[4]

I am charmed that both George Orwell and Jane Austen despise slobs. We puzzle so much about this or that moral *value*, when moral *taste* is frequently more engaging. For example, both Austen and Orwell would prefer the Pink Panther, an efficacious thief, to a crummy slob.

Please write a catty vignette.

Exercise 8: An Essay Pot—A Group *Talking* Exercise

A talking exercise has its uses. Sometimes people in a group are weary of writing thoughtfully. They have been acting like children doing "parallel play"—that is, each of them in the class, albeit in a friendly way, offers writing to the teacher and to the class, but really the student is thinking only of his or her own writing, the way one-year-olds in the same nursery think only of their own play.

The Essay Pot gives group members a chance to pay attention to what is going on in others' minds. They need not write a critique, but they must respond to something that someone else jotted onto a 3-by-5 card. Yet—since it's all just talk—this is a sociable exercise to do together. I use this, usually, for the last session of any weeklong writing class because by then most participants have stirred themselves out of the viscous self-centeredness of isolated writers. The Essay Pot might be useful to middle and high school writing groups and community-education groups, even at the beginning of a course. In the course of this exercise, students hear their own voice responding courteously to others' impressions. Their own voice models some intellectual courtesy.

This is a *talking*, rather than a writing, exercise.

Each class member gets two index cards and writes a few lines on two subjects, one subject for each card. We shuffle and spread out these cards along the edges of our tables.

Everyone walks around the tables, looking at all the cards, and finally chooses *one*—not two. Then we each jot down a few notes in response to the card we chose. We will be speaking, in turns, from these notes. Suggested timing: ten minutes for getting our ideas or anecdotes down onto the cards. Five minutes for walking past all the cards and choosing one. Four minutes for jotting down our responses.

Give these instructions to the class: anyone may either accept or oppose the proposition the card writer wrote—or use it merely as a jumping-off point. The important thing, because this is *not* a joke or a game, is to respond as earnestly as you can. *Add* thoughts. Use anecdotes from your own life to illustrate whatever points you make. Make those anecdotes as vivid as you can. This enriches the experience for everyone. Remember this: a problem of beginning writers is being *chintzy*—not giving enough plain, pure *reading interest* to the reader or listener. Be clear about places and times. If the idea on the card you chose isn't elegant or complex enough, generously help out the original author by giving him or her the benefit of the doubt. Take that author's ideas at the most meaningful level you can. Don't go shallow with it.

Next, each person will speak and host a little discussion for *only four minutes.* The timekeeper must be firm, *not even waiting for the end of a speaker's sentence.* The class may flinch at the brutality of someone barking, "Time!" but it is the only way.

Exercise 9: Writing about Work

In the passage quoted below, from Herman Wouk's *The Caine Mutiny*, we will see a common habit of young people—disrespecting other people's work—or not so much disrespecting it as simply failing to see and acknowledge how marvelous it is.

A worse habit of Americans in particular is to praise terribly *simple* work, but to be indifferent to *complicated* work. The most sentimental things get said about quilt-making, even fairly sloppily stitched quilts or quilts in which the blocks and shades of color have not been planned—whereas I have several times listened to a professor of philosophy do the most patient, charming job of explaining how the ancient Greeks distrusted pi—yet not one of the fifteen or sixteen people in the room stayed to thank him! People praise the simplest religious pedagogues but refuse to admire psychologically exciting theology. Why?

Even people with dreadfully low self-esteem manage to love themselves a good deal better than they love others; they are unlikely to praise others' work if it is sophisticated work. It is OK to be self-centered if it's only a matter of (a) living one's life as just another human life, and (b) writing one's autobiography. But self-absorption serves the writing of creative nonfiction very poorly.

Here we see Ensign Willie Keith's failure to praise Captain De Vriess's ship handling in a tricky Pearl Harbor channel.

> Captain De Vriess came up the ladder. He paced the bridge slowly, leaning over the bulwarks to look at the lines, estimating the wind, peering astern at the channel, issuing brief orders in a dry pleasant tone. His bearing was very impressive, Willie admitted to himself, because it was natural, perhaps unconscious. It was not a matter of a stiff spine, squared shoulders, and a sucked-in stomach. Knowledge was in his eye, authority in his manner, decision in the sharp lines of his mouth.
>
> "Well, hell," Willie thought, "if a destroyer captain can't get a ship away from alongside, what *is* he good for?" He had already adopted the *Caine* mode of shading the truth toward

the glamorous side by regarding the ship as an honest-to-goodness destroyer.

His meditations were interrupted by a shocking blast on the ship's steam whistle. The stern of the destroyer next to the *Caine* swung away sluggishly, pulled by a small tug, leaving a narrow triangle of open water bubbling under the rain.

"Take in all lines to port," said the captain.

A goateed sailor named Grubnecker, who wore headphones, reported in a moment, "All lines taken in fore and aft, sir."

"Port back one third," said the captain.

The fat ship's yeoman at the engine telegraph, Jellybelly, repeated the order and rang it up. The engine-room pointer answered. The ship began to vibrate, and slowly to move backward. Willie had an intuitive flash that this was a historic moment, his first time under way aboard the *Caine*. But he pushed it from his mind. This ship was not going to be important in his life—he was determined to see to that.

"Stand clear of the bulkhead, Mr. Keith," said De Vriess sharply, leaning over the side.

"Beg pardon, sir," said Willie, leaping aside. He mopped the streaming rain from his face.

"All engines stop," ordered De Vriess. He walked past Willie, remarking, "Don't you know enough to get in out of the rain? Go in the pilothouse."

"Thank you, sir." He took shelter gladly. A stiff wind was slanting the rain across the channel. Drops drummed on the windows of the wheelhouse.

"Fantail reports channel buoy a hundred yards dead astern," called Grubnecker.

"I see it," said the captain.

Maryk, in a dripping mackintosh, peered down the channel through binoculars. "Submarine coming down the channel, Captain. Making ten knots. Distance one thousand."

"Very well."

"Fantail reports battle wagon and two tin cans coming up-channel past the gate, sir," said the telephone talker.

"Forty-second Street and Broadway out here today," said De Vriess.

Willie looked out at the choppy channel, thinking that the *Caine* was in difficulties already. The wind was moving her swiftly down on the channel buoy. There was little space to maneuver between the bobbing buoy and the ships in the docks. The battleship and the submarine were rapidly closing from both sides.

De Vriess, unperturbed, issued a swift series of engine and rudder orders, the purpose of which escaped Willie. But the effect was to swing the minesweeper around in a backing arc, heading down-channel, well clear of the buoy, falling in line behind the departing submarine. Meantime the battleship and its escorts passed down the port side with plenty of room. Willie observed that none of the sailors commented or seemed impressed, so he assumed that what had appeared knotty to him was a matter of course to an experienced seaman.

Maryk stepped into the pilothouse and swabbed his face with a towel hung on the captain's chair. "Damn! Puget Sound weather." He noticed Willie standing around, looking uncommonly useless. "What the devil are you doing in here? You're supposed to stand lookout on the starboard side—"

"Captain told me to get in out of the rain."

"Hell, you probably were under his feet. Come on out. You won't melt."

"Gladly, sir." Willie followed him out into the weather, irritated at being in the wrong whatever he did.

"Learn anything," asked Maryk, peering down-channel, "from that backing maneuver?"

"Seemed pretty routine," said Willie.

Maryk dipped his binoculars and looked at Willie, showing all his teeth in a mystified grin. "You ever been on a bridge before, Keith?"

"No, sir."

Maryk nodded, and resumed his search of the channel through the glasses.

> "Why," said Willie, wiping rain from his eyes, "was there anything remarkable about it?"
>
> "Christ, no, no," said Maryk. "Any ensign could have handled the ship the way the old man did. I thought maybe you were impressed for no good reason." He grinned again and walked to the other side of the bridge.[5]

Please write a paragraph explaining in some detail a kind of work—handwork or intellectual work or artistic work or criminal work or religious work or any other kind of work except animal work (no beaver-damming theory). Be so clear and detailed that I can imagine that work even if I have neither done it nor ever watched it being done.

Then add a few of the following elements, in an informal, conversational way, as if you were talking to someone at dinner, or cheerfully gossiping:

- some history of the work you are describing
- where this work is done or isn't ever done, or shouldn't be done
- bad fallout from this work, if any
- invisible blessings of this work, if any
- horrible people who do this work, if any
- marvelous people who do this work, if any
- utterly dispirited people who do this work, if any, and so forth

Exercise 10: Attending to Other—Specifically, Attending to Relatives, Nonhuman Creatures, or Plants

Especially with children's writing it's best to take the group through these eight questions orally—conversationally—to diminish the feeling of orders being given or examination questions being asked. I ask children to imagine a well-loved dog or cat or other animal, and then I show them by example how items 1–8 would apply to that animal. You can let them discuss their animals in small groups. They follow that very well. Soon people see that one can tell anecdotes from one's personal life all the while staying focused on a particular person, plant, or creature. They get quite excited. They go at the writing without fear, with the same avidity people bring to solving puzzles.

1. What is the first thing you noticed about your person or creature or plant?
2. Which quite wonderful qualities does he, she, or it practice or show?
3. Which bad qualities does he, she, or it practice or show? You may want to divide bad-for-people qualities from bad-for-nature qualities. For example,

> The mountain goats of Sogndal, Norway, cut up the steep grassy mountainsides. They yank up the grass, and cause rilling everywhere. But they do *us* no direct harm.

4. Who or what are his, her, or its natural or human enemies? If you name some, what are the characteristics of these enemies?

> I once asked a nature-walk leader in southern England if the little plants at our feet would grow better at lower latitudes. "No," he said. "Well, then," I said, "if we weren't stepping on them all the time?" "No again," he said. "That little fellow you pointed out is thriving for the very reason that we *are* stepping here. We are killing off the bullies in his life. Larger broad-leaved plants that can't withstand human footfall are

absent, so this little fellow doesn't complain at an occasional bruising from us. He likes the path."

5. Who or what are the blessings in your person's or creature's or plant's life? What *qualities* made those blessings blessings?
6. What's missing in his, her, or its life, if anything? Henry James, although a cool-hearted author, compassionately recognized how some people get locked out of the great glamours of life. They, too, would have loved a trip to Europe, but they never got there. They, too, would have loved to insult their boss, but they were too poor or inexpressive to do so. Both James and Nicolai Gogol were geniuses on exactly this point.
7. This relative or creature or plant you are attending to: does it live elsewhere in the world differently from how it lives here? Did it or some of its genus live long ago, making out differently from how you see it here? Is or was its relationship to people quite different?
8. Which aspects of life is your relative or creature or plant gumming up? Might he, she, or it be managing some of those specific issues differently? Any discussion of what's being gummed up can vary from a puppy's refusal to become house-trained all the way to some obdurate characteristic of an older relative that so offends the family that it wrecks any chance for easy affection.

Exercise 11: Increasing One's Affection for Utterly Ordinary People

We are all creatures vulnerable to new thoughts, new attitudes.

—Howard Zinn, *You Can't Be Neutral on a Moving Train*

Our job as makers of beautiful literature is bravely to clear off *any* cultural slick. We should cut lies out when we can. Someone says, "I see you are going to the Boundary Waters for your holidays. [The Boundary Waters of Minnesota and Ontario are to Minneapolis and St. Paul residents what the fall coloring of New Hampshire and Vermont are to Boston and New York suburbanites.] What a wonderful, spiritual journey for you!" It is awfully hard to say, "Actually, in my case, I do not do spirituality." If you ever calmly explain to anyone that you don't like music, they always reply, "Of course you like music." It is infinitely worse with spirituality, even though this use of the word *spirituality* is only twenty years old.

We live in such a tolerant-minded and corner-cutting culture that writing out-of-style truth divides a writer from a support groupee. Sometimes when someone reads aloud just any out-of-style truth to a literary audience, joy flies across people's faces. They look the way people would look who have had an alien membrane cleared away from their throats so that they can breathe again. Here is the humane historian Howard Zinn on nearly the same subject:

> But as dogma disintegrates, hope appears. Because it seems that human beings, whatever their backgrounds, are more open than we think, that their behavior cannot be confidently predicted from their past, that we are all creatures vulnerable to new thoughts, new attitudes.[6]

Imagine someone you know well who mildly bores or even disgusts you. Your temptation will be to see that person only *sociologically*—as a stereotype of his or her habitat. List three or four meaningful occasions or heartfelt goals in that person's life. Imagine, as well as you can, that you *are* him or her, and write up a thought or two of that person.

Arrange the list of facts or occasions you've jotted down about that person's life chronologically. Even add dates if you can. Exactitude does not block imagination, though U.S.A. folk wisdom supposes it does. Exactitude, to tell the truth, intensifies imagination.

If your person did some rare thing or ever had a great moment, write it down. Perhaps this was his or her finest hour. Keep clear of sarcasm. Be very respectful, no matter how tiny the stakes in that person's finest hour. Pulling off the smallest act of heroism feels marvelous to the person doing it. Our greatest temptation is to treat everything we write about first sociologically, ignoring the individual triumphs and individual tragedies that lie inside someone's personal life. A second common mistake is to undervalue courage and wistfulness, longings, love, and feelings of triumph when they appear *on the small scale.* That is, if it's not Winston Churchill keeping England from being overrun by Nazis, then it doesn't count as courage and ingenuity. And if it's not Nabokov or Sir Richard Francis Burton, it hasn't got critical mass as serious news of child molesting. And if it's not Aristotle teaching Philip of Macedon or Charlemagne getting in Alcuin to smarten up his court, it doesn't count as serious tutoring. It's important to make a conscious effort to respect *little people.*

Here is a microscopic instance from my own life that amazingly gratified me at the time. But to anyone else it is so picayune that one would hardly consider it for a piece of literature. I have not yet been arrested for opposing the School of the Americas. I was not at Da Nang. Still, it's one of the driving memories inside my mind.

My college has neo-Tudor, or fake English Tudor, buildings. They are beautiful. The public rooms are tall and full of the daylight from many-paned, clear windows. The dining room of my house looked more like a sixteenth-century clerestory than a dining room. Some of the windows were hinged to the steel mullions; others were lead-soldered shut.

One day a bird got in during lunch. It flung itself in panic from window to window. Clearly its little bird brain couldn't distinguish glass from clear sky. This was a women's college in the 1950s. People did nothing but give tiny screams and act hysterical—something which, thanks to the spunky women's movement, I bet no roomful of educated women would give in to now even if a hundred rats dashed in.

I stood up from my place and went slowly toward the bird. I didn't want to take it into my hands. I had had live mice and live birds in my hands. I wasn't keen on feeling their disgusting little claws against my palms—not to mention the wings' pulsing. I got this bird cupped into my hands and then walked it over to a window that would open, and I put the bird out. Everybody cheered and clapped in their genial, friendly way. Inside myself, I was terribly pleased. Here's why: this was the first time when others had lost their heads that I was able to move on a problem. I had expected myself to be medium intelligent because I got into an Ivy League college. I expected myself to solve problems that other people were solving, but I did not expect to solve a problem that others were *not* solving. It gave me a very strange turn.

What incident could be more minor or less significant than putting a distraught bird out a window? Nonetheless, it meant a lot to someone living a *little life*, the Prufrock sort of life.

As you lead writers in this exercise designed to help them increase their affection for utterly ordinary people, it helps to remind them to bear in mind that other people watch the burgee of their lives as fervently as an armada commodore receives weather reports. (A burgee is a small flag or wind bag at the mast top. It tells dinghy sailors which way the wind is coming so they can trim their flimsy craft accordingly.)

People who live little lives have long memories for their own better moments. They use those memories to quell apprehensiveness. When they see the wind coming from a given quarter, they remind themselves that when the wind came from that direction before they'd met it and corrected for it. They don't fear the wind coming from that direction again because they know they can do it again.

If your utterly ordinary person has any enemies, or any occasions that frighten him or her, mull them over.

And finally, every so often people do something amazingly out of character, or so it seems to their relations and acquaintances. What might such a break be that your person might make?

Exercise 12: A Writing Exercise for Extroverts

Most creative-writing exercises are designed by introverts, so of course they suit introverts. Such exercises are enormously unfair to extroverts, who tend to look outward. This exercise is suitable for idealistic people who thrive on gathering impressions as accurately as they can from the *outside* world.

The diagram for this exercise was offered in a course in reflective leadership at the Hubert Humphrey Institute, Minneapolis, Minnesota, by Robert Terry, director of the Reflective Leadership Program.[7] Terry offered it as a tool for assessing organizations. A troubled organization can painlessly invite in consultants from *outside* to come help. These consultants analyze, diagnose, and then, on the big day, advise. If the top brass don't care for the consultants' conclusions, the whole lot goes to the shredder, and few are the wiser.

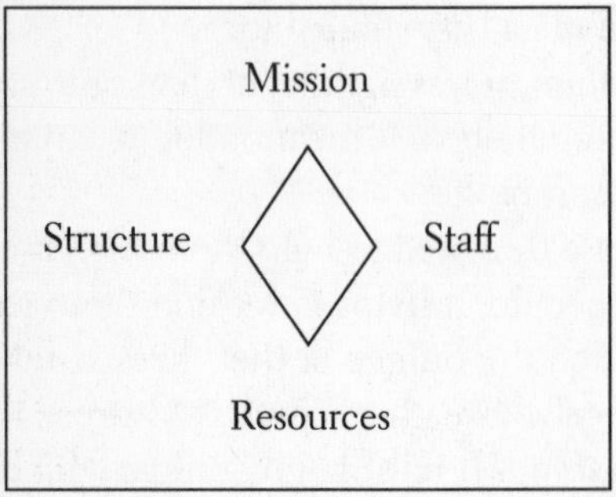

Terry noticed that most organizations report each perceived grief *at one level lower than where the cause of the grief lies.* Typically, an organization will call in consultants saying, "Please pay attention to our structure and our staff. Tell us if anything strikes you; tell us some changes you think we ought to make." Not only do the upper management of most organizations report a perceived grief at one level lower than the true cause, but *individual members* of the organization also report their grief existing one level lower than where the true cause lies.

Robert Terry gave a heartbreaking example. Typists at an organization to which he was consultant and troubleshooter told him that they had a problem with *resources.* Resources lie at the base of any organization. They are usually its first consideration in doing business at all. They are also the only *passive* element in running a business—as graphed by Terry. It's easy to collect and interpret data about resources. If someone is trying to make money mining molybdenum in the Bay

Area, any consulting geologist would quickly recommend a corporate move to Colorado.

The typists told Bob Terry that they arrived at work at 8:30 in the morning. Their supervisors didn't come in until 9:00. The typists did not have a key to the stockroom, so if they needed paper, they were unable to work until 9:00, when executives at the level just above them arrived with the keys. The typists perceived this as a problem with the *stockroom*, which was a resource. Bob Terry saw the problem as being rooted in a shabby, even unkind management style. Why should the typists, just because they're paid low wages, not be trusted with a key to the stockroom? If there were proper respect for the typists' work, managers would have ensured that at least one of the typists held a key.

Those typists' reporting their grief at a lower level than the true cause has a parallel in psychotherapy. Beginning psychology clients typically tell their therapist that they are "just tired," instead of saying that they feel "depressed." One learns to look for that word *just* when used as a limiting adverb. It's an unconscious plea from the client: the plea between the words says, "Leave it alone. Don't look further—it's *just* this." As soon as a therapist hears "just," he or she wonders: "Oh? Why can't I look at it? How do we know it's 'just' such and such? Maybe it's something bigger."

Robert Terry picked up the same signal from the typists.

After two weeks' work, Terry made his report to the organization. There they were, Terry with his flowcharts and his transparencies and all the other wonderful regalia that corporate consultants use to make sense of a troubled enterprise. And Terry showed them the diamond-shaped chart, too.

He in so many words told the leaders of this organization that they didn't need to fire anybody or initiate jazzy quality control or move to Colorado. What was at fault was the top of the diamond, he said—their mission.

"What!" they said irritably.

Terry told them that they were not a kind and loving organization. They were simply not loving *enough*, he told them. He suggested that their various dips in efficiency translating to fluctuating profit/loss balance came not from structural problems nor from incompetent staff nor from dearth of resources. Their failures, he assured them, came from mean-heartedness.

They were furious.

Terry's extroverted scheme for looking at organizations is a translatable tool for unearthing clues to people, any creature in nature, including trees. In fact—one can ask about any creature, "What are its resources? What is its mission? Are its resources good enough for its mission? Is its base of operations OK? What's its staff? Who are its friends? Who are its enemies?"

For this exercise, then, think of a person and analyze that person's structure, staffing, resources, and apparent mission. Unless that person is you yourself, you will have to do some thoughtful guessing. You will have to hypothesize. You will be practicing empathy of a sort empathy at second hand.

Exercise 13: An Irritating Person Exercise

A blessing of this exercise is that it gives us two quite opposite gifts at the same time. It lets us be serious about a negative opinion, and it lets us put our feeling toward a particular person in humorous perspective.

In general, deciding to write a humorous essay is not a very good practice. For every writer who does it without resorting to shallow cheap shots, dozens fail. Because they are being flip or cagey and are not inquiring into their own earnest feelings, they slide into making lightweight remarks designed to please a reader. Every so often, however, it is wonderful to be deliberately lightweight.

Please write up an individual or a group who has irritated you beyond belief. *State your irritation only once, in a single sentence.* That done, present the irritating person or group by showing us only what this irritating person does and says and where it happens. Somehow, get in some sense of that person's values—some sense of what is driving him or her. If you haven't the least idea of what drives him or her, where (as they say) he or she "is coming from," now is a good time to make an intelligent guess or two. The guess that you make is your *theory* about the person. If this person is a problem that needs solving, such as a personnel problem in a workplace, you might include any solutions you've thought of in your essay.

Are there surprises about this person? Do some people admire or love him or her? Are you alone in feeling such dismay or disgust or irritation? Example: did this person's existence recently ruin a perfectly good canoe trip you have been looking forward to—maybe the other paddlers incessantly praised this person all the way to Hudson Bay. When you demurred (just once!) your bow paddler turned back with a brilliant, forgiving smile crying, "Oh, no! You would love him [or her] if you just knew him or her better!"—all the while you would nearly prefer hanging yourself to knowing that person better. You don't need to argue for *why* this person irritates you. All you need to do is present a situation, or two or three situations, showing what this person does that so vexes you.

You need not make only favorable remarks either. This person's principle or principles may have seriously offended you. Say so in a peaceful tone. We may be catty, but we are civil when we are at peace.

Essayists do not shriek. Their tone is, "I have to tell you if there is one thing I could not stand about That Person it was her religion. She had a way of folding her hands that made me shudder."

One needs courage to confront an irritating person. When I was a young married person I used to visit my grandmother-in-law at the Madison (Minnesota) Lutheran Home. I was the garden-variety agnostic you see on American college campuses or hanging around the Church of England. I told my grandmother-in-law to relax about evolution; Christianity would not be hurt by science. I assumed that she would admire my affable remarks. She did not.

She loved me, but she hated my lack of religion. She was glad enough that I came to visit her nearly every day—I was the only family member with the time or inclination to do so. On Sundays I took her to our farm for noon dinner and the long afternoon.

After I had made my rosy remark about religion and evolution that repelled her, she said, "*You* may be descended from monkeys. I am not!"

Then she grinned—no doubt glad that she had told me off, finally, finally! It takes guts for anyone in a nursing home to tell off a frequent visitor. What if that visitor gets cross and won't visit anymore? And will never again take him or her out to see how this year's fieldwork is coming along? She and I went on being good friends until she died.

Exercise 14: A Nearly Impossible Writing Exercise

Not only is this writing exercise nearly impossible, but it falls naturally into two parts, and both parts are nearly impossible in their own individual ways. People find it so difficult not to sneer at someone whose tastes they regard as lower than their own or, ironically enough, at someone whose tastes they regard as better than their own. This sneering seeps into their manuscripts without their noticing.

This is an exercise in consciousness-raising—of being aware of how your own mind can keep you in a narrow mind-set. For this exercise I give most M.F.A. candidates grades like F/A. (Giving an F/A has a tremendous advantage. It reflects total failure in content and good work in writing at the same time. And because the grade is so arch and idiosyncratic with the slash, it needn't redound unfavorably in anyone's record of marks, and writing students know that.) I explain the grading system to the class when I give those papers back.

We need chances to channel psychological truths in a light vein. I explain that nearly everybody in the class got an F for content and an A for writing, if the writing was good. The F is awarded to students who allowed scorn into their material. When students read their work aloud to the class, they hear that scorn. Maybe they had not read their manuscript aloud to themselves, or they did, but did not listen carefully, and therefore the scorn festered.

Sometimes we read aloud some of these failed F/A papers in class. People laugh because the grading is ridiculous. Or they laugh at the intense scorn the author was perfectly unconscious of. My own feeling is that it's bracing to get an F now and again, especially if the better part of a class got Fs. It's bracing to be collegial in this particular way—everyone deciding with satisfaction that their teacher is insane.

Part 1. A Person of Different *Taste*

Describe someone whose taste in nature, in books, in television, on the Internet—in anything—is quite *other* than, quite *different* from, yours. Make clear the fine points of that person's pleasure, too. Say, for example, that person loves to pour catsup onto a hard-fried beefsteak. Describe their joy without scorn, even if you are a cilantro-loving vegetarian.

Be particular. Do not allow even one drop of scorn to enter into your writing, not one *drop* of superiority! You will have to imagine what the kick is that your person gets out of this predilection. This writing lesson stops our saying, "I just can't understand how so and so could *do* . . . ," or "I just can't understand where such a person could be *coming* from who would like something like that!"

People who have the hardest time with this writing exercise are knee-jerk liberals. Arts administrators, in particular, tend to have certain endemic opinions on public subjects. Just as conservatives have other opinions on those certain subjects.

A common piece of conventional wisdom among arts administrators is that professional football in the United States is a bad thing. Another is that boys in high school who devote a good deal of effort to playing football are training for life in a bad way. A few years ago I proposed to The Loft, the Minneapolis-based writers' organization, that we start a statewide competition in which athletes of both genders would describe their various moods as they tried to improve their playing in given positions—in football, in soccer, or in track or any other sport. The Loft board laughed this idea out of our meeting room, the other directors being agreed that no good could come of paying attention to something like football. Intellectuals sometimes refuse outright even to *imagine* the courage it must take to receive a pass when you know it means you will be hit very hard. Running back a kickoff I know I would signal fair catch one foot from the goal line, even if there were no one within twenty yards of me. Most liberals, however, feel such scorn for football that they have no intuition on the subject.

Note what little rats the minor characters in Alice Munro's and Anton Chekhov's work are. Yet those authors bother to imagine little rats. They make intelligent guesses about their characters' goals and hopes and dismays. They give them a right to live in literature. Besides, ignobility is a long-standing part of the human personality. We should be able to write about it.

Here is an example of a failed piece of writing by a famous author. We don't know what Natalia Ginzburg's mission was in writing the essay "He and I," from which this passage is taken, but if her mission had been, let's say, to do the Nearly Impossible Writing Exercise—that is, to describe someone else's taste without any tone of superiority—then she would get an F/B on this writing. (F/B rather than F/A because the essay structure itself is not very personable.) The author is indirectly insisting on her superiority.

> He always feels hot, I always feel cold. In the summer when it really is hot he does nothing but complain about how hot he feels. He is irritated if he sees me put a jumper on in the evening.
>
> He speaks several languages well; I do not speak any well. He manages—in his own way—to speak even the languages that he doesn't know.
>
> He has an excellent sense of direction, I have none at all. After one day in a foreign city he can move about in it as thoughtlessly as a butterfly. I get lost in my own city; I have to ask directions so that I can get back home again. He hates asking directions; when we go by car to a town we don't know he doesn't want to ask directions and tells me to look at the map. I don't know how to read maps and I get confused by all the little red circles and he loses his temper.
>
> He loves the theater, painting, music, especially music. I do not understand music at all, painting doesn't mean much to me and I get bored at the theater. I love and understand one thing in the world and that is poetry.[8]

Part 2. *A Person of* Superior *Taste*

Describe someone whose tastes in behavior or media or literature or anything are *probably better* than yours. Don't think for even a minute that some tastes are not better than others. Forget for the moment all the nonjudgmental cant about "not better—just different." A cat, for example, torturing a mouse, experiences genuine pleasure. A real swine of a cat can keep a wounded mouse (just) alive for a good twenty minutes. Such a cat's pleasure is not "equal but different." Its pleasure is plainly low. If you could tell that cat that you know some people who, frankly, are above torturing mice—people who listen to Mozart, say—the cat might answer, "Torturing mice is just as good as listening to Mozart—it is different, that's all. Look, torturing mice is in my line. Mozart's in yours. So what's your point?"

Try to hypothesize what your person's pleasure might be in some pastime that is so superior that you scarcely understand it. You will have to guess at it since you yourself haven't that quality of mind yourself—not so far, at least. Do not imply for a split second that the person is crazy. See if you can write respectfully about someone whose sensibilities, for now, anyhow, are more elegant than yours.

A job of writers is to *try* to understand, instead of making rhetorical exclamations while feeling superior.

Pitfall: be sure not to choose some beastly occupation for this person of "superior taste." Often beginning writers deceive themselves into thinking that they are writing respectfully of someone who has excellent taste, when what they're really doing is assigning to that person excellent taste all right, but excellent taste in some minimal field of endeavor: students point out that this person dresses so much better than they themselves do. In such essays we understand by the second sentence, if not by the end of the first, that the author has deep inner qualities of sensitivity and literary taste whereas this other person thinks of nothing but clothes. Often writers don't even hear that manipulation until it's pointed out, or until the paper is read aloud to the group. We need to learn to discern when we are sneering, when we are praising.

A personal example: I can hardly do the simplest logic problems. Yet some people can. For years I had any number of defensive things to say about those people. I told myself, "Oh, but they are such limited, linear thinkers!" I told myself, "Those people are imagination killers." It took me literally decades to realize and to say, "That person's logic is so fine it makes us all glad. And it is just plain beyond me, too."

Exercise 15: The Andover Format: Writing Your Life at Two Levels—One the Usual Sort of Memoir, and the Other Secret and Profound

Both kinds of memoir are good. The usual, family-celebratory memoir is good; the secret, deep writing about your own life is good.[9]

Here is what people tend not to understand: these two kinds of memoirs are *very different projects.* Let's distinguish between them, honor both, and then learn how to do the secret, deep memoir. You may not always want that memoir to be secret, *but it has to be secret while you are writing it.* Your mind has to know that it is writing with total confidentiality.

The Usual Sort of Memoir

We are the experts in our own lives. We can write an affectionate, particularized, vivid memoir. When we get old, our children ask for affectionate, particularized, vivid memoirs from us. Just outside or just within our hearing they murmur, "We should get Mama to do this *now,* before . . . before . . . " They're right.

Should Mama decide to do a family history—or the less intellectual task of tracing her genealogy—there are Web sites, libraries, reading rooms, short writing retreats, and whole courses designed to serve her. Grown children may gratefully pay for printing your book. An age group that loves people's memoirs is eleven-year-olds. Eleven is the age at which people commonly begin to separate the old self from the new, *contemplative* self. At eleven one steps outside oneself and sees oneself from a step away. One loves biography at that age, because reading biography is a psychological parallel to stepping outside oneself and looking back in. Eleven is an appropriate age group for "finding one's roots." Age eleven is actually a much more appropriate age group for someone to spend time finding his or her roots than at some of the older ages when people more commonly go about it. Eleven-year-olds are the age group who fantasize whole, imaginary countries. They are the age group that thrived on *Dungeons and Dragons* twenty years ago. *Dungeons and Dragons* allowed even children who had never been read to aloud the joy of navigating an inner world made separate from the outer world.

There are limitations to what one's family members *want* when they encourage you to write up your life. They do not always want what is best for you as a thinker and a writer.

Families like to know sensational stuff. They want to know about what it was like when there was only black-and-white TV, if any. They like to know about outdated farm equipment. They want to hear about childbirth in a snowstorm and other vivid physical sorts of experiences. They do not want your autobiography or personal history to start: *How odd that all my life I have respected honesty and talked about it and praised it, and yet two lies I told caused two deaths—my own father's, and later a young soldier's. I managed for four decades not to feel galled by those lies, but now they are in my mind's eye all the time, as if someone each night unearthed those bodies, one in Indiana and one outside Tashkent, and laid them afresh on my doorstep.*

Family writings, or any public writings, have invisible rules you won't notice until you break one. *You* may not have noticed that family members do not want to hear your confessions—not your real ones. But your *mind* knows, and circumspectly it does not suggest improper emotions for you to record. Your mind says, "Hey, be nice to your family. They love you and you love them. Tell them about how your mother, their grandmother and great-grandmother, used to wear a flowered apron for canning, but when she was to bake bread, she changed to an ironed white apron. Tell them how clean-cut the neighborhoods were. If you lived on East 18th Street, you could speak Russian to anyone you saw."

Your children are right. All that sort of thing makes beautiful public memoir.

Getting to a Secret, Meaning-Based Memoir

No matter how loving your spouse or other loved ones, no matter how respectful your clergy or other mentors, no matter how cordially curious other family members and friends are—and especially members of your writers' club if you belong to one—be sure you *do not show your meaning-based, secret memoir to any of them.*

Why? You will base your secret on a list of fifty-four values. If your brain feels you might go *public* with the fifty-four values, it will not reveal your deepest feelings to you. Your brain is not a fool. It knows that once something is said aloud, even if it is said aloud only to a spouse or other loved one, the laws of sociability will stiffen whatever it was you said. What you said is now a *social artifact*, so you can't rethink it. Your mind will be in its social, audience-related mode, not in its inquiring, revising mode.

A second reason not to share your fifty-four values list or any other part of your secret memoir with others: you are asking too much of people if you tell them either painful or wildly joyful truths *that they haven't been expecting*. They will give staccato responses—or none. People caught in deep surprise tend to shrink.

Say you decided to show an intense, very personal memoir to your now grown-up siblings. You expected them to be interested. Yet only one said something on the core subject: he said, "Well, obviously you saw such and such an incident in our childhood completely differently from how it struck *me* at the time!" The other siblings only asked if you weren't mistaken about the route for the old streetcar you recalled. Or they praised minute, completely external points. They said, "You got that right about how the dogwood blooms come out before the trees leaf out." Or they said, "Thank you for sending the memoir. Mike and I will be writing you as soon as we get time to read it." You never hear from them. Later you learn that they had already read it when they wrote you, but presumably they were stymied at the prospect of responding to your ideas, so they lied.

What can it mean that people so commonly give scattershot, superficial, or lying responses to someone's trustful sharing? My guess is it means only that most people live unreflectively. You offered them a *reflective* piece of writing as opposed to a book of anecdotes. You showed them intense, *gathered* feeling. They couldn't manage it.

If you felt angry at them because their only response was to fidget or lie, that anger might later back up and become anger against yourself. Such an insult to your own soul is hard. An even worse outcome: sometimes, after our dear ones have inadvertently insulted our soul, our own mind gets cynical. It says to us, "Obviously there is no point to all these deeply felt truths. Take a break. Go change the filter on the wet-dry vac and clean up your shop in the garage. You've been wanting to lay out the tools in a different order. So do it. Forget writing."

Step A: One starts with a serious *list*—a list of fifty-four named feelings. Lists are impervious to outside pressures. Someone making a list of what's needed at the store is not deflected by the neighbors' opinions about what's needed. Lists—if you can stand hearing this sort of thing!—pull information from the interactive layers of the upper cortex in our brains. Lists are codifications that your brain loves to make, and willingly, even if piecemeal, over years and years, has put together for you. It is helpful to realize that the brain doesn't really do a process you could call "storing memories." What it does do is make, and then cheerfully remake, *categories.* When our eyes or ears or skin or other sources of information tell us something new, our mind revises the categories. Much of what we call "memory" is better described as the mind altering its opinion on some new or old subject. The mind does it by feeling. Actually, the mind is a terrific value freak. It feels everything it thinks.

Why fifty-four values? Fifty-four values is so many that long after you have peeled the obvious ones off the top of your head and the generic, cultural ones you've picked up from forty or fifty years' exposure to Newton's Apple and *Sixty Minutes* and *Masterpiece Theatre* and the Pittsburgh Steelers, and long after you have cudgeled your brain to recall values learned in Andover's U.S. History or Abbot's English IV—after you have run through all of the above—you *still* won't have written down, verbatim, fifty-four values. So now you will have to invite the shy, half-conscious parts of your mind to come up with other qualities of life that you hate or love or dread or feel thankful for. These last—the listings for which you had to creep to rarer hearths of your mind—these are usually the most serious and beautiful, or rightly outraged, of the lot.

Perhaps you have spent your sixty-seven or sixty-eight years of life convinced that focusing on the *self* is very nonclassy and introverted and pathetic, a piece of sickness. Do it anyway. After all, no one is going to see this writing. If it helps, do it in the third person. "Once upon a time," you can write, "there was a man who did ten years' good work, and then he did twenty-odd years' mixed bad and good work. Both he and his wife knew this, but they never got anywhere talking about it. For one thing, whenever they felt close and decided to mosey through their feelings about the bad, but—let's say—*profitable,* work he was doing, he would feel profoundly grateful that she was his loyal, empathic partner, his loyal support or loyal opposition. They moved toward each other joyfully. They went upstairs. They left the discussion behind them in the living room. And so he never wrote down his truth—not all of it."

If it helps, try doing even the values list in the third person. For example, "There was a man who despised crime, yet he found himself fascinated by particular criminal cases . . . for instance he once . . ."

Step B: After you have all fifty-four qualities of life written down, choose five or six of them and deliberately recall the *first time you noticed each of them.* Which day, or which year? Because until that moment you weren't aware of that "value." Until that moment you thought that was "just the way life is, I guess. No big deal." Notice how often people say: "I mean, that's the way life is, isn't it? I mean, we're just talking human nature here, aren't we?" Those are people who have never secretly decided on their values. They have not assigned their experiences any configuration—anything you could call *moral configuration.* For them, things just happen: "A happens. Then B through G happens. Oh yes, and then I guess H and I happened. Hey. And J. And L. You know how it goes. Hell, after L what do you get? M and N. It figures." They don't connect and interpret.

When you have chosen your five or six values, don't explain them or argue for them. Give the *scene,* the place, the people there, if any, the animals, if any, even the weather, if you noticed it. *Be careful not to lie.* Don't fabricate what you don't remember. Don't decide to sketch in a snowstorm if there was none.

The idea here is that when you start with a personally felt concept (one of your five listed insights) and tie to it a vivid anecdote, you are practicing what is called writing literature.

Step C: After you have written a scene for each of your five or six values, ask yourself: did life offer me any *challenges* to those values? What was one occasion when one of my values was challenged? How'd it go? Describe the place, the time, the people, the weather, the animals, and so forth.

And did you fail any of your beliefs or values? Were you false-hearted or mildly slothful about any of them, on one or another occasion? Did any of those values seem vital to you at one time, but less so at another? Describe some scene when you did not do battle and now wish you had done.

Describe a scene in which you *did* the really good thing. You stood for a value. "Stood for" usually involves "sacrificed something for." Sometimes one loses friends over a value. Sometimes one loses a good deal of money over a value. One loses cachet. Look at all Winston Churchill lost in the 1930s by standing up for the idea of rearmament and building up the RAF when others in the British government were appeasers or they covertly didn't want to shackle Hitler, in the hope that his strong Nazi Germany would attack the Soviet Union.

A sad example: A young astrophysicist named Halley urged and helped Newton to write the famous *Principia.* Halley even put up major money. Newton didn't pay him back. What's more, Newton fudged some figures. (So what else is new?) We have the great *Principia* mainly because of Halley. And does the world appreciate young Halley's generous work on behalf of the old scientist? No. We think Halley was just some guy who figured out the route and schedule of a visiting comet.

In your life, have you done some quite wonderful, disinterested work like Halley's helping Newton, that may never be noticed or recalled by others? *Write it down.* Remember: you are not boasting because this is a secret memoir. (My personal huge hope would be that you eventually make this particular material public. We all, young and old, need true stories of people stalwart enough to endanger their careers for a principle.)

Step D: Here is a psychological fact. Once you have written down heretofore secret, thoughtful, probing, truthful material, you yourself are slightly changed. In pop culture, such change is variously called "being transformed" or worse, "finding out who you are," or still, much, much worse, "having made a spiritual journey." Never mind the beastly language. The experience is splendid. The good effect on one's own mind and one's happiness in life is unmistakable.

I used to wonder how clergypeople could be so patient listening to their parishioners using all that same tinny jargon (transformation, spiritual journey, and the like). Now I realize that clergypeople forgive the language because they are so gratified by the change of mind that that language is trying to describe.

Step E: When you have written a secret memoir, you may feel that after all *some* of it could be moved over into your own more ordinary memoir: you might find yourself willing to put some of its ideas and anecdotes into the narrative about the old tools and giving birth in a snowstorm and the black-and-white TV. The two memoirs might combine very well.

But for now, absolutely keep those memoirs on two separate disks or in two separate portfolios.

A Final Remark

The experience of honoring one's own insides, one's own personality, is for everyone. Serious recording is nature's gift to us all. Homo sapiens is a species that delights to write history—some of it shallow or glinting with lies, but some of it profound. Lions, gorgeous as they are, do not takes notes on life. We do.

One certain outcome of private record keeping is this: anyone who writes down his or her fifty-four-item list, and adds true, not fudged, not fictionalized, not shined-up, anecdotes for five or ten of them, will see, sometimes for the first time at age sixty-seven or sixty-eight or seventy, what a human, serious, humorous, and meaningful life he or she has had—and is still having.

Appendix II

Usage Sheets

Usage Sheet No. 1

To lay and to lie:
2 verbs, one transitive, one not

a) *To lay:* a transitive verb. It always takes an object. It always lays *something* or *someone.* Its principal parts are **lay** (present tense), **laying** (present participle), and **laid** (past tense) and **laid** (past participle). Therefore,

> **Whenever I tire of it, I lay down my work.**
> and
> **Norfolk Englishmen like laying hedges—that is, bending or cutting the growth so vertical new rods grow up between the horizontal branches, making such a geometric tangle that a bull can't break through.**
>
> **Yesterday I laid bread to rise under white cloth.**
> and
> **The bricklayers had already laid a course.**

b) *To lie:* an intransitive verb. It never takes an object. In its sentences there is only the subject and a word or phrase telling wherever or whenever or however the subject does or did the lying down. The verb's principal parts are lie (present tense), lying (present participle), lay (past tense), and lain (past participle). Therefore,

The balsams lie where the fallers have left them.
Down timber left lying soon becomes cover for voles and rabbits scared of hawks.
Fussell describes how his squad lay all night among dead German soldiers without knowing it.
The young Germans had lain there so long their faces were mottled white and green as marble.

Usage Sheet No. 2

Distinctions among various singular and plural possessives in English

The possessive form of collective nouns.

Of the people = **the people's**

That government didn't care two cents' worth about the people's welfare.

but *of the peoples* = **the peoples'**

French is an OK language for the French people, but it isn't all those other peoples' language, so no wonder they spell it so variously.

Of the children = **the children's**

Plural possessives when not collective.

The Harrises live on that street. (the plural takes no apostrophe)

The Harrises' house is lovely, but there is no insulation at the electrical entrance. (plural possessive)

Singular possessives ending in s.

Actually, Louisa Harris's tastes are strange. Actually, both Harrises' tastes are strange, James's as strange as hers. And Charles's are plainly aberrant. He did over both dogs' houses.

⇨ The possessive form of *pronouns*

> Short fiction is lovely, its blessing being that it takes you into imagined other. . . . It's too bad about Charles's redoing the doghouse in neo-Tudor. That suited only *his* taste. *Hers*—the dog's—was simpler. She had asked for perpendicular-cathedral, but she might as well have barked at a stone wall.

Usage Sheet No. 3

Two Words with Two Spellings and Two Uses Each: *affect* and *effect*

First (ideally) memorize the two words and two uses. Failing that, keep this sheet handy. Every time you use one of these words, check its use against this sheet. Do not be cross with yourself if you have trouble memorizing usage. A mature mind hates doing rote work just as a skilled cathedral builder hates mixing and carrying mud for the masonry.

- *Affect*, a noun. Pronounced AFFect. *Affect* means "feeling or emotion" in contrast to cognition or thinking. The word is usually pejorative.

> When she snapped, "Add two and two," he began to tremble and show a lot of affect, but he didn't seem to be *thinking* about the arithmetic at all.

- *Affect*, a verb. Pronounced af*FECT*. Means "have an influence on." There are also two or three archaic meanings for the verb "to affect." An example: Shakespeare said, "Study, Sir, what you most affect," meaning major in something you enjoy. Another meaning: *to fake:* "She affected ladylike ways but everyone knew she had the most fulsome, unscrupulous private life imaginable."

> Terry DeBruyn had been a bear hunter. Getting actually to know a given mother bear affected his mind's philosophy. He developed from hunter to advocate.

- *Effect*, a noun. Pronounced ef*FECT*. Means "result."

> The effect of playfulness in human beings is an encouraged imagination, and an effect of imagination is or can be the ability to empathize with others.

An arithmetic teacher said, "If ten expectant bears successfully forage for and find berries, vegetables, greens, honey, fruit, and fish, and then nest down in good shelter for the winter, what effect will that have on their cubs?"

- *Effect,* a verb. Pronounced ef*FECT.* Means "to implement or make happen." It does *not* mean "to influence."

That arithmetic teacher made kids cry and talked a lot of teaching theory but she effected neither love nor grasp of math in her students.

Appendix III

Abbreviations and Notes for Referencing Margin Comment on Students' Papers

ca	around, approximately—from Lat. *circa*
re	about (a subject)—from Lat. *re*
$\therefore$	therefore—from algebra
$\bar{c}$	with—from Lat. *cum*
$\bar{s}$	without—from Lat. *sine*
//	parallel to
=	is or are the same as
$\neq$	is not or are not the same as
POV	point of view of
v	very
fasc	fascinating
fyi	for your interest or possible use
s.t.	something
s.o.	someone
int	interesting
gr	grammatical or usage weakness
subj	subjunctive mood needed here
Grrrr	sound of growling. This appears on a paper (1) when a remonstrance has been made about some point over and over, yet the writer still repeats the mistake; or (2)

	when the author has written too slothfully by far—for example, on an exam, in reply to "How do you understand the character of so and so in such and such a work?" the student wrote, "Give me a break."
e.g.	for example—from Lat. *exempli gratia,* for the sake of a typical instance
i.e.	that is—from Lat. *id est,* that is
A red •	I may ask you to read this to the others in our group
A green •	I assign a revision of this paper

Please do not use slashes such as social/economic and goals/ideals in this course. We would never dodge around in arithmetic the way we hedge about in literature: no one would say, "if I have two apples and someone gives me three more apples, then I have four slash five apples." We would never say, "I am marrying so and so because I like/respect him." It helps a person think bravely if he or she decides never to use any slashes.

Some of the abbreviations here are classic scholars' abbreviations; for example, c̄ and s̄ given for *with* and *without* instead of the social sciences' w/ and w/o. You have the right to know the traditional elegances, just as every high school kid gets to wear a graduation gown instead of a T-shirt. When one marries one gets to say "I do" or "I will" instead of "You got it!" or "Sure thing." When we *know* the tradition and formality in large or little things, we have a choice between being formal or being casual. If we have never heard of the traditions or formal usages, all we can do is be casual. Unfair but common—usually passed off as democratic.

Appendix IV

Formats and Strategies

A Format for Writing an Essay

Note: This is a *content-focused* format. It says: what you kno[illegible] life deserves respect. It is absolutely opposite to a five-p[illegible] techno-fix![10]

This format helps you both draw out and organize ideas. I[illegible] you put your own thinking in perspective with others' ideas on the same subject. It is so flexible you can use it to describe anything from a certain particular change in your own life to the look of a mouse in a trap, with the light showing through its pale ears. This format would do just as well if you wanted to describe some present-day parallel to the time when the Roman Catholic Church forbade the use of the compass for four hundred years.

1. State an idea or a value or merely the name of an object that interests you.
2. What is its purpose or what is its program? What does it want of life?
3. How did it work in your life *before* you changed your mind about it (if you *have* changed your mind about it in some way)?
4. Thicken the plot. How is this idea or value or object, or your having changed your mind about it if you have, more complicated than it first appeared?
5. Who else has looked into this subject, just as you are doing? It is

genial and scholarly to bring in others who care or feel warmly on the same subject. These others may be from other cultures or from the past. I hesitate to suggest to Americans that it would be politic to mention others in the field who have written on the same subject one is writing on oneself. I hesitate to do that because creative writing students are always being told something politic to do and I often don't think it's good for them. In this case, however, in matters of scholarship and matters of courtesy it improves an essay to show that you have read the other people on the same subject.

Sometimes other essays appear to be on the same subject but really, in fact, are on a different subject. If your essay is likely to be confused with material that is really on another subject, this is a good place to say so—to save readers' time and to spare them confusion.

6. Describe the opponents of your idea: (a) Be empathic—that is, imagine the thing or situation or issue from their point of view; and (b) converse a little about how these opponents use, or try to kill, or are in love with, the idea, value, or object. *Civilly* account for how the opponents came to take their stand. Perhaps they get tremendous benefit from the very situation you are trying to change. They may be experiencing any or several of the following:

- serious financial well-being
- comfortable denial of pain—anyone's pain—very often their own
- wonderful ego reinforcement from how things are now
- comfortable religious piety: you and your idea may strike them as the work of the devil, in which case it is their pride and joy to oppose you.

7. How would the world be affected if your idea were universally adopted? Would the world be a better place? If the general world with its people and planet were not improved by it, whom *would* your idea benefit? Or harm? Not all ideas are of equal size. Some have scarcely any scope at all. If your essay is on the subject of a new design for a mousetrap, for example, that is not so important as Winston Churchill's design of a tank to be used during World War I. The idea here is to give yourself a chance to have the right perspective on how important you think your idea is.

8. Draw the conclusions that your own mind has given you. Here is silly-sounding but very important advice: be grateful you had any idea at all! If you came up with several ideas, be severally grateful.

The Vertical-Line Way of Taking Notes

An Example of Vertical-Line Notes—the left-hand column being the note taker's analysis of "The Three Little Pigs," and the right-hand being the note taker's personal responses to the folktale text. [See the discussion of Vertical-Line note taking in Chapter 9.]

Dramatis personae [people in the story] include a straw-buying pig, a sticks-buying pig, a brick-buying pig, a man of the commercial type (sells anything to anyone), a conventional wolf, presumably male.

Author respects M.I.T.-type technical savvy re: beam strengths of materials (e.g., third pig's use of masonry to resist huffing and puffing).
Summary treatment of death (the two pigs' deaths and the wolf's death)
Style and setup: Showing, not telling
Author does not give inward point of view (POV) pigs or wolf or man.
Genre: Exterior magic realism.
Dialogue: crisp, sub-Hemingway level.

What exasperates me about this story is that the wolf might be a mother desperate to bring back pork for the cubs and cub-sitting uncles. She may have promised "the other white meat." She feels a promise is a promise. Animals are tightly programmed: if some procedure hasn't gotten recorded in their brains they probably won't try it out. The mother wolf has no records of ancestors successfully returning from having descended a masonry chimney.
Author tells the story as a morality tale but the moral is so cheap. The moral is "Be Technically Smart."
Story has a heartless, negligent tone to it, if you ask me.
Such a story may not immunize little kids to suffering, but then it might. I mean, in theory this story has a happy ending, but look at whom it isn't happy for.
I don't know. I will think about it. Whatever may be wrong with this story, it sure didn't wreck its market. No one seems to mind it except me.

Analyzing a Literary Work of Art

Preparing Yourself to Look at a Piece of Literature

Your note sheets should be full-sized, not bits of paper or 3-by-5 cards. A proposal—that you divide them vertically in half—is offered earlier in Appendix IV. The left-hand half of the page is for your literary analysis, and the right-hand half of the page is for your personal response to that given work.

Be sure deliberately "to put on your thinking cap," not just your feelings cap. The poet Tom McGrath said that one thing that killed Americans during the Vietnam War era was that hundreds of thousands of us "had no elder (to) put on (our) thinking caps." But remember that although you should think detachedly and be cool, you still have the right-hand side of each note sheet for angry or joyful or disorganized responses to the work. Keep those right-hand-side notes! Some of your responses may be *holy*.

Tell yourself you are going to stay focused on this literary work. At the same time, acknowledge and write down your forthright ideas about the work. Don't dillydally about with fancy phrases. Speak plainly.

Be of a mind to make *lists*. The list-making process makes our brains work with faster spark than does our cordial, paper-writing process.

Keep half an eye out for things to *praise* in the work—but don't lie. Never lie. An odd psychological insight is this: we learn by praising others; what's more, we learn by reading or hearing someone else praising others. I don't know why this is.

Analyzing a Piece of Literature

After you have read the work or have taken a few notes of one kind or another, make a point of asking yourself, "What is this work mainly *about*?" Except for journals and biographies, works of literature have a thesis or issue. For example: D. H. Lawrence's great story "The Rocking-Horse Winner" has a strong point. It has to do with Lawrence's idea that if parents don't love their children, the children will be desperate and will try to love the parents and to feed the parents what they think the parents need, and this will eventually kill the children. It's important to get the main point. I make an issue of this here because it is stylish now to say that a work of literature isn't *about* anything.

Now look at the parts of the work. Analysis means *taking things apart* in order to see what the parts do. In serious literature, all the parts contribute some meaning to the whole. You need to see how they do that. This is not true of journal and memoir writing, where the unity of the whole work lies in its being about one person, not about one universal idea.

Be sure to be clear about what evidence from the text you are basing your deductions on. It's no good saying, "I don't know—all I know is, that's what I got out of it." If you ask yourself, "What in this poem or story or essay made me think?" that will get you started. Points to consider should include the overall plot, gestures, metaphors, dialogue, the tone of descriptions, and the outcome of the plot.

Make your analysis with dispatch. Once your brain has worked for you in turn, it is time to speak up for it. Don't fuzz the issues. Don't lie to please someone in authority. Granted the world isn't a good enough place for us or for the plants, and we are an appalling species. We need to do some new, hopeful thing.

Oddly enough, one place to start is with no-nonsense analysis and truth telling about first-rate literature.

Appendix V

A List of Useful Sentences for Writers in a Tight Spot[11]

Sometimes a mechanistic formula is more useful than several thoughtful paragraphs. This list of useful sentences for writers in a tight spot I got by analogy from my violin teacher. She said, "Get the score memorized ahead of time into your fingers. The brain can't think fast enough to read musical score each time. You need to get it into your fingers, and they will do it by instinct." A use of such small-fix psychology is that it often suggests little shields or tools that one can put to use against the blows of common life. Sometimes one doesn't want a philosophy: sometimes one wants just a good way to defend oneself. I began to think that lots of the problems that writers have in a commercial culture or that writers have with their families would vanish if writers could protect themselves with a few fast, civil but clean-cut remarks.

I have been teaching this list of useful sentences for people in a tight spot for about five years. People make use of it. Sometimes people in class use it against me. When I have said, "Listen, you must learn such and such," the writers have said to me, "You don't know that; we don't know that. We don't know that we need to learn that at all." And that's a direct quotation of one of these sentences. I regard it as a *good* thing.

Defending yourself in a tight spot variously means: (1) holding off someone who is intruding on your thoughts or well-being; or (2) holding off someone who is out-and-out bullying you for any reason; or (3) holding off someone who is trying to stop you from thinking ethically in your group—or, most commonly, (4) holding off someone who is trying to kill your enthusiasm for a new idea that you have made up yourself. A footnote to this: sometimes people use friendly smiles and kidding to control how other people vote or behave in a group. One needs a way to insist on your stance without getting rattled. It can be difficult. They may continue to smile in a friendly way and say, "Hey—will you lighten up a little? Feels awfully heavy around here," or something like that, a remark intended to make you feel like a party wrecker.

1. If someone says, "Who do you think you *are* to be taking all these fancy moral stands in your writing? You could get in trouble!" You might quietly agree. You might say, "You could be right. The whole thing might work out very badly for me."
2. If someone says, "But last month you said just the opposite!" you might say, "That's right! You're right! I've changed my mind about it!"
3. To someone who prophesies, "That won't work!" you might say, "Actually, we don't know that. We don't know if it will work or not."
4. When someone has made an argument for something you are opposed to, you might say, "Actually, I'm on the other side here." Sometimes if the discussion is friendly, the other person will then say, "Oh, I bet we really agree—we just express ourselves differently," and you can say, "No, actually, I understand what you are saying and I really *am* on the other side." (If the person insists further that it's really just a question of semantics—a very common remark, I know—you might say, "No, it really isn't a question of semantics; it's a question of morals.")
5. If someone has just said something that you're not sure you have the point of, you can say—and this is a kind idea: "Let me be sure I understand what you just said. Will you please say that again? And also, could you give me an example of how that would play out so that I can be clear about it?"

6. If someone in authority—an older person, parent, or caretaker, priest or roshi, rabbi, or pastor—says, "Please listen to the voice of experience! If you want to build any kind of a decent life for yourself, you're going to have to learn to go with the flow! Use some common sense." You might say, "I bet you're right! I bet you're right, Dad! I bet you're right, Mom—Professor so-and-so—Aunt Sarah—I bet you're right, Father So-and-so—I do hear your voice of experience. Sounds sensible too. Makes life sound totally meaningless, too. But you're right, it does sound sensible."
7. If someone in authority—or *pretending* to be in authority—says, "Look, what you're proposing here, that's been tried a hundred times, and I *assure* you it doesn't work! It never *has* worked and it's not going to work *now*," you might say, "You may be right. On the other hand, you may be wrong. Actually, it may not have been tried a hundred times, or it may have been tried a hundred times, but I'm giving it a different spin."
8. If someone says, "You really need to mellow out some." If you feel like answering that one at all, you could try saying, "I believe you. I bet you're right. But here's my feeling about mellowing out. I think I only thirty or forty percent want mellowed-out life like what you're talking about. The other seventy or sixty percent of me wants something more meaningful—or at least so it feels for now."
9. This sentence and the ones just following tend to be very useful in workplaces. When a CEO remarks, "Sorry, fellow, but we have the stockholders to think of here too. You've got your ideals, but what they want is earnings." You might say, "Actually, you may not know what the shareholders want. Perhaps forty or forty-five percent of them do not want our firm to pollute the earth. You have not asked them for their opinions, and the proxies, steered as they are to dismiss stockholder proposals on ethical questions, don't give you good stats."
10. This sentence is useful for groups when someone has just proposed some new policy. You might say, "That is OK for me. That is OK for you. Are we missing anyone? If we go ahead with this, is there anyone this won't be OK for down the line?"
11. When a group tries to rush you, you might say, "I need more time on that," or "I'd like to wait on that." If someone then snaps, "Well,

we'd like to get home someday!" you might add, "Right, but I need to think about it some more." If the group continues to jeer or get ugly, you might say, as a very last resort, "Think how nice it would have been if, after dropping the A-bomb on Hiroshima and finding that Kokura* was clouded over, someone had said, 'We need more time to think before going ahead with a bombing of Nagasaki.'"

12. If someone says, "I'm sure we can find some commonality here in this discussion. We need to work to find the common ground," you might say, "That may be true, but also, it may not be true. If we really believe in diversity, we don't need to find commonality or common ground at all times. We need to ask one another questions about our differences and then be content with those differences."
13. If someone, or if a part of yourself, tells a sad or brutal story, but laughs in the telling as if it were a joke, you can very soberly say, "I am missing the point here. Would you repeat that story please?" (Reason: the second time around there is some chance that you or the other person will not feel constrained to make a joke out of something serious—especially as you were grave, not sneering, in asking them to retell it.)

The next two are especially for middle school or high school people who show up in writing classes. Sometimes young people nowadays are so pressured to talk badly, to tell the *story* of a feeling instead of *naming* the feeling, to be inexact and to point at something instead of really discussing it and identifying it, that we have to help them with language. The following two sentences to remember are designed for students who are having a hard time in a writing class. "Hard time" does not mean that they are not able to become writers. "Hard time" means the American culture has not served them well. Here's the first one:

14. To someone who says, "I'm like, what's going on?" you can say, "Well, what's the actual feeling you're feeling?" This helps the person get conscious of how mad or sad or glad he or she may really be. Often when people say, "I'm like, such and such," they themselves are not clear about their stance. But they do know that they're feeling *something*.

*Kokura, the city originally chosen for the second bomb, is now a part of the Japanese city Kitakyushu.

15. And to a student brought up in our careless, cynical society who says, "Look, I'm up to here with sappy classes, sappy group, and sappy empathy, and all the other sappy stuff!" You might say, "Here's one way to look at sappy. Students and English teachers and school social workers are like football players. Some can make a fast move when all the plans have gone haywire and there's trouble on the field. Some just can't adjust. Some are courageous, but some, no matter how much the team needs it, just don't make the block. They can't make themselves hit the person. They can't make themselves receive the catch if they know they're going to be hit. So stick with me for two weeks. Hang in here." The advantage of this conversation is that it moves the conversation from scorn and disdain to a consideration of character—what part fearlessness may play in how much we learn or how much we don't learn.

The advantage of memorizing a few sentences ahead of time is that when you find yourself in a tight spot, there's isn't time to think. If you have the sentence ready you can defend yourself and save face and give yourself a few moments in which to think. My work for the National Farmers Union impressed me with this truth: when there is trouble—for writers or for anybody—that trouble is almost always caused by *someone.* It isn't that the victim has trouble because the victim isn't a good manager. The victim is having trouble because a predator made moves. It has sunk into me that sometimes we need to reason and talk and use metaphor with people, but at other times it's a case of someone having attacked our psyche, and all we need is a small way to fend off the bully.

Appendix VI

Two Examples of Class Agendas for M.F.A. Students

The two class agendas presented below were actual handouts given students in the advanced nonfiction writing course at the University of Minnesota, Winter 1999.

Names of class members appeared in bold type, so students could quickly see if they would be asked to read aloud or illustrate a point. About ten minutes of weekly class time was given to English usage, based on either errors or neat phrasings in students' papers that week.

University of Minnesota EngW 5130
Carol Bly, Instructor

Agenda for January 27th 1999

Handout: Writing assignment for February 3rd
Assignment for Feb. 3:
Please write essay as described on the handout.
Please be thinking up a writing or in-class discussion exercise.
These can be sent to me by e-mail or snail mail. Then the group can choose one or two.

In-class exercise in agility of invention, to be done fast as night:

Please define and describe a little, in not more than four sentences, the following, and we will read it all aloud.

Schlammus / originalis

Three readings aloud to do with ethics in essays:

From *Changing the Bully Who Rules the World*, p. 484 [Further to influence of life spent in groups]
From *The World Wide Church of the Handicapped*, "Wilma Bremer's Funeral" apropos of Good Work.
From *Tobias Wolfe, In Short*, p. 58—and Tom Haley on not lying re: feelings for the dead (later this eve.)

The Discussions

1. Being willing to write in despair or when "still too close to some painful thing." A trick to try: jot down notes on the oppressive subject, in a list at one side of your desk. Refer to it in some essay you happen to be writing, very lightly, perhaps as one of those things people endure. Reason to write mid-despair: your memory won't be very good if you are in pain, so you need writing. Second, if you write mid–disastrous events, you sometimes find other feelings you had not sighted before. Perhaps the pain is only 99 percent and you find 1 percent the pleasure that philosophers have. Philosopher, the word is from "philo" (Greek for "love"). Love of the universe, beastly as it is.

2. It is good to talk about literature by content as much as by authors. For example, the greatest American author on breaking wind is Carson McCullers. Ernest Hemingway, James Salter, Steve Adams have the best imagery on lustful feelings. See "Keeper," in *Glimmer Train*, p. 128.

3. Writing about modest feelings. We are not always silvery and in flight.

Jan Koenen—motivation in jobs dictating how one works . . .

Mary Heng says she changed to a bad job "seeking the usual trappings of short-sighted people: better pay, holidays off, and an 8 to 5 schedule."

Tom Haley's redo of Shallow Place essay [Cemetery]. Also note simile re elderly. Versus writing immodestly and [I think] facilely:

Judith Kitchen[12] "Over Hiroshima, the plane burst through a seam in the sky—a glint, and then a blinding flash. The earth has learned to live with us. It accommodates bone, shadows burned in stone."

Emily Hiestand p. 67—in trouble because started out too lightweight.

4. Imagery in the prose:

   Joe Hart re: the Latinas handling the hamburgers "daintied" "petals"

   Elizabeth Noll remembers conv c̄ sad man and woman. "Then silence sat on the telephone wire" "and their arguments were so many and so fierce they wore their good times down to a skinny thread."

   Mary Winstead re: mother "nosing iron into each frozen ruffle, smoothing the wrinkles with the crackle and pop of a ship's bow breaking through a thin layer of ice."

   Cynthia Ozyck, "I landed in Edinburgh with the roaring of the plane's four mammoth propellers embedded in my ears for days."

5. Being willing to add one philosophical or anecdotal bit to others

   Elizabeth Larsen re: scapegrace Web site job and wedding

   David Littau re: principled and unprincipled workplace behavior

6. Avoiding what is called "self-referencing" in essay, even in memoir

   2 Guinea pigs for this evening **Elizabeth Noll** at the end

   Mary Winstead "it seemed to me"

7. Keeping control of slang and informal English

   Bad if a habit; good if it gives a light non-holier-than-thou touch, as with Marie Williams's wtg re Wilma Bremer's funeral

8. Sentences:
   Starting them with the weak, secondary elements—dependent clauses, adverbial phrases
   Too-long sentences.

Readers Aloud this Afternoon: **Elizabeth Larsen,** Web site/wedding
Bruce Piltz, "Grinder"
Wayne Smith, "Mowing Mr. Troyer's"
Elizabeth Noll, re: Iraq

Small Uses and Grammatical Indignities

"as it were" "if you will" "be it"—Black Tie phrases, usually toney about nothing much

Phrase piling: adding phrases in apposition after a comma. Usually humbug

"a one" "ones" in the predicate—weak language

Flimsy diction: becomes, seems, is, seemingly, it seems

"not . . . much" when what is meant is not at all. "I don't eat much grandmother flesh actually"

Two bad uses of the demonstrative: "all that rich" and "on that October day in Wichita when the whole country club membership got taken down to that station" "I will never forget that day in June when"

"Enough that" is wrong. It has to be "enough so" or "enough so that"

Always bad verbs, Minnesota usage notwithstanding:
grab, pull in, head out, head toward, sits, sat (instead of stands, stood, or lies, lay)

University of Minnesota EngW 5130
Winter Quarter, 1999
Carol Bly, Instructor

Agenda for February 3rd, 1999

Handouts: Agenda
Assignment for February 10, 1999

An answer to Bly on lying in memoir, "On the Need for the Lie," WSO, fyi
On-line newsgroup letter against "craft fascism," fyi
Discussion of gratuitous cruelty by Christian IV of Denmark to women and by Lockhart to John Keats, fyi
Web site pitch for reading what you read for the individual author who wrote it, not as an example of some literary style going around, fyi

In-class 1.5 minute writing:

Please define and discuss or tell an illustrative anecdote about
Schlammus Originalis
in not more than four or five sentences. See what you can do with this fantastical writing. We will read what people write aloud.

The Discussions

1. Surprising insights or some surprising expertise that others are ignorant of. e.g.

Jan "I enjoyed . . . being forced to pay attn to where I walked."
Susan: re: horses shifting around. Also Susan read the whole Pastures wtg:

2. Quick Cures for two- or three-word dead phrasing.

"It felt as though my soul was lifted from my body and unfurled like a silk banner, allowing to fly in the wind." Subjunctive use, too?

3. Good theater and Flat slackness in essays

Present participial attachments slow down any feeling. Short sentences leave us right on the site.
Self-referencing kills theater. It makes it all just talk not presentation.

Bad Theater: He then left his coat on the chair, moving up the aisle.
Wondering what he had in mind, she waited, as she dragged on a cigarette.
Better: He left his coat on the chair. He moved up the aisle. She waited. She dragged on the cigarette.
Worst case: I will never forget how having left his coat on the chair he moved up the aisle. As I recall, she was just waiting, wondering what he had in mind, etc.

4. Leaving the world of childhood behind.

Childish diction: please read all your first drafts aloud, loudly to yourself, like Winston Churchill, so that you hear childish language or deadbeat language and run-ons. The mark of a beginning writer or of experienced writers but only in their first drafts is long sentences. This is not a matter of literary gift. This is a matter of decision making. Childish diction includes words that are not words such as "scoot over" and "squinch" and "squish" and "icky." Deadbeat language is "who I am" "in my perception" "can relate to" and other worn culture littering.

Childish subject matter. For the rest of this course use anecdotes from your and others' adult lives for your essays. Unfortunately, memories of sensitive occasions in one's childhood don't teach one to write well. It is unfortunate, too, because those occasions are immensely meaningful. Nonetheless they leave one writing without much imagination. We shouldn't be surprised: look at the wonderful imagination of adults! They can think up twenty wild plots for every one that a child can think up—because, because. Be sure to stay fixed on your adult life. It is a treasure and you are the expert in it. If an old mean uncle or aunt tricked you into thinking that childhood is when we are gladdest, he or she lied. Tell him that he needs to find his inner warrior and tell her that she needs to work on her perception of who she is.

5. <u>Readers this afternoon:</u>
Bill McDonald, Mary Heng, Elizabeth Noll
David Littau (Susan Taylor, above)

6. For your interest: values listed by this group so far

<u>*Bad*</u>

Need to dominate or always be right (bossiness)
Dishonesty
Ostracism
Losing a loved one
The inevitability of the pain of death
Self-righteousness
Hypocrisy
Fear of God
Adults who terrorize children because they can
Feeling ashamed of a parent
Child abuse
Dread
Guilt
Genocide
Hopelessness
Helplessness
Overpopulation

<u>*Good*</u>

Learning for learning's sake
Joy
Humor
Awareness
Private prayer (really private, not to be advtd to convert friends or any other self-service)
Unexpected kindness from strangers
Creativity
Solitude

Spiritual faith
Romantic love
Birth
Connection

Will everyone who didn't pass in a list of at least 4 horrendous and 4 blessed aspects of life please do so?

7. Small usages. The word *all* can nearly always be omitted, removing inaccuracy from mss. Use of two nouns with "of" between them usually vitiates whatever you meant with that second noun. Such use is good church practice, where people have to get along: one hears people say "sense of spirituality"—but terrible literary practice where we either think an idea or we don't think it but we mustn't molder around half-taking things back. For example, "There's a way in which . . ." a magnificent U.S.A. businessplace expression invented by the human resources departments. One can say *anything* in such a sentence. It is closely linked to "Does that make sense?"—a remark that shamelessly begs the listener to agree whether he or she really does or not. I have tried saying "Actually, no, it doesn't really" and I can't tell you how badly that works.

sort of thing, sense of fear, sense of [anything], kind of [anything]

The word *incredibly* is finished. It started at Cambridge [UK] where people used it to show they were not Teddies. It went to Harvard, where people used it because they herded: others were using it. It showed you weren't a townie. Then it came over here, along with other exhausted British usages such as "chat" and "a bit" and "a tad." A tad, especially when joined in "a tad sticky" is *excrementum gravis* (Roman Empire for serious drivel). Other affectations are "dicey" and "bloody." I know it is v hard to get over the habit of using these horrible phrases. I am stuck with bloody, myself. But do try. They lay a light scrim of posturing over one's prose. They make it hard for the mind to think of metaphors.

Avoid (as was on the agenda last week) old-hat rhetoric such as "Be it." This week's horrible flimsy usage was "Or should I say," which sounds intelligent and pleasantly modest, and is meant that way, yet it is really what George Orwell would call gas and E Hemingway would call "goddamned writing."

From the AOL Writers' Club

There is a problem between old authors and young student writers.* The old authors are always wildly busy. And they like their own generation: who doesn't?—so they often don't give young people's newly published work a careful reading. When they do, they often don't seem to see much good in it. This makes student writers uneasy. Their manuscript seems *perfect right now* to them, and it should be out there in print, right now, or soon, but here is this old writing teacher: maybe this old writing teacher is just a swine before whom I am casting down my pearls? It is a nerve-racking question.

*Please take this to your comfort, as the Episcopalians say.

Appendix VII

The Robertson-Bly Ethics Code for Teaching Creative Writing to Middle and High School Students

The Ethics for Respect of Privacy

In 1987 Brenda Robertson and I took the Code to some Midwest Council of Teachers of English conferences. We still keep amending it. Neither of us is done thinking about it. When you read over the Code, please see it as an unfinished assemblage of constraints that we suggest teachers accept on behalf of their students. But any ethics code for teaching writing needs more wisdom: please weigh in with your ideas.

1. The teacher will treat all students' work as confidential except for getting professional help as requisite by law when suicide or abuse is suggested.
2. The teacher will ask for permission from a student before quoting from his or her work in class discussions.

The Ethics of Human Well-Being of All Kinds of Populations

3. The teacher will model inclusive language and will insist on its use in all papers handed in or used in the course. Not for any reason

will "he" be used to stand for "he and she." When this ethics code was developed we were thinking especially of women, but the same unqualified respect is needed for every possible population, including people whose first language is not English.

4. When new publications or articles on composition and creative writing (such as those from Bedford or in *College English*) use non-inclusive or racist language, the creative-writing teacher will write a complaint in to the editor of such publications to be noted for new editions and for changing consciousness.

The Ethics of Improving Education in the United States

5. The teacher will work to improve language and creative-writing instruction in public schools, private schools, colleges and universities—through private effort and group association. The teacher will not simply take the present customs or situations to be incorrigible. At the high school level, he or she will try to influence *classroom size* and the fact that students' *ideas* are so important that although of course craft must be taught, it must not be taught at the sacrifice of the content of a student's writing.
6. Teachers will attend conventions, read literary magazines regularly (not just education magazines), and keep current with educational theory, listen to speakers, take classes, and engage in dialogue with other professionals in order to keep abreast of new ideas and to keep from "entrenching."

The Ethics of Encouragement to Write

7. The teacher will respond to students' work promptly and kindly, modeling courteous response to others' ideas.
8. The teacher will be as generous in arranging individual conferences as is possible.
9. The teacher will uphold the adage that one learns by writing—by doing the writing itself—and therefore will assign frequent, short

writing exercises to be read and responded to rather than asking for a rough draft and then a final project only.

10. Whenever possible, the teacher will do the in-class writing exercises with the students—this for the sake of empathy and for the camaraderie of the writing task.
11. The teacher will protect the students' self-confidence by not asking too much of any one assignment, especially of revision work.
12. The teacher will write only comment, as such, on the students' work: students' work must remain theirs and not be rewritten by the teacher.
13. The teacher will encourage students to surpass the given assignment when it would make the work more meaningful for them. If a haiku is assigned, for example, but one student would rather write a short story, the teacher will not punish the variance by grade or in any other way.
14. The teacher will keep an eagle eye on the group process of the classroom in order to keep the tone comradely.
15. The teacher will help all the students in a writing class to anchor their self-confidence against *moral drift*. Moral drift occurs when a majority of vociferous people in a room hold one opinion while one student, or a small group, holds another. If the minority opinion begins to weaken and change, either losing its clarity or crumbling over toward the majority opinion, then that minority has succumbed to moral drift. Very great—even valiant—ideas have been lost to moral drift, as is reported frequently and sadly by historians.
16. The teacher will consider himself or herself charged to encourage the less promising writing students as much as the promising students. Learning to write is even more important to the inexperienced or reckless or rigid-hearted student than to a student who is used to thinking on paper. Intellectually foreclosed students usually have a very hard time in middle school and high school and, in fact, an even worse time once they get to college—if they get there. In college, even more than in middle and high school, one must freely consider ideas and let them bump against one's own previous ideas. Just as if we had been rowing when suddenly our bow bumped into

a bizarre object floating in the lake. We shouldn't feel that we must back off and shell it: we learn to look at it simply, take the bump, and decide if this novel object has any significance or not.

The Ethics of Encouragement to Find One's Deepest Personality

17. The writing teacher can be and should be a psychological force to help students develop from supercilious or cynical or shallow thinking levels to more value-laden and serious reflection.
18. The writing teacher can stand for the principle that *writing* is an appropriate and psychologically valuable activity not only for the gifted few but for every single member of our species. We are a writing species. All of us write unless we are physically or psychologically or culturally blocked from it by unfair people or unfair mores.
19. *The Ethics of Getting Children Away from Harm.*

    A few years ago a Minnesota high school boy handed in a paper in which he wrote that he felt suicidal. His creative-writing teacher honored confidentiality and said nothing to anyone. She knew the boy was gay, and no doubt she weighed the pain that he would suffer if he were involuntarily outed by her asking a psychological intake professional for help. He then committed suicide. Two weeks later, his best friend mentioned that suicide in a paper about grief, and shortly after that he killed himself. These deaths no doubt drew authorities' attention to the significant position of English teachers. New legislation came of it.

    Children's and teenagers' creative writing often refer to terrifying or abusive situations. English teachers, like school social workers, get oblique news of cruelty at home. It is hard to know what to do.

    States' child-protection laws vary. Following are the main heads of Minnesota's, just to give an idea of what creative-writing teachers need to think about when coming across grievous signals in students' work.

    The 1999 language is "maltreatment," not abuse. Reports of child maltreatment fall into two lots—maltreatment in schools and suspected maltreatment taking place elsewhere. If the suspected abuser is responsible for a child's care in school as defined by statute—including, but not limited to, teachers, administrators, coaches, counselors, paraprofessionals, and bus drivers—the maltreatment should be reported to the Department of Children, Families and Learning (CFL). In Minnesota this situation falls under the Maltreatment of Minors Reporting Act, Minn. Stat. §626.556.

Suspected maltreatment taking place outside the school should be reported to local law-enforcement agencies or local social service agencies. Typically, the social service agency would be the child protection unit within the county where the child currently lives. If a teacher is in doubt about which county a child lives in, he or she can call the appropriate agency and without revealing names at this point give the general details to the intake people. They will tell the teacher where the report needs to go.[13]

Endnotes

Chapter 1

1. Denis Halliday in a speech at Harvard on November 5, 1998. Reprinted in *Iraq Notebook*, a newsletter edited by Lee Loe, Chair of the Fellowship of Reconciliation of Houston, at 1844 Kipling St., Houston, TX.

2. "G.I.'s Tell of a U.S. Massacre in Korean War," *The New York Times*, September 30, 1999.

3. Gerald Graff, *Literature Against Itself: Literary Ideas in Modern Society* (Chicago: Elephant Paperbacks, 1995), p. 213.

4. Robert M. Liebert and Rita Wicks Poulos, "Television as a Moral Teacher," in *Moral Development and Behavior: Theory, Research, and Social Issues* (New York: Holt, Rinehart and Winston, 1976), p. 284. The author is summarizing reports by George Gerbner of studies he made in 1972 and 1973: "Measures and Indicators of Violence on Prime-Time and Saturday Network Television Drama, 1967–1972." Unpublished manuscript, University of Pennsylvania, 1973; and "Violence in Television Drama: Trends and Symbolic Functions," in G. A. Comstock and E. A. Rubinstein, eds., *Television and Social Behavior, Vol. I: Media Content and Control* (Washington, D.C.: U.S. Government Printing Office, 1972), pp. 22–187.

5. Friedrich Schiller, *On the Aesthetic Education of Man: In a Series of Letters*, edited and translated with an introduction, commentary, and glossary of terms by Elizabeth M. Wilkinson and L. A. Willoughby (Oxford: Clarendon Press, 1967). Schiller's book was published in 1801.

6. Philip Levine, *The Bread of Time* (New York: Alfred A. Knopf, 1994), p. 6.

7. Peter Elbow, "Closing My Eyes As I Speak: An Argument for Ignoring Audience," *College English* 49, no. 1 (January 1987): 50.

8. David Ehrenfeld, *Beginning Again* (New York: Oxford University Press, 1933), pp. 68–69.

Chapter 3

1. This format was partly developed by Mary Peterson, Lic.S.W., and Carol Bly, cochairpersons of the Collaborative of Teachers and School Social Workers.

2. Carol Bly, *The Passionate Accurate Story* (Minneapolis: Milkweed Editions, 1990, 1998, pp 172–75.

3. Denise Levertov, "Like Loving Chekhov," in *Life in the Forest* (New York: New Directions, 1978), pp. 77–78.

Chapter 4

1. Carol Bly, *Changing the Bully Who Rules the World* (Minneapolis: Milkweed Editions, 1966), pp. 166–67.

2. Jane Loevinger, *Ego Development* (San Francisco: Jossey-Bass Publishers, 1987).

3. Richard Leakey and Robert Lewin, *The Sixth Extinction: Patterns of Life and the Future of Humankind* (New York: Anchor Books), ch. 10, 172 ff.

4. Richard Wilbur, "The Mind," *New and Collected Poems* (New York: Harcourt Brace & Jovanovich, 1988), p. 240.

5. Schiller, 171f.

6. George Orwell, "Why I Write," *Eight Modern Essayists*, ed. William Smart (St. Martin's Press, 1985).

Chapter 5

1. William Wordsworth, in "Preface to the Second Edition" of the *Lyrical Ballads* (London, 1802).

2. Dava Sobel, *Galileo's Daughter* (New York: Walker & Company, 1999), p. 19.

3. D. H. Lawrence, "The Elephant Is Slow to Mate," *Complete Poems*, edited by Vivian de Sola Pinto and Warren Roberts (New York: Penguin, 1994).

4. Antonio Damasio, *Descartes' Error* (New York: G. P. Putnam's Sons, 1994), p. 164.

5. Ted Kooser, "King: A Dog of the North," *North Dakota Quarterly*, Vol 62 Number 4, Fall 1994–1995.

Chapter 6

1. I refer to Thomas's humorous and ironic poem "In My Craft or Sullen Art."
2. Natalia Ginzburg, *The Little Virtues*, translated from the Italian by Dick Davis (New York: Arcade Publishing [Little, Brown and Company]). Copyright © 1962 by Giulio Einaudi editore s.p.a. Translation copyright © 1985 by Dick Davis.
3. Scott King, "At the Shore of Snowbank Lake" (Northfield, Minnesota: Red Dragonfly Press).
4. James Salter, *Solo Faces* (San Francisco: North Point Press, 1988). Originally published by Little, Brown & Co., 1979. p. 15
5. Ibid., p. 26.
6. Ibid., p. 84.
7. Ibid., p. 93.
8. W. H. Auden, "Musée des beaux arts," *The Collected Poetry of W. H. Auden*, copyright by W. H. Auden 1940, renewed 1961, Random House.
9. Richard Hoffman, "What's Love Got to Do with It?" Forthcoming in *Flashpoint: Where Art & Politics Meet*, http://webdelsol.com/FLASHPOINT/
10. Salter, p. 18.

Chapter 7

1. Denise Levertov, "Modulations," in *Life in the Forest* (New York: New Directions, 1978).
2. Wordsworth.

Chapter 8

1. C. Fred Alford, *Group Psychology and Political Theory* (New Haven: Yale University Press, 1994).
2. See Alford's "Epilogue: The Wolini," pp. 184–208.
3. Susan O'Hanian, *Who's in Charge? A Teacher Speaks Her Mind* (Portsmouth, NH: Boynton/Cook Publishers [Heinemann], 1994).
4. Scott Russell Sanders, first and only appeared in personal correspondence with the author, reproduced by permission.

Chapter 9

1. Alvarez's collection of short stories is forthcoming from Graywolf Press.

Chapter 10

1. Edith Wharton, "The Young Dead"

2. Cleanth Brooks and Robert Penn Warren, authors of *Understanding Poetry* and editors of *Southern Review.*

3. Irvin D. Yalom, *Existential Psychotherapy* (New York: Basic Books, 1980).

4. Loren Eiseley, *The Night Country* (New York: Charles Scribner's Sons, 1971), p. 3.

5. This narrative was told by Professor John Clark, University of Minnesota Department of English. Clark was an Old English (Anglo-Saxon) teacher with special expertise in historical sound changes in English.

Chapter 12

1. In a review of Emery Halloway's *Whitman, The Nation and Atheneum.* xl, p. 426 [Dec. 1926] copyright *New Statesman,* cited in *Encyclopedia Britannica,* vol. 23, 1967.

2. Sobel, p. 51.

3. Gene Bell-Villada, *Art for Art's Sake and Literary Life* (Lincoln, Neb.: University of Nebraska Press, 1998).

4. Ibid., pp. 8–9. Bell-Villada's footnote refers to Ernst Cassirer, *The Philosophy of the Enlightenment,* trans. by Fritz C. A. Haden and James P. Pettegrove (Princeton, N.J.: Princeton University Press, 1951), p. 275.

5. Jorge Luis Borges, "Blindness," translated by Eliot Weinberger, from *Seven Nights* (New York: New Directions, 1985), p. 107.

6. Rainer Maria Rilke, "The Panther," in *The Selected Poetry of Rainer Maria Rilke,* trans. and edited by Stephen Mitchell (New York: Vintage Books, 1989), p. 25.

7. Rainer Maria Rilke, *Letters to a Young Poet,* trans. and with a foreword by Stephen Mitchell (New York: Vintage Books, Random House, 1987), pp. 72–73.

8. Virginia Woolf, *The Three Guineas* (San Diego: Harvest/HBJ 1938), pp. 62–63.

9. Ted Kooser, "Lying for the Sake of Making Poems," *Prairie Schooner* 72, no. 1 (Spring 1998): 5.

10. M. F. K. Fisher, "I Was Really Very Hungry," from *As They Were* (New York: Vintage Books, a division of Random House, 1983), pp. 43–44.

11. "He hath scattered the proud in the imagination of their hearts . . . and the rich he hath sent empty away."

12. Rebecca Harding Davis, *Life in the Iron Mills,* with a biographical interpretation by Tillie Olsen, Feminist Press Reprint Number One (The Feminist

Press) 1972. *Life in the Iron Mills* was first published in *The Atlantic Monthly* in April of 1861.

13. William Stafford, "The Day After Then" in William Stafford, ed., *Roving Across Fields: A Conversation and Uncollected Poems, 1942–1982*, (Daleville: The Barnwood Press Cooperative, 1983), p. 40.

14. Richard Hoffman, "What's Love Got to Do with It?"

15. Richard Hoffman, *Half the House: A Memoir* (Harvest Books, 1997).

16. Sid Gershgoren, *The Wandering Heron*, Introduction by Thomas McGrath (Northfield, Minn.: Red Dragonfly Press, 1999), pp. 23, 25.

17. Carol Bly, Wednesday, May 13, 1998, America Online Writers Club, Fiction Writing Message Board, "Integrity and Art in Fiction" folder.

18. Celia Dugger, "Fatal Abuse," *The New York Times Book Review*, April 20, 1996.

19. AOL posting, "Integrity and Art in Fiction" folder.

20. William Manchester, *The Last Lion: Winston Spencer Churchill: Alone 1932–1940* (Boston: Little, Brown and Company, 1988), p. 71.

21. Ibid., p. 82.

22. Schiller, p. 173.

23. Ibid., pp. 177, 179.

24. Patricia Hooper, "The Statues," *The Hudson Review*, Summer 1999, Vol. LII, no. 2, pp. 274–75.

25. Richard Eberhart, "The Groundhog," in *Collected Poems 1930–1960* (Oxford University Press, Inc., 1960).

Appendices

1. Freeman Wills Crofts, *The 12:30 from Croyden* (New York: Penguin, 1965), pp. 183–84.

2. David Ignatow, "Above Everything," in *New and Collected Poems, 1970–1985* (Middletown, Conn.: Wesleyan University Press, 1986), p. 195.

3. George Orwell, *The Road to Wigan Pier* (San Diego: Harcourt Brace, 1973), p. 7.

4. Jane Austen, *Sense and Sensibility* (New York: New American Library, Signet), p. 177.

5. Herman Wouk, *The Caine Mutiny* (New York: Doubleday, 1951), pp. 100–2.

6. Howard Zinn, *You Can't Be Neutral on a Moving Train* (Boston: Beacon Press, 1994).

7. Dr. Robert Terry, *Leadership—A Preview of a Seventh View*, External Relations Office, Hubert Humphrey Institute of Public Affairs.

8. Natalia Ginzburg, "He and I," in *The Little Virtues* (Boston: Arcade Publishing, Inc., a Little Brown Company, by arrangement with Seaver Books, New York, 1989). Originally published in Italy under the title *Le Piccole Virtù*. Translated from the Italian by Dick Davis.

9. This format was offered as a means to help retirees structure their memoir writing. I offered it to the fifty-year class at Phillips Academy, Andover, in June of 1997. Please see the discussion in Chapter 7, "Seven General Issues in Teaching Creative Writing," in the section of that chapter devoted to well-educated people taking on some writing for the first time in their lives.

10. This format is a mix of ideas stuck together by Carol Bly, University of Minnesota, and Abigail Davis, University of St. Thomas.

11. This handout called "A List of Useful Sentences for Writers in a Tight Spot" was originally developed as a gift to the senior class of Shattuck–St. Mary's School in the fall of 1997 for their annual fall ethics retreat.

12. In *In Short*, Judith Kitchen and Mary Paumier Jones, eds. (New York: W. W. Norton and Company, 1996), p. 64.

13. This material may be reproduced for teaching purposes. Please credit The Robertson-Bly Ethics Code, © 1987, 1999, by Brenda Robertson and Carol Bly. Reproduced by permission of the authors.

A *Reading List*

Alvarez, Aldo. "Ten Ways to Participate in the Future of Literary Fiction as a Reader or Writer." www.noveladvice.com, message board, May 31, 1997, 05:02 P.M. Professor Alvarez (Indiana University) lists the intellectual and aesthetic tasks of literature and suggests ways not to sell them out.

Bell-Villada, Gene. *Art for Art's Sake and Literary Life.* Lincoln, Neb.: University of Nebraska Press, 1996. Professor Bell-Villada offers a two-hundred-year history of aestheticism as a literary phenomenon specific to Western industrial societies.

Bly, Carol. *Changing the Bully Who Rules the World.* Minneapolis: Milkweed Editions, 1996. An anthology of ten poems, ten stories, and four essays with nine chapter essays by the editor connecting stage-development theory and empathic inquiry in order to understand first-rate literature better. The book argues for literature as a normative, rather than a descriptive field.

Bly, Carol. *The Passionate, Accurate Story.* Minneapolis: Milkweed Editions, 1990. The introduction and Chapters 1, 2, and 9 contain suggestions for nonfiction as well as for fiction writing.

Damasio, Antonio R. *Descartes' Error: Emotion, Reason, and the Human Brain.* New York: G. P. Putnam's Sons, 1994.

Edelman, Gerald M. *Bright Air, Brilliant Fire: On the Matter of the Mind.* New York: Basic Books, 1992.

Gass, William. "The Art of Self: Autobiography in an Age of Narcissm." *Harper's Magazine*, May 1994, 43.

Graff, Gerald. *Literature Against Itself.* Chicago: Elephant Paperback, 1995.

Hall, Donald. *Writing Well.* 9th ed. Reading, Mass.: Addison-Wesley Pub. Co., 1997.

Kooser, Ted. "Lying for the Sake of Making Poems." *Prairie Schooner* 72, no. 1 (Spring 1998): 5.

Loevinger, Jane. *Ego Psychology: Conceptions and Theories.* San Francisco: Jossey-Bass, 1976.

Lukeman, Noah. *The First Five Pages.* New York: Fireside Books, Simon and Schuster, 2000.

Moxley, Joseph M., ed. *Creative Writing in America: Theory and Pedagogy.* Urbana, Ill.: National Council of Teachers of English, 1989. See especially "The Future of Creative Writing Programs," by George Garrett, pp. 47–61.

Oliver, Mary. *A Poetry Handbook.* San Diego: Harcourt Brace, 1994. See especially "Workshops and Solitude," pp. 112–18.

Orwell, George. "Politics and the English Language." *Eight Modern Essays,* 5th ed. Edited and with a foreword by William Smart. New York: St. Martin's Press, 1990.

Rilke, Rainer Maria. *Letters to a Young Poet.* Translated and with a foreword by Stephen Mitchell. New York: Vintage Books, a division of Random House, 1987.

Sanders, Scott Russell. "The Power of Stories." *The Force of Spirit.* Boston: Beacon Press, 2000. p. 113.

Sanders, Scott Russell. *Writing from the Center.* Bloomington, Ind.: Indiana University Press, 1995.

Ueland, Brenda. *If You Want to Write.* Minneapolis, Minn.: Graywolf Press, 1997.

Index

Permissions Acknowledgments

Grateful acknowledgment is made to the following for permission to reprint previously published material:

Aldo Alvarez: Excerpt from "Ten Ways to Participate in the Future of Literary Fiction as a Reader or Writer." www.noveladvice.com, message board, May 31, 1997. Copyright © 1997 by Aldo Alvarez. Reprinted by permission of the author.

Gene Bell-Villada: Excerpt from *Art for Art's Sake and Literary Life.* Copyright © 1996 by Gene Bell-Villada. Reprinted by permission of the author.

Jorge Luis Borges: Excerpt from "Blindness" by Jorge Luis Borges, translated by Eliot Weinberger, from *Seven Nights.* Copyright © 1985 by Eliot Weinberger. Reprinted by permission of New Directions Publishing Corp.

Antonio Damasio: Excerpt from *Descartes' Error* by Antonio Damasio. Copyright © 1994. Reprinted by permission of Penguin Putnam Inc.

John M. Dolan: From "An Approach to Teaching" by John M. Dolan, a statement composed on the occasion of his induction into the University of Minnesota's Academy of Distinguished Teachers in June 1999. Reprinted by permission of the author.

Celia Dugger: Excerpt from "Fatal Abuse" from the April 20, 1996 edition of *The New York Times Book Review.* Reprinted by permission of *The New York Times.*

Richard Eberhart: "The Groundhog," from *Collected Poems 1930–1986,* by Richard Eberhart. Copyright © 1960, 1976, 1987 by Richard Eberhart. Used by permission of Oxford University Press, Inc.

David Ehrenfeld: Excerpt from *Beginning Again: People and Nature in the New Millennium,* by David Ehrenfeld. Copyright © 1993 by Oxford University Press, Inc. Used by permission of Oxford University Press, Inc.

M. F. K. Fisher: Excerpt from "I Was Really Very Hungry," from *As They Were* by M. F. K. Fisher. Copyright © 1937 by M. F. K. Fisher. Reprinted by permission of Alfred A. Knopf, a division of Random House, Inc.

Sid Gershgoren: From *The Wandering Heron* by Sid Gershgoren. Copyright © 1999 by Sid Gershgoren. Reprinted with the permission of Red Dragonfly Press.

Natalia Ginzburg: Excerpt from *The Little Virtues* by Natalia Ginzburg. Copyright © 1962 by Giulio Einaudi editore s.p.a. Translation copyright © 1985 by Dick Davis. Reprinted by permission of Arcade Publishing, New York by arrangement with Seaver Books and Carcanet Press Limited.

Gerald Graff: Excerpt from *Literature Against Itself: Literary Ideas in Modern Society,* by Gerald Graff. Copyright © 1995 by Gerald Graff. Reprinted by the permission of the author.

Patricia Hooper: "The Statues" by Patricia Hooper. Copyright © 1999 by Patricia Hooper. Reprinted by permission of *The Hudson Review,* Vol. LII, No. 2 (Summer 1999).

David Ignatow: "Above Everything" from *New and Collected Poems: 1970–1985* by David Ignatow. Copyright © 1986 by David Ignatow and Wesleyan University Press. Reprinted by permission of University Press of New England.

Scott King: "At the Shore of Snowbank Lake." Originally published in *Pemmican.* Reprinted by permission of the author.